HAMMERS IN THE HEART

**Pete May is a West Ham season-ticket holder
and also the author of:**

West Ham: Irons in the Soul

*The Lad Done Bad: Sex, Sleaze
and Scandal in English Football*

*Sunday Muddy Sunday: The Heart
and Soul of Sunday League Football*

Football and its Followers

*Rent Boy: How One Man Spent 20 Years
Falling Off the Property Ladder*

Ageing Body, Confused Mind

Pete May

HAMMERS IN THE HEART

West Ham's Journey Back to the Premiership

MAINSTREAM
PUBLISHING
EDINBURGH AND LONDON

For Nicola, Lola and Nell

First published in Great Britain in 2005 by
MAINSTREAM PUBLISHING COMPANY
(EDINBURGH) LTD
7 Albany Street
Edinburgh EH1 3UG

ISBN 1 84596 084 X

A catalogue record for this book is available
from the British Library

Typeset in Frutiger and Garamond

Printed in Great Britain by
William Clowes Ltd, Beccles, Suffolk

CONTENTS

ACKNOWLEDGEMENTS

Special thanks to everyone who has helped with this book, and particularly the writers of *Hammer*, the West Ham programme, which, along with the *Sky Sports Football Yearbook* and John Helliar's *West Ham United: The Elite Era – A Complete Record*, has proved an invaluable research tool. Also thanks to Nicola Baird for match-day childcare (I told you that programme collection was essential!) and our daughters Lola and Nell for enduring my unhealthy addiction to all things claret and blue. Others who have prevented fortune always hiding include Bill Campbell at Mainstream, Peter Stewart, Alan Pardew, Joe Norris, Phill Jupitus, Carol and everyone at Ken's Café, Vivian and John at the Newham Bookshop, fanzine editors Shane Barber and Steve Rapport, fellow fans Denis Campbell, Matt George, Nigel Morris, Gavin Hadland and Fraser Massey, and everyone I've ever been to a match with over the years. Come on you Irons!

1

IT'S ZAMORA!

30 MAY 2005
Bobby dazzles . . . West Ham get their own section back on Teletext . . . Pards dances with his daughters . . . the cycle of misery is broken . . . Nigel gets to the Hammersmith Apollo on time . . . order has been restored and West Ham are back in the Premiership.
  Price of programme at the Millennium Stadium: £5

Jimmy Walker has been carried off on a stretcher. It's the biggest game on Earth. The £25 million final. In the huge bowl of sun and shade that is the Millennium Stadium, Preston have a free-kick on the edge of West Ham's penalty area with just five minutes left. The Hammers are 1–0 up. But I just know that substitute goalkeeper Stephen Bywater's first action will be picking the ball out of his net.

It's moments like this when you are tempted to ask for help from any deity going – although if there was a God, then He would surely never have allowed West Ham to be relegated – or pray for a time rift in Cardiff to open up (well, there was one in *Doctor Who*) and allow an alternative universe to seep into this one, one where West Ham don't lose leads and fail to find ever more inventive ways of torturing those with Irons in their souls and Hammers in their hearts. But I doubt if even the Doctor and Rose will be able to save us now.

We've been through a never-ending season of forty-six league games followed by three play-off ties at a cost of another £150 for tickets, travel, programmes and beer. And now everything depends on this. It could be the rebirth of our club. Or it could be a slide into administration. Mattie Etherington would certainly be sold. Probably Marlon Harewood, too. We might go the way of Nottingham Forest, twice European Cup winners, and slide into League One, which in pre-rebranding days was known as the Third Division.

The 2004 play-off-final defeat to Crystal Palace was my worst moment in football: the desolation of knowing that one game had cost £25 million in revenue and a place in the Premiership. But now we are nine minutes away from returning to where we belong, a land way beyond Crewe, Brighton and Burnley.

And now Preston's McKenna is running up towards the ball. He connects well, the ball is thumped past the wall and towards the gaping goal and . . . BYWATER HAS SAVED IT! He's positioned himself perfectly and held on to the ball as well. The faces of Nigel, Fraser, Lisa and me crumple with nervous relief. We might do this. We just might hold on . . .

I've been following West Ham for 35 years, and it's difficult to believe how nervous I am. The cup finals of 1975 and 1980 were tense but there was the glory of having reached Wembley, whatever the result. They were nothing like this: where the very solvency of a club depends on one match. No game should be this important. If I'm honest, then league tables are a much fairer way of deciding promotion.

But, as ever, it's that John Cleese quote in *Clockwise* that applies: 'It's not the despair I can't take, it's the hope.' West Ham have perfected the art of agonising expectation; we've scrambled into sixth place, thrown away a two-goal lead at home to Ipswich and then played superbly to win the second leg. Now we are one game away from the Premiership. Only now everyone is saying that Preston's young boss Billy Davies is the next David Moyes, and, of course, their assistant manager is David 'Ned' Kelly, the legendary former West Ham striker who couldn't stand up for falling down. So they are certain to beat us.

It's been a long day. We set out at seven from Nigel's new house in Kew Gardens, where he lives with his wife Carolyn. I'd stayed overnight; it's a quiet suburban home with no sign of his much talked about Deep Purple memorabilia, bar a cutting about Ian Gillan on his kitchen noticeboard. Judging by his penchant for heavy metal (he still gets very excited seeing Iron Maiden's Steve Harris entering the East Stand), I'd expected something more like Ozzy Osbourne's gaff, with black-painted rooms and crucifixes on every door. He's already warned us that he wants to make a swiftish getaway from Cardiff to watch Swedish axe hero Yngwie Malmsteen (who?) live at the Hammersmith Apollo.

We've made a collective decision that after last year's debacle in Cardiff our routine has to be different in every way. Last May, I went by train and stayed overnight with my pal Sean who lives in Cardiff. This year, it's going to be a one-day car journey, assuming Nigel has kept up his RAC payments in the event of a calamitous breakdown on the M4. My mate Denis Campbell (DC) is taking the train instead of driving like last year. Matt and Lisa are staying overnight in Bristol, but most definitely not Newport, where they stayed last May. Not that any of us are superstitious.

Forget Liverpool coming back from three goals down to win the European Cup final last Wednesday. This is the game that matters. In the car we're careful to qualify all questions with both Premiership and Coca-Cola Championship answers. Nigel asks what new grounds we'd like to visit in both leagues, and I opt for Sunderland in the Premiership and a trip to Hull and back in the fizzy pop league. Although soon we're agreeing that Harewood has to play better this time, and in two years' time we'll be in the Champions League. Providing we don't freeze again. Last year we had more freezers than Iceland.

'At least we can go to the play-off final at Wembley next year,' suggests Fraser hopefully. We pass numerous vehicles with Hammers scarves trailing from the windows: white vans, stretch limos and bizarrely, a fire engine full of Hammers-supporting firemen still in uniform. You can imagine some house in Essex being engulfed by flames as the emergency services operator says, 'Well, caller, we can make it any time after five o'clock; no, better make that six in case it goes to penalties.'

After last season's tales of gridlock, we speed along the M4, pay our toll at the Severn Bridge and find ourselves parked in Cardiff by 10.15 a.m. Nigel even has time to show us his old student house in Cardiff, where Hugh the Judas Priest fan lived downstairs. We pass the flag-sellers and enter Starbucks for coffee and a late breakfast, surrounded by other weary Hammers fans. Then it's down to the Millennium Stadium to buy programmes (including one for my daughter Lola's former class teacher and top Hammers fan Nikki Denton) and join a huge queue for a cashpoint. In the Preston section of town, the white-shirted legions are already drinking pints of beer at 11 a.m.

An hour later, we've tracked down Matt and Lisa at another café, along with Dave from the *FT*, whose boss, Ed, used to be my next-door neighbour, along with his wife and three kids, complete with home-made Trevor Brooking badges. 'They've sold out of programmes already,' I tell Matt. 'They only printed 30,000,' adds Nigel. Matt is a man who fell into deep existential despair after failing to get a programme at Wigan last season. He thinks games don't count unless you get a programme, and, sadly, I quite agree with him. Matt was only saved by Lisa, his amazingly football-tolerant girlfriend, writing to Wigan FC and obtaining the missing programme for his birthday. It must be love. Nigel remarks that Matt thinks we're joking about the programmes being sold out but that 5 per cent doubt factor will ruin the rest of his morning.

Matt's also still waiting for his ticket, which is with DC, who's had the clever idea of taking a train to Bristol and catching the connecting service. Only he has now discovered that the connecting service is a two-carriage Trumpton railway service with several thousand fans trying to board. Matt is an anxious man.

We set off in search of a pub. It's a testament to the devotion of the Hammers' fans that anyone has turned up at all after last year's disastrous day in Cardiff. Yet here we are with another discordant carnival. Klaxons blare everywhere. Play-off final flags are waving. Bouncers bar the way to pubs already full of Hammers fans. An entrepreneurial local is selling cans of Stella at £2 a go, and the empties are stacked on every window ledge.

There are numerous choruses of 'Bubbles' and glottal-stop-free versions of 'Oh, Mattie Mattie, Mattie Mattie Mattie Mattie Etherington!' One group of fans are parading giant cut-out heads of Hammers legends on sticks, looking like refugees from a footballing version of *Vic Reeves' Big Night Out*. They chant 'We've got Paolo Di Canio on a stick!' to the tune of 'He's Got the Whole World in His Hands'. There's Trevor Brooking, Bobby Moore and Julian Dicks on a stick, too. A tray of ten tequilas is being carried outside to the men with sticks, salt and lemon at the ready. Surely not the wisest choice of pre-match drink. Still, maybe it's isotonic tequila.

They lurch into a drunken chorus of 'My name is Miklosko, I come from near Moscow!' which, although a nice tribute to our goalkeeping coach, is perhaps a little inexact geographically, in that he was born in Ostrava in what was then Czechoslovakia.

Last year's choice of pre-match pub is closed. Everywhere else is barred by bouncers wearing black polo shirts. It's estimated each game at the Millennium Stadium is worth £15 million to the city, and the West Ham fans are nobly attempting to up that total through extreme alcohol consumption. But my group are too nervous to drink. So we head to Harley's Café in the Royal Court arcade, the very same place we had lunch last year. This breaks our new rule of not doing anything we did last year, but it's too late now.

DC is here at last and hands over Matt's ticket before retreating to join some prawn sandwich-eating FA types. He's managed to find Matt an extra ticket, so Lisa is going to sit with us while Matt will watch the game on his own. He figures that in moments of acute despair she may need familiar figures around her. Big Joe leaves a message but is lost in the ether of mobile land. It's hard to eat my cheese salad roll. It's wrong that £25 million should depend on any game. It's wrong that the season should go on forever, that Ipswich, who finished 13 points above us in third place, don't go up automatically. But right now we don't care about natural justice or being able to plan summer holidays. I thought we'd lose at Portman Road. But something that smelt like team spirit was discovered that night. And now I've told Tom Watt on Radio London that Bobby Zamora will score again. If not, Hayden Mullins with a 30-yard screamer. For this game could mean escape from Crewe Alexandra. No disrespect to Crewe, as they say.

At two o'clock we head for the ground, past the cinema complex, where it's tempting to escape the tension and watch *Star Wars* instead. Up five flights of stairs, past a heaving mass of lager-drinking 'Bubbles' singers and up towards the light to test our seats. Fraser, the man who finally managed to get through to Ticketmaster, has done well. We're in the front row of the Upper Tier, just to the left of the goal.

We retreat back to the bar for a lager to help ease our nerves and then return to our seats to watch the players in bibs playing keep ball and running past cones. Numerous banners are hanging from the front of our tier. We're next to a huge Cross of St George flag with 'Stratford

Hammers' on it. Luckily Nigel hasn't brought his 'Kew Gardens' Hammers banner, as, frankly, it doesn't sound half as hard as Ilford or Basildon Hammers. One of the best banners, in a *Carry On* kind of way, reads 'Mattie Etherington lays on more balls than Abi Titmuss'. There's 'Look out, Mourinho, Hammers "R" coming' and of course the traditional 'Brown Out'. When you see 35,000 West Ham United fans together, you suddenly realise the potential of this club.

'Welcome to the biggest game in football!' booms the PA, just to ease our nerves. Pardew has opted to play Newton instead of Fletcher, who had a good game in the semi-final at Portman Road, perhaps feeling that the side need greater width on the wide pitch today. Sergei Rebrov, the one-time £11 million striker, has not even made the bench.

Hammers' matchday announcer Jeremy Nicholas has been recruited to help in the pre-match frolics. I almost expect him to announce suddenly, 'We go above Sheffield United! We go above Watford! We're sixth!' But, instead, he plays the 1975 Cup final squad's recording of 'I'm Forever Blowing Bubbles'. The swathes of Hammers fans stand arms aloft, hollering those wistful words about the nature of failure, and it's a moment when throats constrict, hearts quiver and all your sensations tingle.

The Preston DJ responds with a recording of 'Pigbag', which the black-and-white sections bounce about a little to, but it reassures all us Hammers fans that Preston don't have a proper song.

The teams emerge into the Cardiff sunlight, Preston led by their legendary winger Tom Finney. It's a fine gesture by West Ham to agree to this, although Nigel would have liked to see a reciprocal arrangement with West Ham led out by the immortal Steve Potts.

'God Save The Queen' is played, although sadly not the Sex Pistols' version. The teams are presented to Charlotte Oades, the president of Coca-Cola Great Britain (who?) and then they're at the centre circle. Come on, you Irons. We can do this. We can do this.

Preston kick off but West Ham soon gain possession. Etherington immediately runs at the Preston defence and gains a free-kick. He'll be sold if we don't go up and is certainly capable of playing in the Premiership and even for England on the left. But throughout the play-off games, Mattie has played like he wants to get into the Premiership with us. From a Chris Powell cross, Preston keeper Carlo Nash is forced to produce a flying punch to clear the ball. We look much more purposeful than last year. Like we've come to do a job. Like we know this game has to be fought for.

Then Zamora, looking quick and mobile, lays the ball off to Shaun Newton, who runs at the heart of the Preston defence, waits a second then plays a cleverly weighted pass behind the defence to, unbelievably, Tomas Repka. Having played like an overlapping Brazilian full-back at Ipswich, here he is again. Just yards from the Preston goal, shooting and . . . HITS THE POST!

In what is likely to be his last game for the Hammers, Repka has nearly scored his first ever goal. Maybe he should have. But we continue to press. Zamora has a penalty appeal turned down. Eddie Lewis takes some of the pressure off Preston with several good runs, then a clever free-kick routine with a stepover by Nugent ends with Cresswell firing across the box. Hayden Mullins escapes with a booking after motioning with his head at the abrasive Brian O'Neill. But back come the Hammers. It's encouraging that Elliott Ward is showing no sign of nerves and is winning most long balls in the air, while Anton Ferdinand is a diligent sweeper beside him.

Harewood is wrongly adjudged to be offside when through on goal. Then Harewood flicks on, Zamora controls on his chest, runs across the area and plays in Mattie Etherington, whose fierce shot is parried away by Nash. Nigel Reo-Coker, who is dominating midfield and finally looking like the future England player he's meant to be, plays a great ball through to Zamora, who is dispossessed by Claude Davis, wins the ball back and is about to shoot before being stopped by a fine saving tackle from Davis again.

Half-time arrives and we've had the best two chances of the match so far. 'That wasn't bad!' say disbelieving voices within the mêlée in the gents. Bizarrely, there are no urinals, just cubicles. After a day of alcoholic indulgence, relief is being sought wherever it can be found. Like a gentleman, I queue for the proper porcelain. But, believe me, it's probably best not to wash your hands in the sinks at the Millennium Stadium after a play-off final.

The tension is even worse for the second half. There are the disjointed sounds of horns everywhere, but it's difficult to get a collective song together. Every fan is concentrating on the pitch. Early in the second half, Ward concedes a corner and from it Cresswell's header seems destined for the net, only to be cleared off the line by Shaun Newton. There are collective 'oohs' as the agony continues.

West Ham surge forward again. Reo-Coker plays in Harewood, running on goal, who chips Nash, but the goalkeeper produces a great one-handed save, only for the ball to fall to Zamora, who produces a left-foot half-volley that is heading for the net until, bloody hell, Mawene clears off the line, and now it's come out to Harewood, who does well to turn and volley but it's saved by the goalkeeper again. Sod it!

'What do we have to do to score?' pleads Nigel. My body feels drained after that triple save. If Amnesty International knew about the metaphorical electric shock treatment we were enduring, imprisoned without trial in the Coca-Cola Championship, they would be asking their members to write to the Premier League, pleading for our release from this cruel and unusual punishment. You'd find leaflets with our photos on falling out of your copy of the *Sunday Times* with a request to 'please write to the president of Coca-Cola'.

Teddy Sheringham is warming up on the touchline. Is it time to introduce his experience and guile? Then Harewood flicks the ball on with his head, Zamora cushions the ball and plays a neat pass out to the onrushing Matthew Etherington on the wing. Bobby is running into the box for the return, Etherington heads for the byline and crosses, Preston's Claude Davis slips, the ball comes to Zamora, who connects with a cushioned left-foot volley and IT'S ZAMORA!

There's an explosion of joy and relief from the West Ham fans in front of him. My feet leave the floor, and I'm punching the air like everyone else. Bobby disappears somewhere underneath the warming-up West Ham substitutes and then the rest of the side. The fan behind me is looking for his mobile phone, which he's dropped somewhere under the seats. It's Zamora's fourth goal in three Premiership play-off games. We've scored in the play-off final, which is more than we achieved last year. Could this be it? Could we be returning to the Premiership?

Various versions of 'Bubbles' emerge from different sections of the fans. Huge chants of 'Come on you Irons!' emanate from West Ham's half of the stadium. Then Zamora puts a free header over the bar. That could have settled it. Preston's David Nugent breaks well but fires straight into Jimmy Walker. Cresswell controls the ball on his thigh and volleys wide. A Harewood header skims wide of Preston's goal.

Then Pardew makes a substitution, and it's bizarre. Zamora is coming off to be replaced by Christian Dailly. None of us can understand this, as Zamora has been our best forward. It's a safety-first move that will surely lead to us sitting back and Preston equalising. It seems that Pards is repeating the mistake of last season's final when he took off all our forwards, Connolly, Zamora and Harewood, leaving Deane and Hutchison up front, the slowest forward line in history. Pardew is later to say that Zamora's calves tend to cramp up late in games because of the extra pressure on him as a West Ham fan. Blimey, we're West Ham fans, too. And our bodies must be suffering from enough mystery stress-induced ailments to keep the alternative therapy gurus employed for decades.

But at least it's Christian Dailly, our cult hero, even if you wouldn't necessarily want £25 million resting on his performance as a midfield dynamo. Nigel and myself start up a chorus of 'Christian Dailly football genius!' but, surprisingly, no one else joins in.

Dailly does make several interceptions in midfield, bolstering the bodies alongside Mullins and Reo-Coker. Preston sub Patrick Agyemang wins a corner, but Cresswell's header is gathered by Walker. Then, with less than ten minutes left, Nash produces a long kick upfield. Walker, dominating his area in a way that Stephen Bywater failed to do earlier in the season, races to the edge of the box to take the catch but is dangerously close to the edge of the box. Attempting to pull himself inside the line, he falls very awkwardly on his right leg and, in doing so, drags the ball outside the box. He's down for ever. Then comes the orange stretcher, and he's being carried off. The prone Walker is yellow carded and Preston are awarded a free-kick in a central position on the edge of the penalty area. On comes substitute keeper Stephen Bywater, who hasn't played since 18 March. What a test for the young goalkeeper. This is more than anyone can take.

And then Bywater saves McKenna's free kick, and we all dare to believe again. Lisa, who has been sucked into the maelstrom of emotion that is being a West Ham fan thanks to Matt, is one mass of jumps, screams and yelps, apparently now mainlining on the Hammers. Up comes the board. Seven minutes of injury time. Seven minutes? That's half a game. That's half a century. That's half a footballing millennium.

Preston press on. Ward makes a desperate clearance from his six-yard line. There are choruses of 'Bubbles' and desperate whistles from the Hammers end. It's one of those moments when your facial muscles appear to collapse, the eyes go moist, the heart palpitates. It doesn't matter, of course, not compared with climate change, terrorism, death in Africa, war in Iraq and the search for world peace. But at this moment it does. I'm thinking of my daughter Lola, whose school is opposite Arsenal's new ground. Will I at last be able to tell her that West Ham are at least in the same league as Arsenal? Will I be able to take my younger daughter Nell to Premiership fixtures?

I'm thinking of relegation at Birmingham, when the home fans tried to kick our heads in just to make it a little easier. Of sitting in Pontcanna Fields by the River Taff unable to move after losing the play-off final to Palace last year. The pain of seeing six ex-West Ham players – Frank Lampard, Rio Ferdinand, Joe Cole, Jermain Defoe, Michael Carrick and Glen Johnson – playing for England. Watching us lose away at Rotherham and Gillingham. The reported £30 million-plus debt that if we don't go up will necessitate yet more sales. The people who said I should never renew my season ticket . . .

I've put so much emotional investment into this season, seeing West Ham play Burnley, Rotherham, Ipswich, Notts County, Wolves, QPR away, Stoke, Plymouth away, QPR, Brighton, Watford, Leeds, Notts Forest, Sheffield United, Norwich, Derby, Sheffield United, Cardiff, Plymouth, Preston, Crewe, Leicester, Coventry, Sunderland, Watford away and Ipswich home and away. Reo-Coker makes a break and Mark Noble, on for Newton, is clear in front of the Preston goal and chips agonisingly wide, when really he should have scored. Come on! Nigel and Fraser are looking ill, while Lisa, who is close to emotional collapse, is screaming and pleading. Preston have a throw-in on the left but attempt to play a one–two and simply put the ball into touch when they should have launched it into the box. Repka is taking the throw-in, the ball goes to Etherington and suddenly he's running with his arms in the air and YEEEESSSSS!

Thirty-five thousand East Enders explode with joy and relief. Sod bloody Liverpool! People are hugging and leaping and punching the air. Yes, yes, yes, yes! I'm shaking hands with the man behind me, whom I've never met before. And some people are on the pitch . . . Alan Pardew, the man who's seemingly been one game from the sack all season, is leaping on top of a group of players, the subs are all running on as the squad embraces and there's mayhem everywhere.

'Promoted to the Premiership are West Ham United!' booms the PA, except we can hardly hear it. Next to me, amid all the hysteria and euphoria, Fraser is sitting down smoking a cigar as if auditioning for a Hamlet advert. If we'd known he had that cigar this morning, we would have instantly confiscated it for outrageous tempting of providence.

'WE GET TEN PAGES ON TELETEXT!' I'm shouting dementedly at Nigel. No more messing around on 412 for Coca-Cola Championship news. Our own Premiership club section with ten pages of Hammers news and outrageously priced phone-line offers! Football really has come home in my living room. Being on *Match of the Day* again and not having to trawl through *Sky Sports News* looking for goal highlights! Parachute payments! Having our defence lambasted by Alan Hansen! Not playing 46 games! A season that ends when it's supposed to and not having to explain to Her Indoors that actually it now goes on until 30 May!

Tom Finney! Billy Davies! Richard Cresswell! And, erm, anyone ever connected with Preston . . . WE GAVE YOUR BOYS ONE HELL OF A BEATING!

It's Crewe no more! Brighton and Lewes no more! Friday Sky no more! Hull no more! Burnley no more! Preston no more! Millwall no more! When you go, will you send back a letter from the Championship? No longer do we have to roam this league to prove how much it hurts.

Marlon Harewood is sitting on the turf, punching the air. Mark Noble – who really is a West Ham fan, unlike the majority of new signings who claim to be one – has his shirt on backwards for some reason; Bobby Zamora, another West Ham fan, is deliriously punching the air; Elliott Ward is draped in a flag and looking more like a Billy Bonds/Tommy Taylor era '70s player than ever; Anton Ferdinand is dancing and doing the shuffle he perfected after scoring at Watford – these young players look like they still want to play for West Ham. Sod bloody Defoe, Cole, Carrick and the rest. They got us relegated. Now we've a new generation coming through and we have to keep them. In the Premiership! And they've won something with West Ham!

As if to emphasise the togetherness of the squad, Jimmy Walker is back on the pitch being carried by Stephen Bywater and Ludek Miklosko. The PA is playing 'Is This the Way to Amarillo?', which, unless Amarillo FC are in the Premiership, has nothing to do with West Ham, but we bounce along to it anyway. But sha-la-la-la-la-la-la hey!

Then it's 'I'm Forever Blowing Bubbles' again, and for once, our dreams haven't faded and died. I try to phone my partner, Nicola, but can't hear anything and leave a message telling her that West Ham are in the Premiership.

And now the players are gathered around the podium on the halfway line. Mattie Etherington is wearing a West Ham flag sarong-style around his waist. Chris Powell is wearing a '70s-style West Ham scarf around his neck. Etherington rushes up to the play-off winners' trophy and kisses it. It's only about a foot high and looks like something Coca-Cola bought on Saturday night from some cheap jewellery store in Cardiff, but it's a trophy nonetheless. All the West Ham players are wearing winner's medals around their necks. I'm sorry I'll just write that again. The West Ham players are wearing winner's medals around their necks! We don't need the PA system; a proper chorus of 'Bubbles' comes unaided from the fans.

Some woman no one recognises is holding the trophy, about to present it. She hands it to our young captain Nigel Reo-Coker and club captain Christian Dailly. Dailly, who has been injured all season, whose father has recently died of cancer, who might not be a Rio Ferdinand but always gives everything he has and says he wants to play for us whatever division we're in.

And now Nigel and Christian are hoisting up the cup. There's a roar that knocks the Millennium Stadium's retractable roof somewhere towards Swansea and a cascade of claret and blue streamers shoot into the air. And the West Ham players are lifting a trophy! I've waited 24 years for this. If we forget about the Inter-Toto Cup win when I was on holiday in the Lake District for the away leg, and anyway it was in France, then this is the first time I've seen a West Ham captain lift any sort of trophy since Billy Bonds collected the FA Cup in 1980 followed by the then Second Division championship in 1981.

The players perform another lap of honour and the obligatory team dive. The PA plays 'It's Zamora', the tribute record to Bobby from Mark Adams, the star of the Dean Martin musical *The Rat Pack: Live From Las Vegas*. Eventually, we retreat from the stadium, satiated and mentally exhausted. Acting most irrationally after the euphoria, I spend £7 on a play-off flag for daughters Lola and Nell.

I get through to Nicola, who's staying at her mum's. Amazingly, Nicola, who never listens to football on the radio ever, turned the radio on just as Zamora scored and listened to the rest of the game. Apparently, she seemed to believe that my mental health and emotional stability depended on this result. Four-year-old Nell is very intrigued by the injured West Ham goalkeeper. 'Did he die?' she asks. Thankfully, I'm able to reassure her that Jimmy Walker is still with us and was indeed carried onto the pitch at the end.

Nigel is keen to reach his car and complete his perfect day by being home in time to see Yngwie Malmsteen. In his eagerness, he takes us through hordes of disgruntled Preston fans outside pubs. 'Well done, lads. I wish you all the best,' says one polite Preston fan, proving that sportsmanship still exists in football. 'Bastards!' glowers another less Corinthian-spirited fan.

We make it to the car and find we have beaten most of the traffic back to London. There's a quick call to DC to see if he stayed for the final whistle or left early to catch the Silverlink, as is his usual Upton Park match habit. It seems he might have missed the end, as he's already in Newport. It's a joyous ride down the M4 accompanied by Radio 5 Live. It's huge fun listening to whinging Preston fans on the phone-in. 'I'm absolutely sick of West Ham fans phoning up and saying "We're back where we belong,"' moans one caller. 'They didn't win it, we lost it!'

'Those players on huge wages froze!' moans another. They seem to forget that players are also human beings, and can be affected by nerves and psychological pressures like all the rest of us.

It's been an incredibly un-West Ham-like end to the season. Snatching victory from potential disaster. How good it feels to be talking about buying players rather than selling them. We can now join the predators circling relegated or still-in-the-Championship clubs. Our wish list goes through Kelvin Davis, the Ipswich goalkeeper (assuming Walker is badly injured), Andy Johnson, Dean Ashton, Peter Crouch, Kevin Phillips, Phil Jagielka and many more. 'That Shevchenko isn't bad either,' suggests Fraser. In fact, it's obvious that with Man United now hugely in debt having just been bought by Malcolm Glazer, Arsenal spending £400 million on a new stadium and Roman Abramovich likely to tire of his plaything at Chelsea, the axis of supremacy is surely shifting towards West Ham as the dominant power in world football. And if it isn't, then at least we can wipe £10 million off the debt and rely on two years' parachute payments.

We glide into Hammersmith, Nigel parks up a back street and runs for the Apollo. He texts me to say he's got in a minute before the set starts. West Ham winning promotion and seeing Yngwie Malmsteen in one day. Nigel hasn't been so happy since he ticked Rotherham off his groundhopper's list.

Fraser and I retreat into The George for a couple of pints. Then it's the Tube home to an empty house, as Nicola, Lola and Nell are still at her mother's. First I change my answerphone message to, 'Order has been restored! West Ham are back in the Premiership!' over the 1975 cup final squad's recording of 'Bubbles'. Then I pour myself an Ardbeg single malt whisky and sit down to watch the highlights of the game first on *Sky Sports News* and then ITV. No more Andy Townsend or Gabriel Clarke and trying to remember to record *Soccer Sunday* at 10.30 a.m. next season. Zamora's goal looks just as sweet, while the TV replays bring home how horrific Jimmy Walker's fall was.

After the game, Pardew, who had lost previous play-off finals with both Reading and West Ham, tells the cameras, 'There's been a lot of doubters. In all honesty, a lot of people who should have known better have knocked me and the team. Today was about the players. You could see our unity on the pitch; the players come together as a team and that's the only way you're going to win in any league in the world. You've got to be together.'

He also neatly manages to summarise much of my Hammers-supporting life in one phrase when he reflects, 'Two years ago, all I heard was negative stuff. We're not playing this way or playing that way, he's not good enough, I'm not good enough, the chairman's not good enough. It was a cycle of misery, but we have broken the chain. And if we get the stadium positive, we can achieve things together.'

A cycle of misery. Maybe Morrissey was a secret West Ham supporter, too. But heaven knows I'm not miserable tonight. Pardew continues, 'This result is everything for me and our team. It gets our fans in buoyant mood, and we have gone a long way to justifying the fact that I am manager. There was a period when I felt things might have got away from us. I had doubts myself about whether we would make it. That is when you need your family and friends and people in the game, and, luckily, I have good people around me.'

Pardew is also keen to thank chairman Terence Brown: 'When the press kept saying that I was going to lose my job, he stayed solidly with me. He employed me, he headhunted me to come to this club, and it is a vindication for him, because he never gets any good press. He's not very good with the media, he doesn't like to say too much, the fans hammer him and some of the criticisms, to be fair to him, he's held his hands up to.'

We've all been critical of Brown and the board in the past, but the chairman made the right decision in not sacking Pardew after defeat at Reading left the Hammers floundering in mid-table. It was only right that he be given a full season to try to achieve promotion, and now West Ham are back after losing only one of the last thirteen games. Pardew was set a time frame of two years to gain promotion and he's done it.

And there indeed is Terry Brown, blinking in the unfamiliar light of publicity like some rare sighting made by Bill Oddie, being interviewed on the pitch. He claims that it wasn't a win-or-be-sacked game for Pardew: 'He had a plan for the Premiership and a plan for the Championship.' While hoping that Pards has shut the doubters up, he smiles wryly when asked if he's silenced his own doubters, commenting, 'It'll take more than this to shut them up.'

Preston manager Billy Davies gives a brave speech, saying he can't fault his players. He then sportingly congratulates West Ham on reaching the Premiership and says he hopes they enjoy themselves there.

There are more reflections from Pards: 'There were times when you have to keep yourself in check. Maybe the failures I've had have made me a better person. I like to think so. I'm not so exuberant. But I don't want to lose my confidence and my arrogance. José Mourinho has shown you need a bit of that. Hopefully, as I grow as a manager, I'll get that balance right.' Maybe Pards was the Special One all along.

We also see a lovely shot of Alan Pardew dancing on the pitch with his two young daughters and smiling at the fans. He can seem too dour and serious at times, and you just hope he'll be smiling a little more next season.

I also video the highlights and, after it's over, rewind and replay at full volume the moment when Reo-Coker and Dailly lift the cup. I play it again and again before lapsing into the contented sleep of the just promoted.

The next day, West Ham are on the front page of the *Mirror*, *The Guardian* and *The Times* and that evening there's a victory parade in an open-top bus down the Barking Road and on to the Boleyn Ground. On *Sky Sports News* a kid is interviewed who refused to go to Cardiff because he'd made a promise to his dying granddad. Instead he watched it at home beside his granddad's ashes.

An estimated 70,000 fans are on the streets and again you sense what this club still means in the ever-changing community of east London, Essex and way beyond. Mind you, this being West Ham, the microphone doesn't work when the players are finally on the balcony of the West Stand. Pards manages to shout, 'We've come out of the darkness and into the light of the Premiership,' before the system goes down and we hear someone saying, 'Put on the CD!' But it doesn't matter; all you can hear are the fans and the horns and the choruses of 'Bubbles'. We're back where we belong.

TOP TEN WEST HAM-SUPPORTING WEST HAM PLAYERS

- BOBBY ZAMORA: Loves the Hammers so much that the pressure of playing for them gives him tight hamstrings.
- TEDDY SHERINGHAM: Stood on the North Bank watching Billy Jennings and was still dreaming of the Hammers even when winning the Treble for Manchester United.
- IAIN DOWIE: The Mr Incredible lookalike grew up as a Hammers fan; sadly, that didn't stop him coaching Palace to play-off victory.
- CHRIS POWELL'S DAD: Chris Powell's dad was always a Hammers fan, which made young Chris feel he was finally coming home when he signed for the Hammers.
- SERGEI REBROV: Ignored Dynamo Kiev to always look out for West Ham's results while growing up in Ukraine. Allegedly.
- MARK NOBLE: His whole family are West Ham supporters, and he still plays like he's one, too.
- ROBERT LEE: Finally made it to Upton Park at 37. We should have signed him ten years earlier. Despite endless media

mentions of him wanting to play for his beloved West Ham, we dithered while Keegan moved in.

- TONY COTTEE: Loves the club so much he apparently tried to buy it. Still keeps a scrapbook of all his goals. And probably his Soccer Stars stickers, too.
- STEVE WHITTON: Grew up in East Ham and was enticed back to his home club by John Lyall. The prodigal winger returned and was, erm, not really very good.
- PAUL KONCHESKY: Dagenham lad who stood on the North Bank as a boy and idolised Julian Dicks.

2

SIDEBURNS AND SINNERS

1970–74
Bill Remfry discovers 'rock' music . . . Trevor Brooking grows his sideburns . . . Hammer ponders the problems of beating custodians behind 'tight defensive structures' . . . Bryan 'Pop' Robson can't stop scoring . . . Billy Bonds gets piratical and is one of only two things that won't ever let you down.
    Price of Hammer *in 1974: 5p*

My first West Ham game was against Blackpool on 31 October 1970. It was a different era, when teams like Blackpool were in what would now be called the Premiership. There was a brass band on the pitch before the kick-off that day, which my dad liked because it wasn't this new-fangled pop music.

At the back of *Hammer*, the West Ham programme, was a column by Hammers DJ Bill Remfry in which he referred to Rod Stewart as having 'been around for quite a time in the "rock" world': it was a time when the word 'rock' had to be placed in inverted commas. Bill Remfry also thanked Miss E. Baker and Miss M. Weston of Camberwell, who had written some words to be sung to the tune of 'The British Grenadiers'. He published the lyrics for the fans to sing, which went:

Some talk of Derby County,
And some of Coventry,
Of Spurs, Arsenal and Southampton,
Of West Brom and Chelsea,
But of all the world's greatest soccer teams,
With all their cups and glamours,
With Bobby as their captain,
The best are called the Hammers.

It was a time when two generations were colliding: those who'd lived through the war and their children, who were into rock music, sideburns, crops and Dr. Martens boots. Strangely enough, a song about West Ham's 'glamours', sung to the tune of 'The British Grenadiers' didn't prove too popular with the skinheads on the North Bank, who preferred 'Oh, we don't give a widdle and we don't give a wank, we are the West Ham North Bank!'

I wasn't a West Ham fan as yet. At the age of 11, I'd decided to follow the other boys at school and take an interest in football. The 1970 World Cup finals had been on television that summer, and I wanted more. My dad, a tenant dairy farmer in Great Warley, Essex, who liked beer, Beethoven and lodge meetings, but had no previous interest in football, dutifully started taking me to matches.

At first, we were promiscuous football followers. I'd started off liking Manchester United because they had George Best but, slowly, the lure of a local team took hold. The very first game we'd attended was Stoke v. Ipswich while visiting my aunt Audrey and uncle Arthur in the Potteries. It was a 0–0 draw, but being a sad anorak, I've kept the programme from every game I've attended ever since. There's an interestingly dated advert from the National Coal Board in that Stoke City programme offering 'unrivalled prospects in mining and the other branches of engineering'. At least until Arthur met Maggie.

Next, we tried Arsenal v. Nottingham Forest and Tottenham v. Liverpool and then made our first visit to the Upper West Stand at Upton Park. John McDowell was making his debut at right-back for West Ham. Tony Green had put Blackpool ahead, but West Ham won 2–1 with goals from Jimmy Greaves and Peter Eustace (whose name lent itself, I noted, to endless shouts of 'Useless Eustace!'). It was the pace of those early games that struck me: how hard you had to concentrate to remember who crossed for a goal. Plus the smell of football: embrocation on the players' legs and fried onions from the burger stalls on Green Street.

Fittingly, in view of the many struggles to come in a lifetime of supporting West Ham, that season was all relegation battles and dodgy signings. The club was third from bottom of Division One (although back then only the bottom two went down, Burnley and Blackpool being the unlucky ones that term). West Ham had also just sold World Cup-winning star Martin Peters to Spurs and received Jimmy Greaves in exchange. Spurs had got a player who was, to quote manager Ron Greenwood, 'ten years ahead of his time'; we'd got a player who was ten minutes beyond closing time. Although Greavsie scored the winner that day, he was, unbeknown to this 11 year old and 26,238 other fans watching him, also an alcoholic and set to call time on his career at the end of the season.

As was to become the pattern, that West Ham side seemed too good to be struggling. It was an old cliché that, under purist manager Ron Greenwood, West Ham 'won friends and lost matches'. Bobby Moore was still captaining the side after winning respect from Pelé for his superb performance against Brazil in the 1970 World Cup and remaining magnificently unruffled after being wrongly nicked for stealing a bracelet from Ratner's of Bogotá; a young centre-half with fine sideburns and ruffled blond hair called Tommy Taylor had just been recruited from Leyton Orient; and 1966 World Cup hat-trick hero Geoff Hurst was up front alongside Greavsie.

Looking at that first programme, it's also interesting to note that back in 1970 people were saying that football had lost its soul. *Hammer* reproduced a page and a half of press comment, and in the *Daily Telegraph* Donald Saunders moaned:

> League football seems so determined to tear its tattered image to shreds that with a third of the programme completed, good games are almost as rare as tax cuts and bitter controversy has developed into a weekly occurrence.
>
> During the past month, those who have a high regard for English soccer must have become reluctant to pick up their newspapers or even tune in to local radio. Occasional controversy probably

stimulates interesting soccer. An atmosphere of constant strife could provoke public disgust.

During that season, my dad and I made further visits to home games against Crystal Palace (0–0) and Manchester United (2–1), which would confirm West Ham's perpetual ability to raise their game to the standard of the opposition. West Ham beat a side containing Denis Law, George Best and Bobby Charlton. The goals came from Geoff Hurst and Bryan Robson, a new forward signed from Newcastle, who was a superb finisher. In another era, Robson might have been an England regular. George Best scored for United.

West Ham goalkeeper Bobby Ferguson saved a penalty that day, but even that fine save couldn't completely erase the image of West Ham being a club that was principled to the point of folly. For in 1967, Ron Greenwood was given the opportunity to sign the best goalkeeper in the world, Gordon Banks. However, he had a gentleman's agreement with Kilmarnock that he was going to purchase Ferguson, so Greenwood signed the young Scot instead. Ferguson had some good games for West Ham and possessed a prodigious goalkick that my dad and I would view from behind the North Bank goal, but he was only an average Division One custodian (as *Hammer* insisted on calling all goalkeepers), and we could have had the best.

My fourth trip to West Ham was the final home match of the 1970–71 season against Huddersfield. The comments in *Hammer* could have applied to numerous seasons yet to come. 'It would be no understatement of fact to say that in many respects we are heartily pleased that today's match is the last of the 1970–71 league season,' began the 'Hammer's View' page in its peculiar Micawber-esque style. It continued:

> For the greater part of the last nine months we have been fighting a rearguard battle against relegation . . .
>
> In his report at last week's Annual General Meeting of the club, our Chairman stressed this point of tension, and emphasised the strains upon players, managers and administrators in modern-day football . . .
>
> During the current campaign, we have set a new 'all low' record by winning fewer games at home than in any of our previous 44

seasons of league football, and our away record in the past couple of campaigns contributed much to our low placing. Like many other clubs we have found it increasingly difficult to penetrate tight defensive structures, and our style of play had to be adjusted accordingly.

Quite what a 'tight defensive structure' was remains unclear but *Hammer* makes it sound something like the Maginot Line. In those early years, *Hammer* was probably my major reading matter, along with *Goal* and *Shoot*, and I was to grow to love its verbose style. Even in 1971 it appeared a little dated. Presumably, much of it was the work of editor John Helliar. Any event occurring after 45 minutes was 'after the resumption'. Words like 'axiom' and 'kudos' and complex treatises on the nature of success, were proffered to the perhaps not completely receptive denizens of the North Bank.

The following season, my dad and I would stand at the front of the North Bank, just to the left of the goal. Before matches, a man in a brown coat would wander through the North Bank muttering, 'Peanuts. Roasted peanuts.' After matches, the terraces were covered with shells from Percy Dalton's finest peanuts. Behind us was a dark, forbidding territory, where people sang rude songs and forward surges would occur whenever West Ham nearly scored. If West Ham scored, the police would wade up the gangways and eject at least ten youths, often holding them in painful-looking arm-locks. It was never clear what they'd done apart from being part of a crowd surge. In fact, the whole routine seemed to be a theatrical ploy accepted by both fans and police: the police could claim to be ejecting troublemakers, and the youths in arm-locks were made to look hard in front of their mates.

From the back of the cavernous terrace, a chant would go up of 'Harry Roberts is our friend, is our friend, is our friend, Harry Roberts is our friend, he kills coppers!' I didn't know who Harry Roberts was, but, in later years, I was to discover that in August 1966 he had participated in the infamous 'Braybrook Street Massacre' outside Wormwood Scrubs prison in which three unarmed policemen were shot dead. The case had caused national outrage. After 90 days hiding out in a wood near Bishop's Stortford and a huge manhunt, Roberts was arrested and found guilty of murder. He is still in prison today.

For a child living on a farm on the outskirts of London and attending school in middle-class Shenfield, it was a mysterious, enticing, urban world. It was a short drive from home to Upminster station and then either a fast train to Barking and two stops on the District Line to Upton Park, or the full Tube journey taking in Upminster Bridge, Hornchurch, Elm Park, Dagenham East, Dagenham Heathway, Becontree, Upney, Barking, East Ham and Upton Park.

There was something magical about those Tube trains: the way they felt warm in all weathers, the slow, sliding motion of the doors, the search for other supporters, the fact they could take you all the way to Fulham Broadway for an away game at Chelsea.

While queuing to go through the half-price turnstile for 'Boys/OAPS', I'd see policemen confiscating high-leg Dr. Martens with steel toecaps from skinheads. At the time, there was a chant of 'Tiptoe through the North Bank with your boots on, get your head kicked in!' But somehow the skins didn't look quite so hard in just red socks, braces and tight Levi's.

There were skinhead girls, too, with short cropped hair and wispy bits at the side. Some of the real hard lads wore white lab coats with the names of West Ham players written on the back in felt pen and had scarves tied around their wrists. The other occupants of the North Bank consisted of youths with sideburns and longish hair, who looked like potential members of Supertramp, older men in suits and ties and a few middle-aged women at the front with flasks and home-made scarves.

From behind the goal, it was easy to see that Bobby Moore was still an imperious presence in defence. His tackles were all about timing and anticipation. Even after a few lagers with Greavsie and the like, he still looked unruffled, rarely having to break his stride. He would mark one of the posts at corners, his sideburns showing only the merest hint of sweat.

Another crowd favourite was Harry Redknapp. Inspired by the Hare Krishna chants of the time, the North Bank never tired of chanting: 'We've got 'Arry 'Arry 'Arry Redknapp on the wing, on the wing, on the wing. We've got 'Arry 'Arry 'Arry Redknapp on the wing, on the wing – 'ARRY 'ARRY REDKNAPP, 'ARRY REDKNAPP ON THE WING!'

Harry was a local lad who could exhilarate the Chicken Run – otherwise known as the Lower East Stand – with his runs down the right flank, and, more importantly, his name scanned perfectly for the 'on the wing' song. However, he rarely scored and I can still recall one of his shots actually hitting the corner post. I also remember 'Arry racing 40 yards down the right wing once to cross for Geoff Hurst to score a great goal against Liverpool in the League Cup.

West Ham's fortunes improved a little in the 1971–72 'campaign', as *Hammer* would have called it. My dad and I became regulars, often accompanied by my school friend Nick Toms, a Man United fan. Upton Park was a compact ground, and with the fans so close to the pitch, it was easy to imagine yourself taking a corner or sending over a far-post cross. You could hear the calls of the players and sometimes even share jokes with them.

The obscene jukebox on the North Bank terrace was still providing illicit fascination, too. Here were adults using the 'f' word with enjoyable regularity. 'You're going to get your f***ing head kicked in!' would greet chants from opposition fans in the South Bank, while any sliced shot at our end was serenaded by 'He shot, he missed, he must be f***ing pissed! Number nine!'

That season, the side finished 14th but were never in serious danger of relegation. A young Bermudian forward called Clyde Best scored seventeen goals, plus six in the cups. My uncle Arthur in Stoke had watched Best on *Match of the Day* and picked him out as a great prospect. Best was big and skilful but, a little like Emile Heskey today, sometimes appeared too diffident and reluctant to use his strength.

West Ham were one of the first sides in the country to include black players like Best, Clive Charles and that season a new young striker called Ade Coker, who scored on his debut at Crystal Palace. Having seen Pelé and the great Brazil side in the 1970 World Cup on TV, I couldn't really understand why there was any novelty in having black players. But there were jokes in the school playground about hanging bananas on the crossbar, and you'd hear shouts from the fans of 'Go on Clyde, have him with your spear!' It's thanks to the bravery of those early black players like Clyde Best that such remarks seem so stupid and anachronistic today.

I started to realise that, although West Ham were floundering in the bottom half of the league, the home games were nearly always entertaining. That season saw a thrilling 3–3 draw at home to Brian Clough's Derby. Frank Lampard scored in that match with a great volley, the sort his son converts with disturbing regularity for Chelsea. Bryan Robson also scored with a fine effort, with Best involved in the build-up to both goals. Another 3–3 draw came at Southampton, only this time West Ham had been 3–0 up. On *Match of the Day*, Barry Davies' voice rose several octaves as the Saints completed their unlikely comeback and proved the old adage that 'goals are guaranteed at either end' whenever West Ham play.

A young number 10 called Trevor Brooking was emerging as the fulcrum of the team and in that 3–3 draw with Derby he scored a memorable goal. When Bobby Moore's cross was half cleared, Brooking picked up the ball on the edge of the box, shimmied past three Derby defenders and unleashed a curling shot into the far corner of the North Bank goal. He ran away with his arm in the air, muttering something like 'blooming marvellous' to himself. Brooking made football into art. He had impressive *Onedin Line* sideburns, too, which now that I was shaving I did my best to emulate. And he also lived in Shenfield. Some of my schoolmates claimed they had seen him in his garden washing his car.

Trevor had a way of simply dipping his shoulders and letting the ball run past him that invariably fooled opponents. He was two footed, and I read that he'd practised with his weaker foot against a wall for hours as a boy. So I did the same, booting the ball endlessly against a wall on our farmhouse, knowing that a career with West Ham would surely result. When he reached the byline Brooking could seemingly wrap either foot around the ball and whip over a telling cross. And he had such equanimity, never appearing to be unsettled by crude fouls. He was never booked. Off the pitch, he was unfailingly modest and polite. In short, he was class.

Billy Bonds was an inspirational ball winner in midfield and Bryan Robson was proving to be a top finisher. That season, my dad and I tried some away games, even travelling to Old Trafford on a football special to see George Best beat the great Bobby Moore before scoring a memorable goal in a 4–2 defeat. West Ham wore their away kit of light blue with claret hoops and countless fans now associate that kit with old footage of West Ham losing away. At home, though, the Hammers beat United 3–0, with goals from Robson, Best and a Hurst penalty in front of 41,892 fans. Footage of the match even featured later in an Alf Garnett film.

There was also an epic struggle in a League Cup semi-final against Stoke City that season. West Ham had won the away leg 2–1 at the Victoria Ground, with Clyde Best scoring a great winner after a run and cross by 'Arry Redknapp on the wing. West Ham had not won a trophy since the Cup-Winners' Cup in 1965, but now it seemed they were heading to Wembley again. At Upton Park, with Stoke winning 1–0, West Ham gained a late penalty when Gordon Banks hauled down Redknapp. If Geoff Hurst had scored, West Ham would almost certainly have been through. Geoff puffed out his cheeks, blasted the ball high and hard towards Banks' right and somehow the Stoke custodian managed to tip it over.

The game then went to two replays, this being before penalty shoot-outs or even substitute goalkeepers. I watched the second replay at Old Trafford late at night on my sitting-room TV. When Bobby Ferguson was injured, Bobby Moore had to take over as keeper. His first act was to save a Mike Bernard penalty, only for Bernard to fire home the rebound. Billy Bonds epitomised West Ham's spirit that night, scoring with a deflected shot after winning the ball through sheer determination and then setting up Brooking for a superb finish.

Only without a recognised goalkeeper did the tired Hammers eventually succumb to goals from Dobing and Conroy. Stoke had never won a major trophy before and at least it made Audrey and Arthur, my aunt and uncle in the Potteries, happy. They would proudly show me their 1972 League Cup winners' mug after Stoke went on to beat Chelsea in the final.

In 1972–73 West Ham had a great season, finishing sixth but, as was to become their habit even when successful, still managed to slightly frustrate their supporters by missing out on qualification for the UEFA Cup. (In fact, the administrators of all European competitions have spent years developing sophisticated rules to find ways of stopping West Ham getting into Europe: third in 1986, fifth in 1999 and still no qualification.)

When I was 13, I was allowed to go to midweek games, and when West Ham beat Coventry 1–0 early in the 1972–73 season, followed by a 5–2 thrashing of Leicester, it became apparent that we were in for a fine season. There was something romantic about Upton Park under the lights: the seething mass of humanity that seemed to speak with one voice, the drama, the mud, the heightened atmosphere. It probably helped that most fans had drunk several pints of Watney's Red Barrel beforehand, too. An illicit shandy with my dad in the Moby Dick off the

Eastern Avenue on the drive home after the game seemed the epitome of sophistication. Soon, football was to merge easily with adolescent beer-drinking opportunities.

Going to West Ham games became a satisfying routine. It meant missing *Doctor Who*, but we were home in time for steak and chips and later a glass of my mum's cider. While my young mind struggled with issues such as the likelihood of lunar colonies in 2001 and the strange sensations engendered by see-through dresses on the sleeves of Roxy Music albums, football presented certainty.

I stopped going with my dad and started attending with my mates instead, because at that age your parents seem to be about 900 years old and were certainly never young – ever. It was tough on my dad, but he kept going to his same spot on the North Bank and ended up as a season-ticket holder in the East Stand until he moved to Norfolk in 1986. Today, awkward male silences are still ended by discussion of West Ham results.

There were always games to look forward to, results, scorers, attendances and tables in *Hammer* to study. And there was something special about West Ham. We entertained. The club was owned by one family, the mysterious Cearns. And as Denis Fenton, a boy in my class who had a Tommy Taylor-style haircut, told me, 'West Ham don't sack managers.'

On Sundays, ITV's *The Big Match* would often feature the Hammers. So away defeats in hooped shirts at Midlands grounds accompanied by Hugh Johns' commentary became indelibly associated with my mum's roast beef, gravy, Yorkshire pudding, roast potatoes, peas and carrots. Brian Moore, whose voice would reach incendiary levels whenever West Ham scored, covered games at Upton Park. 'OHWHATAGOAL!' would greet even a three-times-deflected shot that trickled over the goal-line. It was hard to believe that Brian wasn't a West Ham supporter, although I later discovered that he was Gillingham's only celebrity fan. Occasionally, Moore would entice Ron Greenwood into the *Big Match* studios, where, like an avuncular old uncle, he would say something nobody really understood about angles and playing the ball into space.

Bryan Robson scored 28 goals that season, and Trevor Brooking still insists that he is the best finisher he has ever played with. Winger Dudley Tyler, who had starred for Hereford in the famous FA Cup upset against Newcastle United the previous season before his team were knocked out by West Ham in a replay, was then at Upton Park and for half a season was superb. Brooking was still great, and Bobby Moore responded to the improvement in his teammates. A long trip on the District Line was rewarded when I saw a stunning Moore goal at Stamford Bridge as West Ham won 3–1. Even Tommy Taylor managed to score that day.

But at the heart of West Ham was Billy 'Bonzo' Bonds. My mum sometimes referred to him as Billy Bones, or 'that one who sounds like a pirate'. So many newspaper reports used the word 'buccaneering' that he could have registered it as a trademark. Sporting huge sideburns and soon a beard, the hirsute number 4 looked like he'd been shipwrecked for a decade on a Pacific island and then immediately dressed in a claret and blue shirt. During that season, *Hammer* ran a back-page advert featuring a full-page picture of Billy Bonds looking like someone from an aftershave promotion: arms folded, chunky watch on his wrist, medallion dangling over his chest exposed through an unbuttoned '70s shirt with a huge collar. The copy read, 'There are only two things that never let you down, whatever the conditions, week in week out, season after season, especially when the going gets tough. The other's a Ford from Reynolds.'

It was all true. Bonzo was a huge man and the unofficial minder of the side – if Pat Holland or Trevor Brooking were ever manhandled, he would run across the pitch to grab the assailant by the collar – but his skill was often overlooked. He could pass and play one–twos with the rest of the soccer academy, had a great volley, was good in the air, scored goals and could play in defence or midfield. But it was his effort that really endeared him to the mainly blue-collar supporters. Often surrounded by 'Fancy Dans', he put in an honest day's work and performed to the same level every week, even in the grim outposts of the north where we invariably lost. Billy Bonds never gave up.

Yet off the field, Bonds was first to leave the ground after a game, carrying a pack of beer ready to spend a night with his family. He was so decent that in his autobiography, *Bonzo*, the one person he criticised was former striker Ted MacDougall, for being rude to waiters. He 'carried on as if waiters, receptionists and the like were just menial workers instead of ordinary, decent people doing a job', wrote Billy. His other great hobby was birdwatching. An unlikely twitcher, he could have been the next Bill Oddie with the right guidance.

After finishing sixth, West Ham provided proof of their eternal capriciousness by failing to win any of their first 11 games the next season. It was on 20 October 1974 that they eventually won 1–0 at Coventry thanks to a goal by John McDowell.

That season also saw much debate about hooliganism. In an early home game against QPR, *Hammer* quotes Len Shipman, president of the Football League, calling for the birch to be brought back. *Hammer* printed a picture of some 'Hammers Rule' graffiti found at a motorway service station in Berkshire, causing the programme to fulminate:

> The feeling still prevails that the highest authorities have yet to realise (as in so many instances) that the general public is fed up with the lawlessness that is eroding standards which were accepted as a matter of course before the days of the so-called 'permissive society'. The writing is truly upon the wall!
>
> Unfortunately it does not so far appear to have penetrated as far as the Solent or the Scilly Isles [presumably a cryptic reference to Prime Minister Harold Wilson]. When it does we may get some positive action!

Ted MacDougall, signed from Manchester United at the end of the previous season, was misfiring up front and annoying Billy Bonds. Mervyn Day had taken over from Bobby Ferguson and Ron Greenwood had predicted that he would be West Ham's goalkeeper for the next ten years. He wasn't and my early memories include many Day/Taylor mix-ups and Mervyn being lobbed from the halfway line against Everton. Undoubtedly talented, if erratic, he went the way of Kevin Lock, Alan Dickens, Stuart Slater and numerous other West Ham starlets over the years. Mervyn Day was eventually dispatched to Orient but did manage to revive his career at Leeds and then go into management assisting Alan Curbishley at Charlton.

For the early part of the 1973–74 season, my interest declined. Fatigued by adolescent angst, I missed several games, preferring to visit Mr Byrite and Romford Market or watch *Doctor Who*. But it left a gap, and on 8 December I returned to the West Stand to see West Ham's first home win of the season against Man City. Before the game, the Hammers were second from bottom, above Birmingham on goal difference. The hard-working striker Bobby Gould had just joined from Bristol City to try and provide some penetration up front, while Dudley Tyler had been sent back to Hereford, who would go on to knock the Hammers out of the FA Cup that season. Another new signing, Graham Paddon, had a good game in midfield and possessed a great left-foot shot. That midfield trio of Bonds, Brooking and Paddon was to prove one of the club's best.

Typically, West Ham then went unbeaten for the first ten games of 1974. On New Year's Day Paddon scored twice against his old club Norwich in a 4–1 home win. That day's *Hammer* kept referring to 'a national emergency'. No, it wasn't West Ham being crap but something called a miners' strike. Due to power shortages, the planned 7.30 p.m. kick-off had been brought forward. The following Saturday's FA Cup tie against Hereford kicked off at 1.45 p.m.

We then beat Man United 2–1 at Upton Park in front of 34,000. I watched the game from the North Bank with Paul Dennison, a classmate at school whose mum and dad in West Horndon had proper East End credentials. His mum remembered the Blitz, which we both agreed was a very boring thing to keep going on about as we played *Quadrophenia* by The Who.

'Look, it's the ICF [Inter City Firm] steaming in!' declared Paul, as we watched the flailing arms of psychopathic-looking geezers steaming into the Man United fans in the South Bank. We were safe in the home end and could treat it all as a spectator sport. Paul spoke knowingly of the Mile End mob. The mere mention of the name Mile End sounded hard. Back then, Man United fans were considered incredibly hard, rather than blokes working for TV companies living in Battersea, and this was a top-of-the-table bundle between rival firms.

''Allo, 'allo, West Ham aggro! West Ham aggro!' intoned the North Bank to the tune of Gary Glitter's 'Hello, Hello, I'm Back Again!', followed by 'Come and have a go if you think you're hard enough!' Billy Bonds scored with a great volley, McIlroy equalised and Patsy Holland headed the winner to bring a cascade of unfurling bog rolls on to the pitch in front of the North Bank.

In the first season of three clubs being relegated, West Ham continued their unlikely charge away from the bottom trio. Bobby Moore was injured and his replacement Mick McGiven, despite the questionable hairstyle of a ginger Afro, was in inspired form. There was an epic win against Everton, complete with Bob Latchford, the most expensive footballer in the country. West Ham were two goals down, then went ahead 3–2, were pulled back to 3–3 and then Billy Bonds scored the winner with five minutes to go. Bonds scored a hat-trick in the 3–0 demolition of Chelsea, while he scored his greatest ever volley in a 2–3 home defeat to Coventry.

We beat top-of-the-table Leeds, unbeaten for several millennia, or so it seemed, 3–1 at Upton Park. Bryan Robson scored one of the best headers I'd ever seen, the ball flashing into the top corner from the edge of the area. Then, in a crucial relegation fight, two goals from a revitalised Clyde Best helped West Ham win 4–1 against Southampton. In the final game of the season, West Ham drew 2–2 with Liverpool at Upton Park: Frank Lampard scored with another stupendous shot, and from Clyde Best's knock-down, Trevor Brooking hit home an exquisite curling shot. West Ham were every *Match of the Day* fan's second favourite team. In the final table, West Ham finished 18th, just beating the drop.

A pattern had been established. The Irons had gone from relegation certainties at Christmas to playing like a top-six club. They'd also managed to lose at Hereford in the FA Cup, causing a horde of small boys in anoraks to invade the pitch at the final whistle. The Irons even lost on penalties to Bristol Rovers in the Watney Cup (remember that?). West Ham were either dire or brilliant but always tried to play entertaining football, and no one could predict what would happen the following season.

TOP TEN HIRSUTE HAMMERS

- BILLY BONDS: Patented the pirate look with his buccaneering beard and flowing hair. Would have run 60 yards to grab Captain Bligh round the neck had he threatened Patsy Holland.
- DAVID CROSS: Psycho was always more psychotic when he had a full black beard. The clean-shaven era of punk and new wave meant nothing to him. His retro black beard scared defenders throughout the early 1980s.
- FRANK LAMPARD: A man who was truly inseparable from his beard. If only Frank Lampard Junior would also grow a beard he might develop into a player capable of running round corner posts instead of the lacklustre midfielder he is today.

- TREVOR MORLEY: Was that some form of large furry rodent on his upper lip? The General Kitchener of early '90s football. He came from up north, so perhaps such fashion crimes were understandable.

- KEITH ROBSON: Became even scarier when he grew a beard. He resembled a man marooned on a remote Pacific island for ten years after an air crash, whose sanity had slowly dissipated and who now lived on a diet of raw defenders.

- GRAHAM PADDON: Blond hair and trimmed beard made for a smoother hirsute combination alongside the unkempt Bonzo. Was possibly the fourth Bee Gee.

- ALAN DEVONSHIRE: A thin moustache completed the wartime spiv image. Probably passed on several pairs of nylons to Frank McAvennie to help his pulling power.

- PHIL PARKES: That moustache never altered, along with his shaggy-dog mane of blond collar-length hair, all held together with Cossack grooming products.

- NEIL ORR: Midfield ball winner in the 1985–86 season when West Ham finished third, Neil Orr had a thin ginger moustache that later helped him earn a role in *Shoestring*.

- JULIAN DICKS: Liked to accompany his shaved head with a trendy early-'90s goatee that made him look a little like Carlos in *Desperate Housewives*, but harder. He would have known where all the bodies were buried in Wisteria Lane.

3

TAYLOR MADE

1974–76
Jennings, Robson and Taylor save the season . . . taking the Arsenal
North Bank . . . Whippet Taylor races to Wembley glory . . . Brian
Moore says, 'Oh, a great goal!' a lot . . . Brooking batters Eintracht
Frankfurt . . . and the Hammers lose the Cup-Winners' Cup final to
Anderlecht . . . while failing to win any of their last 16 league
games.
  Price of Hammer *in 1975 and 1976: 10p*

'Oh, Wanky Wanky! Wanky Wanky Wanky Wanky Worthington!' An
unusual masturbatory homage to Leicester City's Frank Worthington was
emanating from the rear of the North Bank. Frank had just put Leicester
ahead, and the away fans were lustfully chorusing, 'Oh, Frankie Frankie,
Frankie Frankie Frankie Frankie Worthington!'

Worthington smiled at this much ruder tribute, made a 'who, me?'
gesture and won applause from his tormentors. Happy times. West Ham's
season really started in that match against Leicester in September 1974.
In the previous seven games we'd won just one. Bobby Moore was now at
Fulham, and a homesick Bryan Robson had opted to return to his native
North-east with Sunderland.

The season had started with a 0–4 reverse at Manchester City. Striker

Bobby Gould was yet to score and being barracked by some fans (which immediately made me want him to succeed). Ron Greenwood had moved upstairs to be general manager, and John Lyall was now team manager. Astonishingly, Greenwood had never had a contract, preferring to deal with the chairman 'Mr Pratt' on a basis of mutual trust. When Ron suggested the change the board simply said, according to Ron, 'Well, if you think that's what's best, we'll go that way.'

John Lyall had been Greenwood's assistant since giving up the game early because of injury, and was the only man in 1974 still sporting a quiff. West Ham were now running the club on Continental lines, some 25 years before Spurs thought of the same thing.

It looked bad again against Leicester, but then West Ham's season turned. General manager Ron Greenwood had instigated the signings of Billy Jennings from Watford and Keith Robson from Newcastle, both playing alongside Gould up front. Lampard played a one–two with Brooking and sped towards the North Bank end. From the byline he crossed and there was Bobby Gould, diving full length to head home. I remember him then standing arms aloft directly in front of me. There were no TV cameras to capture every game back then, but that was one image that remained burned into my memory.

It got better. Gould scored from another cross from the left, and the lively Jennings netted again before half-time. He scored again after the 'resumption' and goals from Bonds and Robson, a skilful and strong left-winger, put West Ham, incredibly, 6–1 ahead. Wanky Worthington pulled one back towards the end, but a truly memorable game ended with a 6–2 home win. Suddenly West Ham were unstoppable. Four days later the Hammers beat Birmingham 3–0 at Upton Park, and the following Saturday they beat Burnley 5–3. I could hardly believe James Alexander-Gordon as he read the result out on *Sports Report* that September afternoon. Keith Robson had scored twice, along with Bonds, Brooking and Jennings. That was 14 goals in a week.

We went on to go seven games unbeaten. By this time I was playing for the Shenfield School Second XI as a firm but fair centre-half, sometimes nicknamed 'Animal May' or 'Cruncher May' for my honest endeavours. I saw myself as Billy Bonds, but really wanted to be Trevor Brooking curling a shot into the corner of the net against Derby. It was only a tragic lack of skill that prevented me from being spotted by Lyall and

Greenwood. After playing for Shenfield School in the morning, I'd head off to Upton Park for matches, my knees still bloodied from the sharp flints that encrusted our school pitches.

Towards the end of October 1974 I travelled to Highbury, where the Hammers got stuffed 3–0, ending their fine run. My companion at the game was Paul Dennison, and it was my first close glimpse of football hooliganism. We went in the Arsenal North Bank because nobody seemed to bother segregating crowds then, and it was rumoured that West Ham were going to 'take' it. Indeed, a large contingent of West Ham fans were already singing 'Bubbles' in the middle of the North Bank.

Then half an hour before kick-off a gap opened in the crowd, there was the sort of silence you probably get before a tidal wave, and then we saw a line of Arsenal skins, one of whom was carrying a bicycle chain. These days they're probably all busy at book launches.

All I could feel was fear, and any prospective career as a writer of hoolie literature was over. The two crews steamed into each other, and I joined the surge forward from those trying to escape, probably joining a young Nick Hornby, who was thinking that if only he could get those nasty skins interested in books about making lists, one day football stadiums would be peaceful havens for the literary middle classes. 'Bloody animals!' shouted the harassed-looking copper in front of me.

The *Big Match* cameras were there to watch the next two home games, when West Ham beat Middlesbrough 3–0 and then thrashed Wolves 5–2. It was always special reliving the previous day's excitement after Sunday roasts.

It's all still there on my *Official History of West Ham* video. Featured are Keith Robson flicking home Gould's cross ('Oh, what a goal!'), Boam scoring an own goal and Paddon driving home a free-kick ('Oh, what a goal!') against Boro and the five against Wolves: Bonds' penalty, Brooking dinking home an airborne ball after Gould's knock-on, Jennings' tap-in after a great Brooking shot, Brooking flicking up a free-kick for Frank Lampard to volley home another stunner, causing three synchronised bog rolls to stream from the North Bank, and then Bobby Gould scoring against his old club and memorably rolling his eyes to the cameras. What I'm left wondering is did Brian Moore ever greet a goal by West Ham without saying either 'Oh, what a goal!', 'Oh, a lovely goal!' or 'Oh, a great goal!'?

From January, West Ham embarked on an FA Cup run. I'd got used to the Hammers always losing to rubbish lower-league sides; we'd even lost to Bobby Moore's Fulham in the League Cup. But that season we couldn't stop winning.

After a 2–1 victory away to Southampton in the third round we beat Swindon after a replay and then recovered from a goal down to beat QPR at Upton Park. Against Rangers, Holland headed in from Brooking's clever chip ('Oh, a great goal!' enthused Brian Moore), and then Keith Robson scored with a trademark header at the back post from Jennings' cross. Robson was a winger with the build of a striker. As well as a fine left foot he added a huge aerial threat to our otherwise diminutive attack. He was loved by the fans because he got stuck in, too.

In the sixth round, we were drawn away to Arsenal. Getting tickets necessitated queuing for a couple of hours outside West Ham's ticket office on a Sunday morning. No one seemed to mind. There was no Ticketmaster, no such thing as mobile phones, nor even credit cards. Legs and cash were what you needed. I'd queued outside the Finsbury Park Rainbow to get tickets to see Rod Stewart and The Faces and I'd queue again.

I was back in the Highbury North Bank but this time stayed sensibly closer to the front. It seems amazing now that football fans could just mingle at will. Occasionally, a copper might ask you who played left-back for Arsenal, but as I knew it was Bob McNab, there was no problem pretending to be a Gooner.

The pitch looked like a series of north London vegetable allotments, which had then been trampled on by a herd of cows. Even the dead donkey that died during the construction of the Arsenal North Bank and was buried beneath the foundations would have refused to perambulate on that sodden quagmire. Yet back then we asked footballers to perform on it.

West Ham had signed a young striker called Alan Taylor from Rochdale. He was nicknamed 'Whippet' because of his speed, footballers being a literal lot. He'd shown early promise and had already scored against Burnley and Birmingham in the league.

Highbury was full of fervent fans who created, as Motty might have said, a real cup-tie atmosphere. The pitch played a huge part in West Ham's opening goal. After Robson poked it on, the ball stopped dead in the mud of the penalty area leaving Arsenal keeper Jimmy Rimmer nowhere. It was like playing pinball in glue. Rimmer recovered to smother Robson's effort, but the ball broke to Paddon on the left who crossed to Alan Taylor at the back post, and the young striker tapped home from one yard out – causing a huge surge from the West Ham fans in the North Bank, there only being about one crash barrier per end in those days.

Later in the first half, Mervyn Day made a great save to tip a John Matthews shot around the post. West Ham were then incredibly lucky. Bonds' back pass stuck in the mud and Arsenal were denied the clearest penalty ever seen when Day practically cut a Gooner in half. In the second half, Day again produced a thrilling one-handed save to tip a Matthews shot around the post. 'Goalkeeping supreme!' extolled commentator David Coleman in his best Alan Partridge voice on that night's *Match of the Day*.

There was time for one final foray into the muddy recesses of Arsenal's half. Brooking played a one–two with Taylor, ran towards the edge of Arsenal's box and tucked the ball back inside to Taylor, who then passed the ball into the corner of the net. No one had really expected to win. We'd beaten Arsenal away in front of 56,742 fans and were in the semi-finals of the FA Cup.

The semi-final against Ipswich at Villa Park was ruined by nerves. West Ham were in all white and Ipswich in yellow, and both sides' performances were as insipid as their away kits. The replay on a Wednesday night at Stamford Bridge was a different game entirely. With the game in London, a huge contingent of Hammers fans travelled down the District Line to take over the open away end at the Chelsea ground.

Before the game, the PA played 'Yeah, I Can Do It' by the Rubettes, a flat cap and silly white suit-wearing outfit who supported the Hammers. It became the anthem of the evening. West Ham took an early lead through Taylor again, when he headed in from one yard out after a cross from the left. Ipswich equalised thanks to a Billy Jennings own goal: a horrible slice past Mervyn Day. Ipswich then had two goals disallowed by referee Clive Thomas, and their manager, Bobby Robson, was left fuming by the decisions. But this was to be our year.

With a few minutes remaining, Taylor latched onto a misplaced clearance on the edge of the box and crisply placed the ball in the corner of the net. Thousands of blokes with flared trousers, wide-collared patterned shirts and Paul McCartney sideburns surged forward, jumped up and down, and hugged each other. There was general pandemonium and disjointed choruses of 'Bubbles' until the final whistle and a huge roar. Yeah, we could do it, as the Rubettes might have put it.

Paul Dennison and I listened to blokes with transistors to their ears as we queued for the Tube home. Fulham had beaten Birmingham. It was to be a London final! Up against Bobby Moore. Reaching the FA Cup final meant more than winning the league then. It was the world's most famous cup competition. The game was screened live, and for a whole day, the nation watched your team on TV. Plus the players got the chance to be asked silly questions in their hotel by Barry Davies and maybe even have their fans embarrass themselves in *It's a Cup Final Knockout*.

West Ham's league form had collapsed in the build-up to the final: the side failed to win for eight games until beating Arsenal 1–0 at Upton Park on the last day of the league season. Later, I was to discover that this always happened when the Irons reached a final. But the league didn't really matter to me with Wembley ahead.

On 3 May 1975, I was there. There had been another day queuing to get tickets, but it was the cup. Paul Dennison and I made our way from Baker Street to Wembley Park on the Tube. I was wearing my traditional West Ham scarf round my neck and a silk West Ham scarf round one wrist. Wembley Way was full of colour: scarves, hats, banners and drunken singing. I bought my cup final programme for 20 pence. The adverts at the back were for Player's No. 6, Double Diamond, souvenir cup final records and 8mm-film soccer home movies, with a Super 8 projector on offer for just £13.75.

Inside the ground the noise was amazing, and an incredible amount of beer was being drunk by the West Ham contingent. Up on the terraces Wembley was a huge bowl of sound. I couldn't believe how loud 'Bubbles' could be when sung by 50,000 fans. The home-made banners, saying things like 'It's Mervyn's Day' added to the spectacle.

Once the game was under way, Fulham had the better of the first half, with Bobby Moore as unflappable as ever and Alan Mullery using all his experience in midfield. West Ham were missing the injured Keith Robson, and I was hoping that substitute Bobby Gould might be brought on, as he always tried and had won my sympathy after his initial barracking, but it was predestined that Alan Taylor would be the man everyone remembered.

On 61 minutes, Pat Holland, in for the injured Robson, dispossessed Fulham's Cutbush, ran down the left and played the ball in to Billy Jennings, who shot for goal. Goalkeeper Peter Mellor couldn't hold the ball and there was the ever-sharp Whippet Taylor, ready to bang the ball into the roof of the net. Three minutes later, Graham Paddon shot, again Mellor couldn't hold the ball and Taylor placed it through the unfortunate goalkeeper's legs and into the net. The West Ham end erupted, banners were dropped, keys lost and flares scuffed with muddy beer dregs as one almighty celebration began. Incredibly, Taylor had scored two goals in the sixth round, semi-final and final of the FA Cup. Wembley was serenaded with 'Bubbles' and then it was all over. The pitch was invaded by thousands of blokes in very wide jeans with flags draped over their shoulders. Trevor Brooking was being carried shoulder high. Eventually, the team managed to make it up the steps to the Royal Box.

Our captain Billy Bonds, who even appeared to have trimmed his beard slightly for the occasion, received the cup from the Duchess of Kent. Billy thrust the famous trophy into the air, and the obligatory roar echoed across north London.

After the game, Paul Dennison and I went to Barking because it was West Ham territory and we thought the pubs would serve us. We drank bitter and lager and sang 'Bubbles' and made our way back to Essex. WEST HAM HAD WON THE CUP. And it really was Mervyn's Day. Perhaps success is wasted upon the young. It would be some years before I realised how rare moments such as cup finals in football can be.

West Ham started the following season in excellent league form. There was another trip to Wembley for the Charity Shield, which we lost to Derby County, but that didn't matter, because after our first four unbeaten games, we were top of the league. I'd been up to Stoke to see Alan Taylor score the winner against the Potters, while visiting my aunt and uncle. Two Alan Taylor goals meant we drew at Anfield, something West Ham never did, and then another Taylor brace had ensured a 3–2 home win against Burnley. Keith Robson's headed goal beat Tottenham at Upton Park to round off the four-match unbeaten streak. I was on holiday at a caravan site in Clacton with Paul Dennison and his parents at the time. We cut the league table out of the *Daily Mirror*, because we knew West Ham at the head of the table was something unique. Being top couldn't last, but West Ham had a fine start to the campaign, beating Manchester United at Upton Park and winning 5–1 at Birmingham. At the start of January, West Ham were still sixth in the league.

However, it was the European nights that were to prove most memorable that season. In November, I'd watched West Ham defeat Russian side Ararat Erevan 3–1 at Upton Park, the highlight being Graham Paddon's opener, which hit a stanchion and bounced out, followed by a Robson header and a clever Alan Taylor chip. *Hammer* even printed a message in Russian for the visiting fans, although finding out how to translate resumption and custodian into Russian must have been a difficult task. Indeed, *Hammer* excelled itself, printing special white covers for the European games with splashes of yellow and gold on the traditional claret and blue.

As our league form crumbled ('West Ham always come down with the Christmas decorations,' I was told) those European nights took on extra importance. After losing 4–2 at Den Haag in Holland, we came back to win 3–1 at Upton Park. Following Bonzo's penalty, Lampard scored another amazing swerving left-footer into the top corner of the South Bank goal and Alan Taylor sealed a trip to the semi-finals.

Keith Robson had now grown a beard and looked like something from *One Million Years B.C.* He looked eminently capable of tossing Raquel Welch over his shoulder and taking her back to his cave after matches. Even Trevor Brooking now referred to him as 'Mad Robbo'. He was certainly committed. Recalling that game against Den Haag, I'm still able to conjure up a mental image of Robbo appearing to very nearly stamp on some poor defender's head.

By now I was in the sixth form at school, and at almost 17 years old, I was old enough to drive my new Honda SS50 moped and ride home from Upminster station. And enjoy illicit under-age pints. Nothing was more satisfying than a post-match pint after a midweek European game. With a dry throat and feeling emotionally battered, I'd return to Upminster station and savour a pint of bitter in the pub next door. Emotion recollected in tranquillity was the way Wordsworth described it.

West Ham followed up that superb European triumph against the Dutch side by losing 6–1 at Arsenal. It was excruciating viewing on *The Big Match*. Even as an optimistic 16 year old I was beginning to have doubts about the professionalism of some of our stars. We hadn't won since beating QPR on 24 January and didn't win any of the final 16 matches that season. As *Hammer* put it, 'Our eventual position in the table was incontrovertible evidence of the general decline which befell us in the latter half of the campaign.' By which it meant we were playing like a bunch of toerags.

But terrible league form was forgotten on a marvellous night against Eintracht Frankfurt on 14 April 1976. After a 2–1 defeat in the semi-final first leg we needed to win at Upton Park and did so in thrilling style. Brooking scored with an unusually emphatic header into the top corner. Standing in the South Bank that night I was cursing when Brooking played a great ball to Robson, who turned back from goal and appeared to have taken the ball a yard too far, only to unleash a stupendous 30-yarder into the top corner of the net ('Oh, but a great goal!' exclaimed Brian Moore). And then Taylor played a long ball on to the breaking Brooking, who turned inside an Eintracht defender sending him running halfway into the Chicken Run before neatly side-footing the ball into the corner with one immaculate movement. Eintracht pulled one back, but we held on to reach the European Cup-Winners' Cup final.

I thought about trying to go to the Heysel Stadium in Belgium for the final against Anderlecht, and even applied for a temporary passport. But having never left the country before and being an impoverished sixth-former it was a step too far. So I watched the live coverage of the game from my living room.

It started well, with Patsy Holland racing in to score from a Billy Bonds' knock-down. But then Frank Lampard made a dodgy back pass and Anderlecht's Rensinbrink equalised. A great finish from François van der Elst (later to play for us) then made it 2–1, only for Robson to score with yet another header from Trev's cross.

West Ham had shown commendable character to equalise but lost the game when Holland conceded a penalty. In the final moments, van der Elst bamboozled McDowell and Day to make it 4–2. We'd lost, but it was the second year in succession that we'd reached a cup final. I was starting to assume that we'd get to cup finals every season now, while ignoring the fact that we'd not won for 16 games in the league. Unfortunately, good form can't be turned off and on and that side was to prove even more suspect than Keith Robson's driving.

4

GIVE US A GOAL, RADDY . . .

1976–78
John Radford is the latest non-goalscoring sensation on 'the Upton Park scene' . . . Kevin Lock isn't the new Bobby Moore . . . Keith Robson almost goes inside . . . Psycho Cross arrives too late . . . just relegation for the Claret and Blues.
   Price of Hammer *in 1978: 15p*

'A quotation from Shakespeare's Richard III is possibly an apt description of the present situation in English football in general and Upton Park in particular: "Now is the winter of our discontent."' The *Hammer* editorials were becoming ever more eloquent as the team's fortunes crumbled.

West Ham were bottom of the league after 17 games and due to play Liverpool at Upton Park on 18 December 1976. After the previous 1–0 home defeat by Middlesbrough, John Lyall commented, 'It's going to be a long, hard haul. We've got to pick ourselves up again and continue battling, continue working hard.'

Hammer, now edited by Jack Helliar, did offer some hope though:

> Our endeavours to obtain new players for certain positions have
> met with some rebuffs, although offers more than matched those
> from other clubs. However, the search patiently continues, and we

hope our efforts will be rewarded as we were expecting to confirm the signing of John Radford of Arsenal last Tuesday. If so we will probably publish a photograph of John, together with his previous 'history' in our next issue. Meanwhile there is quiet confidence that the 'Upton Park scene' will soon improve.

John Radford! Yes, John Radford was our great hope of salvaging the season. The name still causes many West Ham fans to suffer dangerous flashbacks or reach for hip flasks illicitly smuggled into the East Stand. Whenever there's some particularly dire defeat my pal Nigel can still be heard mumbling 'and John Radford didn't score once in 30 games!'

After the opening match of the season it was clear that West Ham had problems. We lost 4–0 at Aston Villa and John Lyall gave one of his familiar nicest-man-in-football post-defeat summaries. Something like, 'We lost 4–0. It was a bit muddy/windy/rainy/Midlands-ish for the lads, but we learned a lot.'

Miraculously we beat QPR in the first home match of the season thanks to a Graham Paddon goal, but then the side didn't win for ten games. It was clear that the terrible run of not winning for the last 16 games of the previous season was not an aberration caused by pursuing the Cup-Winners' Cup.

West Ham did end their winless run by thrashing Spurs 5–3 at Upton Park, but it was the season when Spurs were relegated and seriously rubbish. John Lyall attempted to remedy all this by re-signing Bryan Robson (who always seemed to move away from West Ham just before we won something) from Sunderland and recruiting Bill Green from Carlisle, a player with an iffy moustache who looked like a trainspotter. He was seriously tall and was meant to be a lighthouse at the back; however, he often played with the mobility of a lighthouse, too.

Keith Robson, who should have been a great player for West Ham, was taking both liberties and motors. The saintly Trevor Brooking would later recall, 'If he had a couple of bevvies he was bad news: very aggressive and he liked a gamble.'

After a night at the Room at the Top disco in Ilford, Robson, already banned from driving, had asked a teammate if could borrow his car keys as the music was too noisy, and he wanted to talk to the girl he'd met. Almost inevitably, Robson took the car for a drunken drive and was arrested for driving the wrong way down a one-way street. General manager Ron Greenwood then had to go to court and plead for a non-custodial sentence with his fourth-from-bottom amendment, arguing that Robson was needed for West Ham's fight against relegation.

The attack looked increasingly lightweight and blond strikers Jennings and Taylor were declining forces. At the back, Kevin Lock was living down his one-time tag as 'the new Bobby Moore'. A measure of our injury-depleted desperation in attack was the fact that early on in the season John Lyall played Tommy Taylor as an emergency centre-forward. The Hornchurch-born centre-half's form was increasingly erratic, and one thing he was never going to be was a centre-forward. It was a bit like trying to turn the *Titanic* into the USS *Enterprise*.

It seemed that fortune was hiding alongside our old kit. That season West Ham had dumped the traditional kit in favour of an Admiral outfit with four claret stripes across a blue chest. Not even DJ Bill Remfry's rallying call of 'Today is ours – it must be the start of a great Hammers revival. All you fans out there on the terraces must really roar our team on to victory. The fight is on! Support and survive!' offered that much hope.

And then in December, John Lyall decided that John Radford was to be the saviour of our season. Raddy ranks as a colossus in the Upton Park annals of goalscoring impotence. John Lyall seemed to spend much of his time waiting for 'the right player at the right price', who would invariably turn out to be the wrong player at the wrong price. Raddy was the first of many such failures in the transfer market. After signing, he played against Liverpool and had a reasonable game. Somehow, bottom-of-the-pile Hammers managed to resurrect some of the old traditions of stylish football and defeat the Reds with goals from Brooking and Jennings. But, for the rest of the season, Radford just never scored. Lyall persevered with him for a few games the following season, but by then it was a law of football physics that he would never score in a claret and blue shirt.

The man was an England international. At Arsenal he was a talented forward who had been part of the Double-winning side of 1971. He had scored 149 goals in 482 appearances for the Gunners. It was just that now he was a bit old for that kind of thing: a kind of Victor Meldrew of the old First Division.

In a way, you could see what Lyall was thinking of. Radford was a target man and a physical presence up front. He took a lot of the pressure off Bryan Robson, who was now scoring with some regularity. Whenever we scored, Raddy was always close to the incident, but never quite close enough. He always worked hard, won headers, held the ball up, but never actually did what he was primarily there for – score goals. At that time, everyone in the sixth-form common room was quoting from *Monty Python and the Holy Grail*, and we had a striker who was as effective in battle as John Cleese's Black Knight.

I did witness Radford head the ball into the back of the net once in a home victory against Coventry. The referee quickly disallowed it for some obvious pushing, but at least I could say I was there when he almost scored. It wasn't as if Radford missed that many chances. He just never got there. Looking back at my programme collection, I can deduce that I failed to see Radford score in games against Liverpool, West Brom, Tottenham away, Man City, Everton, Birmingham, Coventry, Derby, Man United and the following season Norwich and Man City. In all, he played 30 games for the Hammers but never once troubled the goalscorers list in *Hammer*. Even club historian John Helliar was later to write that this was 'surely a record for an international striker'.

Some years later, I read Richard Dawkins' *The Selfish Gene*. In one chapter he attempted to explain the massive scale of time needed for life to develop on Earth, but waiting for John Radford to score for West Ham was surely enough to give any fan an insight into the aeons required for evolutionary change.

West Ham's form had improved in the second half of the season, however, and we gained 23 points of the 38 points available from the final 19 games. That was archetypal West Ham: only ever able to play for half a season. We secured survival by recovering from a goal down to beat Manchester United (preoccupied with the FA Cup final) 4–2 in the last home game of the season. West Ham had escaped relegation by just two points.

The start of the 1977–78 season was equally disappointing. West Ham lost their first three games, but then came back from two goals down to win at Newcastle. What was evident during a 1–0 home defeat by Manchester City, though, was that a young midfield player called Alan Devonshire had immense promise. The former fork-lift-truck driver was skilful, able to glide past players at high speed and linked well with Brooking on the left. But we were still dropping points.

While at a scrambled home draw with QPR, accompanied by my

sixth-form mates Mark Crouchman and Tim House, I recall being a little embarrassed by West Ham's efforts; that had never happened before. Kevin Lock scored at both ends that afternoon.

A fan had run on the pitch to attack Manchester City's Willie Donachie in an earlier game, and there was much debate about installing fences. In the QPR programme, John Lyall proved himself prescient with his argument against the introduction of that particular crowd control measure:

> Fences can turn the occasional lunatic back into the crowd. There could still be a lot of trouble on the other side of those fences. They are an insult to the overwhelming majority of decent fans; they prevent the pitch being used as an escape valve in case of fire or other emergency.

That October I began a degree course in English at Lancaster University. Suddenly my supply of games had been truncated. There could be spells of West Ham-watching at the start of the season and during Christmas and Easter holidays, but otherwise, it was an expensive trip back on the train to London to see a match. Football matches had become something precious. I joined the legions of supporters who had to wait powerlessly by radios or watch *Grandstand* in the County College TV room, waiting for their fix of football results.

John Radford had signed for Blackburn Rovers in Division Two, and a university friend of mine and Rovers fan, Keith Nicholson, kept me informed of his form. I very nearly collapsed on the floor of the TV room when I heard that he had scored on his debut for Rovers. Thirty games for us and no goals, one game for Blackburn and one goal. Raddy had a column in a local Blackburn paper in which he wrote things like, 'I said right, Raddy, you're on for a hat-trick, and then, damn, the hamstring went!' He didn't score that many more for Blackburn, moved to non-league Bishop's Stortford and then retired.

Supporting West Ham certainly helped boost my street credibility and gave me an identity at university. With the explosion of punk governing my musical tastes, it was suddenly hip to come from the Essex badlands immortalised by Ian Dury on *New Boots and Panties*. Any northern student would hear my Essex accent and assume that I was the son of an East End docker brought up in Plaistow.

West Ham were struggling again and only won three out of twenty games before Boxing Day, although one of those was a 2–1 home win against Man United, with new-signing Derek Hales scoring the winner. Being in the North-west allowed me to visit Anfield to see the Hammers go down 2–0. Hales didn't look bad, although with his big black beard you wondered if he'd been signed primarily to add to the hairiness quotient of Bonds, Lampard, Green and Co.

Finally, I returned to Upton Park on Boxing Day to see the lads beat Birmingham City 1–0 with a late goal from a promising young midfielder called Alan Curbishley. John Lyall was now official manager, Ron Greenwood having departed to take over England. Like all irrational football fans I knew the reason that we hadn't been winning before: it was because I hadn't been there. Only my next game saw us lose at Chelsea to a crap goal after equalising thanks to Bryan Robson, although a bearded John McDowell returned from injury to score the winner in a 3–2 home win over Leicester in the next match. I celebrated by playing Elvis Costello's *This Year's Model* at full volume.

A major boost from that game was the goalscoring performance of the new bearded striker David Cross. Bought from West Brom he was everything John Radford wasn't, and his CV even included scoring for West Ham. At last we had a proper centre-forward. Even better, we'd often see Cross drinking a half in the Eagle and Child pub in Shenfield, it being a distant time when footballers went to normal pubs and all without *Hello!* photographers anywhere.

It was reassuring to be back with fellow West Ham fans, people who understood my pain. By then there was a solid Brentwood contingent mainly called Steve – Steve Savill, Steve Flory, Steve Day, Alison O'Brien and University of East Anglia student Paul 'Gaffer' Garrett formed the nucleus of the matchday crew, usually driving to games in Steve Savill's ancient Austin accompanied by reggae or punk on his car stereo.

After the Christmas break, it was football famine again until the Easter vacation. It still looked ominous for the third-from-bottom Irons when I returned for the home match against Ipswich in March. Bobby Ferguson was back in goal, replacing the error-prone Mervyn Day. We won that one 3–0 with a hat-trick from David Cross, who was now being greeted with great big booming chants of 'Psycho! Psycho!' from the North Bank, because at last, unlike the fragile Taylor and Jennings, here was a West Ham striker who got stuck in.

We beat fellow strugglers Chelsea 3–1 at Upton Park, mainly thanks to their keeper going off after diving at Tommy Taylor's feet. We were 1–0 down and the game had been mainly notable for a risqué chant from the North Bank of 'Walker Walker, show us your cock!', a reference to Clive Walker's conviction for indecent exposure.

With Chelsea striker Bill Garner having to play in goal, Brooking scored direct from a corner, Bill Green and his moustache nodded his only ever Hammers goal and Pat Holland added a third. In the next home game, we beat Coventry, and a young centre-back called Alvin Martin made his debut, showing tremendous confidence and poise. He kept his place and with Alvin at the back and Cross up front our team finally had a decent spine. Add Devonshire and Brooking, and we had a good side again.

We won at Leeds, beat Derby at Upton Park but then lost 3–0 away to Man United. Two goals from Psycho at Middlesbrough then earned an unlikely away win and seemed to have secured West Ham's survival. All we had to do was get something from the last game of the season at home to Liverpool. West Ham always got out of trouble in the final game. The game was so important that I paid what seemed to be a huge British Rail train fare to return to London. I was confident that there was going to be no relegation for the Claret and Blue, just celebration.

Only we didn't win. We went down 2–0 to the Scousers on 29 April 1978. We had finished third from bottom, one point behind QPR. The enduring image in my mind is of a big skinhead sitting down in tears on the terracing of the South Bank. For the first time in my life West Ham had been relegated.

WEST HAM'S TOP TEN NUTTERS
- JULIAN DICKS: Once tried to slice a Derby player in two on the halfway line for no particular reason during the 1992–93 season when he was sent off three times. Shaved head, Tasmanian Devil tattoo, a liking for heavy metal and a nickname of 'The Terminator'.
- TOMAS REPKA: Four red cards and 49 yellow cards in 163 appearances for the Hammers up to May 2005, plus an on-

pitch pushing match with David James. Too-tight shorts restricting the blood flow to the brain and seriously demonic shaved head to be taken into consideration.

- JOHN HARTSON: Used both a plant pot and Eyal Berkovic's head as a football. Also sent off for punching Derby's Igor Stimac while a Hammer.
- KEITH ROBSON: Took a teammate's car for a test drive while drunk and was disqualified. Loved to clatter defenders and grew scary desert-island beard. Referred to as 'Mad Robbo' by Trevor Brooking.
- STUART PEARCE: Well, would you look him in the eye? Or take his Sex Pistols CD off the team ghetto-blaster?
- FRANK McAVENNIE: Fearless in attack, happy to punch rogue Sheffield Wednesday defenders and snort cocaine, but never less than 48 hours before a match.
- DAVID CROSS: When Psycho was about no goalkeeper was safe. Threw himself at anything that came into the box, be it ball, defender or keeper.
- BILLY BONDS: Would run halfway across the pitch to defend Pat Holland – the ultimate West Ham minder.
- NEIL RUDDOCK: Admirable nightclub bouncer routine, barging into Patrick Vieira when the Arsenal man was sent off, and then performing a bizarre statuesque pose of supposed innocence.
- MARCO BOOGERS: Tried to cut Gary Neville in half when red carded on his second ever appearance. Boogered off to Holland, declared himself mentally unfit for Hammers duty while allegedly living in a caravan.

5

WE'RE ON THE MARCH WITH LYALL'S ARMY

1978–80
West Ham get thrashed at Shrewsbury . . . the ball comes over, and Frank falls over and scores the f***ing winning goal at Elland Road . . . Trevor uses his head . . . John Lyall has another fag . . . Willie Young gets cynical . . . Paul Allen gets tearful . . . and West Ham win the FA Cup.
  Price of Hammer *in 1980: 25p*

West Ham had lost 3–0 at Shrewsbury on 15 December 1979. Yes, a side that contained Trevor Brooking, Alan Devonshire, Billy Bonds, Alvin Martin, David Cross, Ray Stewart, Paul Allen, Geoff Pike, Stuart Pearson, Jimmy Neighbour, Frank Lampard and Phil Parkes (seven of whom were current or future internationals) had somehow managed to lose 3–0 to Shrewsbury Town, newly promoted to Division Two. In contrast to our list of footballing icons, Shrewsbury boasted a player called John Dungworth.

Down by the river, in a place called Gay Meadow, it seemed an aeon away from Green Street. Having conceded the first goal to Town's Maguire in the 58th minute, West Ham then let in another two in the final five minutes. The home fans in the 8,513 crowd were so excited that they probably danced around their scythes afterwards.

An old pal from Shenfield, Will Finck, had been on a training course near Lancaster and had offered to drive me back to Essex for the Christmas holidays, taking in Gay Meadow on our route home – we wished we hadn't. West Ham were down to ninth in the Second Division. John Lyall's rebuilding was suffering from subsidence. As we wearily listened to *Sports Report*, the live draw for the FA Cup third round was being broadcast. 'And West Bromwich Albion will play West Ham United . . .'

'We've lost that one,' I muttered to Will, seeing no hope in the cosmos of beating a First Division side containing Cyrille Regis, Derek Statham and John Wile, for West Ham were a side worthy of a collective doctorate in underachievement at that time.

In the 1978–79 season we'd finished fifth in the Second Division, despite having Trevor Brooking, who had nobly decided to stay despite relegation possibly affecting his England chances. The season had started excellently with a 5–2 demolition of Notts County at Upton Park. Psycho Cross scored a hat-trick with a Devonshire strike and an own goal completing the rout on a sunny August afternoon. It was also the first time that I'd attended a game where someone I knew had been arrested.

Following one of West Ham's goals, there was the usual surge forward in the South Bank. In the days of terracing, the police would sometimes stand among the fans. One of the Steves was grabbed by a policeman and arrested. He was charged with obstructing the police, and in a court case some months later the policeman claimed that he had tried to knee him in the groin and push him over. It was all plainly ridiculous, as the copper was about twice as big as the diminutive alleged assailant.

I was called as a witness and under cross-examination the prosecution immediately told me that only hooligans would go in the South Bank, as this was where the away fans were penned in at one side. Luckily, being an anorak who even then kept handwritten soccer annals of every Division One and Two side's results, I was instantly able to rebuff his crude smear. Firstly by quoting the very low average gate figures of Notts County, and then by pointing out that such a sparsely supported side were unlikely to bring a huge away crew to Upton Park. A university student in a suit who could quote Notts County's average gates clearly impressed the magistrates (and Alison O'Brien's mum Val), and the case against Steve was deemed to be 'not proven'.

West Ham followed up that thrashing of Notts County with an excellent 3–0 away win at Newcastle (with goals from Cross, Devonshire and Pop Robson) before the Brentwood crew travelled to Crystal Palace to see Alan Taylor, now in midfield, score in a 1–1 draw. Seven points from three games; clearly, making the top three was a certainty. But this was West Ham.

We lost to Fulham at home and Burnley away in the next two matches. There was time to take in two September wins against Bristol Rovers and Sheffield United before returning to university. Marooned in the North-west in a soccer desert, I'd watch games such as Bolton v. Coventry and Preston v. Sunderland trying to believe that it mattered, always wondering what was happening at Upton Park. There was a little relief when the *Match of the Day* cameras caught us beating Preston 3–1 with goals from Cross, Devonshire and Lampard.

Vacations were always a chance to do as much West Ham watching as possible. The Hammers were mirroring my punk/new wave musical taste nicely, too. We'd stop on the way before games to buy army greens (then an esoteric fashion item) from an army surplus shop near the Eastern Avenue. A Harrington jacket, DMs, claret and blue rugby or Fred Perry shirt made up my usual match and gig uniform. The likes of the Jam, Stranglers and Buzzcocks all played the university circuit in those days. Sham 69 were said to be West Ham supporters and at the end of their 'If The Kids Are United' there was a chant of 'United! United!' Their gigs were a bit like a football match: at the Rainbow rampaging right-wing skinheads ran through the foyer knocking me over. At the Reading Festival, Sham's drummer had a West Ham scarf on his kit, before the inevitable riot started.

Driver Steve Savill would always park in Hubert Road, and we'd stop at the same chippy on the way home, although it had lately been superseded by a newly opened exotic eatery called McDonald's. I much preferred proper chips. Then we'd discuss the game at The Castle in Ongar Road later that night.

Christmas 1978 summed up the West Ham enigma: I saw the Irons beat Charlton 2–0 followed by the worst Boxing Day performance ever witnessed from a West Ham team. A lunchtime kick-off and a dire 0–2 home defeat to Orient sparked the inevitable hangover jokes. Then four days later we thrashed Blackburn 4–0 at Upton Park. Blackburn had John Radford up front – he didn't score.

We lost away to Newport in the third round of the FA Cup, but then we always lost to crap lower-division teams in the FA Cup. However, John Lyall showed commendable ambition when he bought England international Phil Parkes from QPR for £500,000 that March. It was a world record for a goalkeeper. The club had not bought a player for 12 months, but that was a big signing. The right player at the right price.

Having alternated with Ferguson and Day, he had finally opted for proven quality. It seems astonishing now, a Second Division club buying one of the top four keepers in England. Parkesy was also noticeable for his enduring shaggy-dog hairstyle and 1970s porn-star moustache which, in the era of punk, looked ridiculous. At least he put these attributes to some use when he appeared in an advert for Cossack natural hair control. ('The conditioners in Cossack will put his hair back into top shape, and the gentle holding agents will keep it manageable. Looking natural. For the rest of the day.') With Parkes in goal we would surely go up. And with our side's hair neatly in place, too.

After the Christmas holidays, it was soccer abstinence followed by an Easter stint watching the Irons thrash Newcastle 5–0, with John McDowell, now sporting an Afro, scoring twice and causing Brian Moore to test his octave range on the following day's *Big Match*. As *Hammer* was to put it:

> The manner in which the Magpies were 'taken to the cleaners' was comparable to the unfortunates who were thrown to the lions in a Roman amphitheatre . . . The Novocastrians had no effective reply to the onslaught which first made impact in the 20th minute when Alan Devonshire opened the score after a tremendous individual run.

Predictably we followed that up by drawing at home to Leicester. We then drove to Cambridge where the lads could only draw 0–0. That game was most notable for the West Ham contingent who found a hosepipe, stretched it around the newly erected fences, and spent most of the match trying to heave them down. We could only draw at the old Valley against Charlton, and then I was back at university, where I was able to see a defeat at Blackburn, in which Duncan McKenzie scored a 30-yarder. My mate Keith, a Rovers fan, was excited enough, but West Ham's promotion hopes had been extinguished.

The next season, the year of the Shrewsbury debacle, was my final year at university and West Ham made a terrible start, only winning two out of the first seven games and losing four of them. Lyall attempted to rebuild the side, buying Ray Stewart from Dundee United, a combative Scottish defender who was a good athlete and possessed a great shot. He was to become our penalty taker. Ray's general technique was to blast the ball so hard that it went through the back of the net and decapitated several small children behind the goal before emerging somewhere in Tudor Road. Lyall also purchased Stuart Pearson, a quality one-time England international centre-forward from Manchester United, whose knees were going a bit, plus Jimmy Neighbour, a skilful winger from Spurs who was very much a confidence player.

Returning from a month-long Inter-Rail trip around Europe in the summer of 1979 (during which I had noted that on the Berlin Wall the Europeans had written political slogans, whereas someone from England had simply written 'West Ham') there was time to see the Hammers beat Sunderland 2–0, the goals coming from a crisp finish from Cross and a neat side-foot from Stuart Pearson following a burst down the right from Alan Devonshire. I could only see us surging up the table.

Ah, the optimism of youth. Shrewsbury was a defeat too far, but following that game the Irons did at least beat Cambridge 3–1 at Upton Park, although we needed a blizzard to do it. It was a terrible night of snowstorms, and most fans either expected the game to be postponed or couldn't get there due to transport problems. Only 11,721 fans were present – West Ham's lowest league gate since 1957. At half-time it was possible to imagine Upton Park being caught in pack ice like Shackleton's ship the *Endurance* and being slowly crushed over a long winter, at which point us frozen fans would have to camp on ice floes in the North Bank penalty area and survive by catching and eating programme sellers before trying to sail in a makeshift boat to Plaistow.

Bill Remfry tried to warm us up at half-time. He played Mike Oldfield's 'In Dulce Jubilo' and the fans around me in the lower West Stand were so cold they started to jig. Soon all 11,721 fans were dancing on the terraces – even my dad. Bill Remfry never forgot the night he had finally encouraged mass audience participation by playing a song from 'the pop music scene'. He did his stuff from a wooden box attached to the front of the West Stand, meaning you could only see him from the waist upwards, making him look a little like Davros from *Doctor Who*. For the rest of his DJ-ing career, Remfry would always put on Mike Oldfield whenever he hoped to create a spectator frenzy.

We went on an eight-game unbeaten run after that. I even made a midweek trip to the cobbled streets of Burnley to see Alan Devonshire score the winner and managed to make the last British Rail train back to Lancaster, but promotion still seemed unlikely. It didn't matter too much, though, as instead of getting knocked out by someone useless, West Ham were going on a cup run. Despite my prediction of demise at First Division WBA, we drew 1–1 at the Hawthorns. Pearson scored and then Phil Parkes played superbly, no doubt aided by Cossack natural hair control. We were winning until Albion's last-minute equaliser.

The replay was one of those great Upton Park nights: 30,000 fans under the lights and a winner from that underrated workhorse Geoff Pike. We beat Orient 3–2 away in the fourth round thanks to two goals from Ray Stewart and an own goal and then beat Swansea 2–0 at Upton Park. Young Paul Allen, only 17, scored in that game. Things were getting serious. It was back on the coach from Lancaster for the fifth-round tie against Aston Villa at Upton Park.

The game was heading for a goalless draw when West Ham were awarded a penalty in injury time. Villa fans took up the whole of the South Bank and our Brentwood crew were standing in the West Side. I can still feel the tension as Ray 'Tonka' Stewart placed the ball on the spot. Geoff Pike couldn't look. Being a literal sort of fellow, Ray responded to his new nickname by 'tonking' the ball at something more than light speed into the back of the Villa net, and then everyone in the West Side hugged one another and waved their woollen scarves. We were through to the semis, where we would play Everton.

The whole stadium was singing, 'We're on the march with Lyall's army! We're all going to Wembley! And we'll really shake 'em up, when we win the FA Cup! 'Cos West Ham is the greatest football team!'

The Villa fans were not happy. Walking back towards the car in Hubert Road, the Steve who escaped the police obstruction charge was kicked to the ground by a group of away fans standing around their coach. Steve's girlfriend Alison shouted at them, and we managed to pull him away, shaken but fairly unharmed.

Between the sixth round and the semi-final, I can recall sitting in a pub on a Saturday night in the west end of Morecambe wondering how it was possible that West Ham had lost 3–2 at home to Fulham. The following week we lost 2–1 at Swansea. We were staying down.

Football violence was getting silly that season. Before the semi-final there was a plea in *Hammer* that was notable for its continued obsession with inverted commas and a tone which sounded a little like a housemaster trying to address the ICF: 'Good natured rivalry is readily acceptable and no cup tie would be the "true thing" without such partisanship,' began the editorial. 'Please do not let us have any mayhem, destruction, and all that "aggro" which is regarded by an irresponsible minority as the "in" thing. Make it a "good" day, please.'

Outside Villa Park we saw two frightened Everton fans being chased by a group of twenty or so West Ham fans. It all seemed so cowardly and pathetic. Inside the stadium we were standing in the Holt End segregated by a line of policemen and a wire fence from our Everton counterparts. Coins flew over the divide, and there were many choruses of 'In your Everton homes, you look in a dustbin for something to eat, you find a dead cat and you think it's a treat, in your Everton homes.'

The game was tense and close. Phil Parkes made a great save to tip an Eastoe shot wide, and Everton's Hodge produced a fantastic stop to tip away Ray Stewart's piledriver. Everton took the lead in the first half, Brian Kidd converting a disputed penalty after Devonshire was adjudged to have pushed an Everton player in the box.

West Ham pressed in the second half, in no way intimidated by their superior-grade opposition. (If it was Shrewsbury we'd have had problems, though.) Ray Stewart managed to knock out Everton's Ross with another shot, then came the moment that showed what West Ham were all about. Alan Devonshire took the ball wide on the left in his own half, played a lovely pass with the outside of his left foot into the space where Trevor Brooking was instinctively running. Trev let the ball run on, crossed first time with his left foot and the alert Pearson swept the ball into the net at the near post. Quality.

The game at Villa Park ended in a 1–1 draw. The one thing I hadn't thought about was a replay four days later at Elland Road, Leeds. I was due to return to Lancaster and wouldn't be able to queue for tickets. Also, there was no late train back from Leeds to Lancaster, and hotels were not something I even thought about on a student budget. So, reluctantly, I listened to the game on a radio in a room at County College, Lancaster University. The signal kept disappearing into static. The game was goalless until extra time, when Brooking found Devonshire. He played it to Pearson, ran forward to take the return pass and then appeared to skip past 15 Everton defenders before poking the ball into the net. Later that night, I watched the highlights in the college TV room, and Dev's goal caused Barry Davies to exclaim in his squeaky hysterical voice reserved for moments of greatness, 'Can he put it in? Oh, he can! That is a brilliant goal! That is a marvellous goal!'

Late on in the match, Bob Latchford scored with a diving header from a right-wing cross and leapt onto the fence in front of the surging, ecstatic Scouse fans. The game looked to be going to a draw, but there was just enough time for one final attack. Brooking crossed, Cross nodded on and Frank Lampard dived to head the ball into the net, although what he was doing in that position is a mystery. The West Ham end collectively paused to see if this was really happening, then erupted in a state of collective delirium.

Frank ran madly to the corner flag, grabbed hold of it and then ran round and round it in a crazy dance of celebration, his tight 1980s shorts making it look like a bizarre version of early pole dancing for bearded blokes from East Ham. At first I thought that the radio must have been suffering from more interference, but then I discovered that it really was Frank Lampard that had scored. The Frank Lampard who had been in and out of the side, been played out of position at right-back and had looked to have lost his place to Paul Brush.

That moment was later beautifully encapsulated by West Ham fans in a song sung to the tune of 'White Christmas': 'I'm dreaming of a Frankie Lampard, Just like the one at Elland Road, When the ball came over, And Frank fell over, And scored the f***ing winning goal!'

My pals Keith Nicholson, Ann Casey and Steve Healy thought it all a little deranged but got out a bottle of wine anyway. We were going to Wembley. West Ham were going to Wembley.

Cup fever gripped Upton Park – so we lost our next two home games, against Birmingham, in front of 37,000 fans, and then Shrewsbury, going down to a 3–1 defeat at home. Yes, Shrewsbury had done the Double over cup finalists West Ham, beating us 6–1 on aggregate.

The Cockney Rejects recorded their idiosyncratic version of 'Bubbles' and somehow managed to make 'I'm Forever Blowing Bubbles' sound like a threat. My mate Big Joe still uses it on his answering machine followed by, 'We're not in! What's it to you?' The Rejects appeared on *Top of the Pops* and their version of 'Bubbles' made the Top 20. (It was rather amusing when Morrissey invited the Cockney Rejects to perform at the 2004 Meltdown Festival held at the Royal Festival Hall. The B-side to 'Bubbles' was entitled 'West Side Boys', and its lyrics included 'Dr. Martens and iron bars! Smash the coaches and do 'em in their cars!' Just what would the average Morrissey fan or indeed the classical-music-loving RFH patrons have made of that?)

My only problem regarding the final at Wembley was that my final exams were coming up at university, and a period of frantic revising was required. I couldn't be in London to queue up for tickets, and none of my phone calls home to Brentwood Irons came up with anyone who could get me a ticket. The FA Cup final edged nearer. My finals were set to start on the Tuesday after the game at Wembley. No sensible student would jeopardise their final exams for a mere football match, but as Bill Shankly might have put it, football isn't a matter of life and desks – it's much more important than that. Three days before the final I made a decision. I was going to Wembley even though I didn't have a ticket. My revision had gone reasonably well, half the degree depended on the coursework anyway, and if I didn't know it now, I never would. It would be the cup final I'd remember in future years, not my degree. I took out the rest of my term's grant (about £40) from the bank and resolved to get a ticket from a tout or by any means necessary.

Maybe I was deluding myself; maybe an extra three days of revising would have ensured that I obtained a first-class degree and became a top professor of English Literature or editor of *The Guardian*, or even *Hammer*. But then I'd have missed Billy Bonds walking up those steps, and would have had nothing to sustain me through 25 years of watching the likes of Steve Whitton, David Kelly, Mike Small, Gary Charles and Titi Camara.

That Friday I was given a lift down the M6 with Ev Ivey, a Gunners fan who was going to the game and had a ticket. On the Saturday morning, I caught the Tube to Wembley with Steve Day and Steve Flory, who both had tickets. Soon after noon I was busy muttering 'anyone got a ticket?' at groups of fans. Wembley Way was its usual mass of scarf hawkers, flags, burger bars, beer bottles and urinating fans, while the air reverberated with the sound of horns and 'Bubbles'.

The touts were asking around £50 for tickets, face value £3.50. My search was futile until after an hour or so a West Ham fan and his young son came up to me and asked if I needed a ticket. He suggested that he would sneak his son under the turnstile, and then I could use his son's ticket. I asked him how much he wanted for it, and he said a fiver would be fine. We tried his scam and, thanks to his literally ducking-and-diving son, it worked. I thanked him profoundly, walked through the turnstiles, held my ticket up towards the sunlight and kissed it. I'd done it, I was in! I never found out the man's name, but if he's reading this now, I owe both him and his son a drink or seven.

In the bowels of the Wembley stands it was a cacophony of noise. Beer was everywhere, and I wondered if some of the fans would even make it to kick-off time. I walked up the steps to my section behind the goal, the sky emerged and then the circular stands and that vast expanse of luminous green grass were revealed.

At ten to three the sides entered the field, John Lyall leading the West Ham players out. With his dark quiff, black slacks and beige jacket he looked a little like a 1950s music impresario. The band played 'Abide With Me', which gave me a tingling feeling of emotion and expectancy. Numerous banners were being waved, reading 'Devonshire is the Cream', 'Hitchcock's Dead but Psycho Plays On', and the more Edward Lear-ish 'The Greatest Players in the Land are Captain Billy and his Band. That's Frank the Lamp, Alan Dev, Paul and Stewart and Tricky Trev'. Watching the game on my own, I looked at the cross-section of fans around me and thought that these were good people; whatever else was happening in their lives that day, there was hope that their dreams might not fade and die.

West Ham were at the tunnel end, wearing their all-white Admiral away kit and playing towards the far goal in the first half. After 13 minutes, Devonshire used his pace to leave Rice lunging at air, raced to the byline and put in a cross. Arsenal keeper Pat Jennings flapped the ball away, Cross attempted a shot at goal but the ball was blocked. Pearson then blasted the ball back across goal, and Trevor Brooking, waiting in the six-yard box, stooped to send a header flashing into the net. In the West Ham end we had no idea who had scored until a voice over the PA told us, but it didn't matter. The scoreboard clicked to 'WEST HAM 1 ARSENAL 0'. I knew I would be looking at it for the rest of the game.

Lyall had pulled a clever tactical trick, playing Stuart Pearson in midfield and leaving Psycho Cross alone up front. The big Arsenal defenders only had one forward to mark, but West Ham dominated the midfield. The Hammers boss smoked another fag in his dugout.

Brooking was skilful, creative and also hard-tackling in midfield. In the pre-match build-up Brian Clough had said that although Trev floated like a butterfly 'he stings like one too'. At Wembley, Brooking proved that he could be a thoroughly tenacious midfielder. Cross worked tremendously hard in the heat, young Paul Allen competed well in midfield and at the back Alvin Martin (back in the days when he had hair), Billy Bonds and Phil Parkes were immaculate.

With only a few minutes left, Brooking and Devonshire played yet another one–two, Trevor slipped the ball inside to 17-year-old Paul Allen, who turned inside Price, past the lumbering Willie Young and had a clear run on goal. It looked like it must be another goal, but Young cynically hacked down Allen on the edge of the box with a 'professional foul'. It was before the days when such offences were automatic red cards, and he escaped with a booking. Ray Stewart blasted the resulting free-kick into the wall.

Every West Ham fan in the ground then whistled for what seemed like the duration of another match in an attempt to prompt the referee to call time before George Courtney finally obliged. We might have lost to Shrewsbury, but Arsenal was easy. 'ONE TEAM IN LONDON, THERE'S ONLY ONE TEAM IN LONDON!' sang the Hammers fans.

John Lyall hugged his men, and Paul Allen collapsed onto the turf, head in hands. Trevor Brooking jogged around the pitch like he was mowing his lawn in Shenfield. Geoff Pike was wearing one of those '80s Hammers scarves, white with claret and blue stripes, and several players had donned claret and white caps. Then Billy Bonds, this time clean-shaven, made his way up the famous steps to the royal box, being patted and hugged by fans as he went. He received the gleaming old trophy from the Duchess of Kent and held it up to a huge roar. He was followed by Frank Lampard, Ray Stewart, Geoff Pike, Alvin Martin and a blubbering Paul Allen. West Ham chairman Len Cearns cast a concerned paternal look at the boy, perhaps wondering if he should have told Paul's mum that he wouldn't be home until gone seven o'clock.

Then came the lap of honour and the team photo with Alan Devonshire holding a claret and blue teddy bear. I took one last look at Wembley and then left to meet Steve Day and Steve Flory in a pre-arranged spot by a hotdog stall outside. We celebrated by heading for Trafalgar Square, where groups of Hammers fans were singing around the fountains. Then we went really wild by going to the new McDonald's in Haymarket, followed by a Tube ride to Upton Park to pay homage to the Upton Park gates and then on for pints in The Boleyn pub. Motorists on Green Street were sounding their horns, while inside the pub someone had the idea – perhaps not approved by the Fire Brigade – of burning an Arsenal scarf in the centre of the lounge.

University finals be buggered – I got a 'gentleman's' 2:2 anyway. That night, walking the two and a half miles back from the station to my parents' house in Great Warley, the only revision was the song going on in my head: 'We're on the march with Lyall's army! We've all been to Wembley! And we really shook 'em up when we won the FA Cup! 'Cos West Ham is the greatest football team!'

The next day I watched the highlights on TV. The various Steves even said that Alison O'Brien's dad had purchased some new device called a video recorder and that he had recorded the game so that we could watch it over and over again.

We had won the FA Cup, yet West Ham finished seventh in Division Two that season. During the build-up to the Wembley game, I remember one woman fan being interviewed saying, 'This doesn't matter, it's the league that counts and we should have got promoted!' At the time I thought her comments were churlish, but looking back, it seems absurd that a team capable of beating Division One sides WBA, Aston Villa, Everton and Arsenal in the cup should finish seventh in Division Two.

In modern terms that would have meant West Ham missing out on the play-offs, and a team that finished seventh in the Coca-Cola Championship getting to the FA Cup final and beating the team that had qualified for the Champions League by finishing fourth in the

Premiership. Based on the 2004–05 season, it would be the equivalent of Reading beating Everton in the FA Cup final. Retaining the services of Brooking, Devonshire, Martin and Bonds for two years in the Second Division would have been like Rio Ferdinand, Frank Lampard, Joe Cole and Jermain Defoe still being in the West Ham side two years after relegation.

Beating Arsenal was a massive achievement, even back in 1980. West Ham could match anyone, except Shrewsbury. We just happened to be stuck in the wrong division.

6

THE BOYS OF '86

1980–86
*Winning the Second Division championship with Psycho and Sarge
. . . beating Spurs 4–0 at the Lane . . . the emergence of TC . . .
thrashing Bury 10–0 and signing their centre-half . . . the
unforgettable wing play of Steve Whitton . . . and Frankie goes to
Hollywood (Romford).*
  Price of Hammer *in 1986: 60p*

West Ham stormed to the Second Division title in season 1980–81. It
was as if they suddenly remembered, after two years of promotion failure,
that any side with Brooking, Devonshire, Martin and Parkes should be
whipping the likes of Cambridge, Shrewsbury and Grimsby. Maybe it was
a tribute to the patience of John Lyall: proof that it takes three years to
build a good side.

John Lyall made a big signing in the summer, buying Paul Goddard for
£800,000 from QPR. Sarge, known as such because of his affiliation to
the Boys' Brigade (you can't imagine too many modern footballers being
in the Boys' Brigade now, can you?), was a quality striker. Goddard
replaced Stuart Pearson, who had done well, but had lost his pace. The
partnership of Goddard and Cross terrorised Second Division defences
that season.

After losing the first game of the season at home to Luton, the side went 15 games without defeat. An early game against Watford summed up the determination of the side: David Cross scored with a fine finish at the near post from a Frank Lampard cross; 17-year-old Bobby Barnes cut inside to score a dazzling goal from the edge of the box on his debut and suggest that he might be the next Harry Redknapp (he wasn't); while Trevor Brooking, buoyed by his Wembley winner, scored with another header, this time diving like Andy Gray to head in at the near post from a Devonshire cross.

But while West Ham were sweeping the Second Division aside, I was marooned in Lancaster. Having graduated that summer, I'd stayed up north doing various dodgy jobs such as being a summer barman in Morecambe serving drunken Glaswegians all demanding 'a pint o' lagger and a Groose, Jimmy!' while standing eight-deep at the bar.

As the season started, I was working in a branch of Burton's selling unwanted bespoke suits. There was a small room in the back of the shop with a radio, and as news would come through of West Ham beating Bristol City 5–0, I would reflect how incredible it was that some people chose to work in jobs that necessitated working on Saturday. It's one of the reasons that I've never become a proper football journalist – one who writes match reports about games, travelling to different clubs every week. Whatever the career advantages of being a professional sports writer, I could never do a job that prevented me from seeing West Ham every week. That stint in Burton's taught me that.

I did see the lads at Preston and Blackburn, but both games were 0–0. Parkes and the defence did well, but what this exiled Iron was missing was the flowing football on display at Upton Park. At Christmas I returned to Essex, and during a 2–1 home win over Sheffield Wednesday, I was astonished to watch the confidence of the side, the movement and running. Geoff Pike, usually a journeyman midfielder receiving terrace taunts of 'stupid boy!', was proving himself to be a good footballer and in the best form of his career, while Brooking and Devonshire were brilliant together on the left.

However, the side retained a few of its old erratic tendencies. When we visited QPR on Boxing Day the Irons were thrashed 3–0 by Terry Venables' men, but the next day we beat Orient 2–1 at Upton Park in front of 36,000 fans, with Paul Allen scoring a great goal from outside the box and Pat Holland netting the winner.

My temporary job at Burton's had finished, and I was now one of Maggie Thatcher's unemployed millions. When the chance of a shared house in Brentwood came up, I moved back to Essex, longing to visit Upton Park on a regular basis again. A 5–0 demolition of Preston showed West Ham's football at its best. All five goals were excellent: Goddard's classy chip; Cross backheeling to Goddard who jumped over the ball for Pike to race through, round the keeper and tap home; a Frank Lampard special from the edge of the box; Devonshire playing a one–two with Goddard, dribbling to the six-yard box and poking home; Brooking's chipped free-kick controlled on his chest by Dev, who then struck the ball across the keeper and into the net.

There was so much happening that season. As well as running away with the league, West Ham were in the Cup-Winners' Cup (an earlier game against Castilla had to be played in an empty Boleyn Ground after crowd trouble in the first leg – the atmosphere resembled Wimbledon home games of the '80s) and about to reach Wembley again. My return to Essex coincided with a thrilling 2–0 victory over Coventry in the second leg of the League Cup semi-final in front of 36,551 fans. Goddard turned and shot in one movement for a glorious first goal, and in the last minute, Jimmy Neighbour strolled into the Coventry box to take the Irons to the final.

March saw a home tie with Russian side Dinamo Tbilisi in the Cup-Winners' Cup. Bill Remfry made a special effort in his 'Off the Record' column in *Hammer*, mentioning Tchaikovsky, Shostakovich, Chekhov, Turgenev and Gogol, who were all good players, and telling his readers, 'Western "pop" music is slowly becoming accepted in the USSR . . . I shall endeavour to play some Georgian or Armenian music this evening; if not, we shall have to settle for "Georgia on my Mind" (from the other Georgia in the USA).'

West Ham were playing some of their best ever football that season, but Tbilisi were awesome that night, scored some stunning goals, outpassed the Hammers and won 4–1. At the end of the game, the Upton Park crowd clapped the Russian side off the pitch. West Ham had made a small contribution to thawing the Cold War.

Ten days after playing Dinamo Tbilisi, West Ham faced Liverpool at Wembley for the League Cup final. Alan Kennedy scored a disputed goal for Liverpool towards the end of extra time. The goal stood even though an injured Liverpool player was in an offside position. The game looked to be over until the Hammers proved how resolute they were: Alvin Martin rose to send an imperious header towards the top corner, and it was handballed off the line. Ray Stewart dispatched a last-minute penalty at Wembley as easily as if it had been a pre-season friendly.

After the Wembley final came the return leg of the Cup-Winners' Cup-tie against Dinamo Tbilisi in the USSR. The West Ham side were greeted with a banner reading 'Welcome To West Ham United: Sportsmen of England'. In an era of terrace wars in England, it was proof that football could unite, too. West Ham won 1–0 with a Stuart Pearson goal but went out 4–2 on aggregate.

The League Cup final replay was at Villa Park on 1 April 1981, two and a half weeks after the original match. The three Steves, Alison O'Brien and I drove up for the match. Early on, Jimmy Neighbour whipped the ball past a lumbering Alan 'That is diabolical defending!' Hansen, raced down the right flank and crossed for Paul Goddard to score with a diving header. It looked like we might win a cup or two or three or four for West Ham and the Claret and Blue. But slowly Liverpool showed their European class, and in the second half they scored twice at the Holt End where we were standing. Kenny Dalglish netted with a fabulous turn and shot, and a Hansen header deflected in off the outstretched thigh of Billy Bonds.

It was disappointing, but no one could really complain about losing to the champions and eventual European Cup winners. After the game we drove to Coventry. Alison was a student at Warwick University, and we were going to kip at her house. We made the mistake of stopping the car and going into a deserted chip shop wearing West Ham scarves.

As we left with our chips, about 20 Coventry youths suddenly ran from a nearby pub. 'It's West Ham!' they shouted. They started pushing, kicking and punching us and running over the roof of the car. 'Are you the lot that got us last time?' they asked. It seemed we had been mistaken for the ICF. I thought about saying, 'Yes, we're exactly the same people, so please gave us an extra big kicking!' but didn't.

At first I had considered fighting back, but realising that the odds were twenty to five (including one woman) I decided against it, and instead I parried some blows on my back and felt flying boots trying to kick my legs over. It all went in slow motion. Then, one of the pissed-up Coventry hooligans smashed a glass on a wall and slashed one of the Steves on the arm. Luckily, they saw blood, got a little scared and allowed us to get in the car and drive off. Steve's arm was cut, but the glass had missed the veins.

It was frightening and a little ridiculous, too. It was the first time that I'd ever been attacked by fans of a completely different club to the one that West Ham had just played. Coventry band The Specials had a number-one hit with 'Ghost Town' that year, and the song's sense of urban alienation seemed to be summed up in that cowardly incident. And didn't Coventry lowlife realise that we were considered to be the sportsmen of England, at least in Tbilisi? If any of those Coventry fans are reading this today, then no, we were not the lot that got you last time.

After cup finals and European tours we had almost forgotten about the league. But the side maintained a fabulous record by not losing any of the last 18 games that season. David Cross proved that he was more than just a psychotic striker when he scored a beautiful long-range curler at Watford in one of those matches. Promotion was clinched with a routine home defeat of bottom-of-the-table Bristol Rovers on 4 April 1981. A week later, Psycho scored four at Grimsby to clinch the championship. The last five games of the season were almost an anticlimax, but we maintained our form and finished with sixty-six points, thirteen ahead of second-placed Notts County. Billy paraded another trophy, and after three years' exile, we were back in Division One.

In the following three seasons, West Ham re-established themselves in Division One, finishing ninth, eighth and ninth. Those were three very respectable finishes, although we never seemed to take the next step and challenge for a European spot.

The 1981–82 season began with a marvellous 4–0 win at White Hart Lane, with all four goals scored by David Cross. It was a midweek game, and I was inside a packed but ecstatic Paxton Road end. It was back in the days when they let so many away fans into that confined end at Spurs that it was lucky a disaster never occurred. But we didn't care as Psycho destroyed our presumptuous enemy, and the away fans sung a resounding chorus of:

They're turning White Hart Lane into a public lavatory,
They're turning White Hart Lane into a public lavatory,

They're turning White Hart Lane into a public lavatory,
And we all piss up the wall.
Altogether now,
Wanky, Wanky, Tottenham,
Wanky, Wanky, Tottenham,
Wanky, Wanky, Tottenham!
And we all piss up the wall!

OK, it wasn't very subtle, but it was a very satisfying song indeed to sing when you were 4–0 up at White Hart Lane. Psycho scored a lot of goals that season, although his rate dried up after Christmas.

Another great game that season was a 4–2 home win over Southampton in late September. Kevin Keegan and his perm did not love it when the South Bank chanted at him, as many crowds did at that time, 'Keegan lost the World Cup!' He looked so wound up, you could see that such sensitivity might be a weakness, as it was to prove when he managed Newcastle. Paul Goddard scored a hat-trick, and the underrated Geoff Pike, who was to hit ten goals from midfield that season, scored the other. The only bad part of that evening was being sprayed with a flow of urine from a pissed-up miscreant on the terraces behind me.

Cross ended with 16 league goals, Goddard 15 and new signing François van der Elst, who had tormented West Ham in the 1976 Cup-Winners' Cup final when playing for Anderlecht, scored 5 league goals late on. But in the close season the 31-year-old David Cross declined to sign a new contract and moved on to Manchester City. West Ham struggled to replace him.

The 1982–83 season began with new Scottish signing Sandy Clark up front. He looked a bit like a squaddie but after a sluggish start, proved himself to be hard working and capable of hitting the net. I liked his commitment, even if most of the Upton Park purists didn't. He scored a respectable 7 goals in 26 games before returning to Scotland and being replaced by David Swindlehurst from Crystal Palace.

That year, we managed to beat the champions Liverpool 3–1 at Upton Park, thanks to a tap-in by Alvin, Geoff Pike's volley and a third by Sandy Clark, which was set up by Goddard. Finishing eighth in the league, West Ham scored five against Swansea and Birmingham that season but also conceded five at Stoke. On New Year's Day, 17-year-old Tony Cottee scored on his debut as we thrashed Spurs 3–0 at Upton Park. Young Alan Dickens also came into the side, scored six goals, and was hailed as 'the next Trevor Brooking' (he wasn't).

At the end of 1981, I left Brentwood for London, and even though my peripatetic existence took in Turnpike Lane, West Kensington, Hammersmith, Parson's Green, Fulham Broadway and Camberwell during the next six years, I would make my way to the District Line every other week to stand in the North Bank or Chicken Run with my post-student Joy Division long overcoat on. West Ham were still as much a backdrop of London life as gigs by the Psychedelic Furs and The Clash, even if attendances were declining at every club throughout the country.

West Ham had not built on the great promotion-winning side, and by 1983–84, with Frank Lampard retiring and Trevor Brooking playing his last season, the side was in need of some serious rebuilding. So we bought Steve Walford and Steve Whitton. 'Wally' Walford was an erratic left-back signed from Arsenal. The name Whitton may still cause palpitations in many members of the Chicken Run, but he did have a very good start to his Hammers career. Signed from Coventry, Whitton was an East Ham lad who was returning home to lead his beloved West Ham to glory. At least that was the way it was meant to be.

Whitton had scored against West Ham in a 4–2 win at Highfield Road the previous season, which meant he must be good. Except that Lyall had forgotten that everyone scored against West Ham. The Hammers started the season like they were going to annihilate the rest of the division, beating Birmingham 4–0 at Upton Park on the opening day and winning their first five games. Steve Whitton scored his first goal in a 2–0 win at Spurs, turning sharply to score with a good shot as a corner kick fell into the box. In a hugely entertaining game, we beat Leicester City 5–2, after being two goals down at Upton Park. Whitton scored another two goals, the second a 30-yard piledriver that exploded into the South Bank net like it had been fired by a young Bobby Charlton.

However, as the season continued, Whitton and the Irons were to experience far more miserable times. The problem was that although the player preferred a role as a striker or midfielder, Lyall envisaged Whitton as a winger, which would have been fine if he had pace, dribbling ability or the skill to beat a full-back. For those in the Chicken Run used to watching Brooking and Devonshire on the flanks it was a shock indeed to see Whitton charging down the wing with all the subtlety of a rhinoceros being pursued by big-game hunters.

His grace and poise soon earned appreciative nicknames such as Diego, Dobbin, Donkey and Nellie the Elephant. It wasn't just where I was standing either: my dad had a season ticket in the East Stand and would say in a slightly puzzled tone, 'The man in front of me thinks Whitton isn't even up to Third Division standard.'

Who will ever forget those subtle skills as he gently stroked the ball past his man before crashing into the South Bank advertising hoardings taking ball and full-back with him? His crossing was uncannily accurate – not once did he fail to find the defender's outstretched boot, winning corner after corner thanks to his sublime skills.

There were still home highlights to savour that season. Charlie Nicholas arrived with Arsenal at Upton Park, but the Gunners were resoundingly beaten 3–1 thanks to an inspired Trevor Brooking. On the last day of 1983, the Hammers thrashed Tottenham 4–1 with Ray Stewart scoring a glorious long-range volley.

By now I was working in the press office at the National Dairy Council (NDC). Because my employers were sponsoring the Milk Cup, one of the perks of the job was free trips to cup games. My pal Paul Garrett and I managed to blag our way into the West Ham press box for the Milk Cup home tie against Bury. In this inner sanctum there was free tea, sausage rolls at half-time and a press room with bulky old black phones set at desks around the walls for correspondents to phone in their copy.

It might have sounded like a fairly routine Milk Cup tie, but it was to produce West Ham's record score, a thumping 10–0 victory over Bury. Those who have seen the video highlights will remember it most for the Irish commentator, who repeatedly refers to Tony 'Coatey' up front. Just about every West Ham player scored. Tony Coatey got four, Dev two, Trev two, Alvin one and a Stewart pen completed the thrashing. It was all a little embarrassing for poor old Bury.

Having watched his side beat Bury 10–0, John Lyall decided to buy their centre-half, Paul Hilton. This could only happen at West Ham. Hilts was to be turned into a utility player at West Ham: equally mediocre in all positions. He tried his hardest, but even Trevor Brooking looked a little bemused at ending his career alongside Whitton and Hilton.

The long-term problems for West Ham began when Alan Devonshire was seriously injured against Wigan in the third round of the FA Cup, early in 1984. Dev had damaged knee ligaments and was to be out for the next 18 months. The Hammers won only five out of their remaining twenty-one matches after Devonshire was injured, and finished the season by winning just one of their last twelve games.

During a 4–2 home defeat to a Mo Johnston-inspired Watford, age appeared to be catching up with even Billy Bonds. Whitton was injured in a car crash and added to our injury crisis. My old university mate Steve Healy was living in Liverpool and a weekend visit allowed me to see West Ham at Anfield in April. We lost 6–0. Steve Whitton had been recalled as a centre-forward, and even when the Irons were 6–0 down, he was still able to volley past an open goal before the stunned Kop. Bruce Grobbelaar spent most of the game holding up the appropriate number of fingers as the Kop asked, 'Brucie, Brucie, what's the score?' Yet still West Ham finished ninth, thanks mainly to a fine first half of the season, and a combined 28 goals from Cottee (15) and Swindlehurst (13).

Towards the end of the season, Trevor Brooking was sensational in a game against QPR at Upton Park, creating six clear chances, but we still only drew 2–2. As the season ended with a whimper, few fans were expected for the final home game against Everton. Yet 25,452 turned up to say farewell to Trevor Brooking in his last game. West Ham lost 1–0, but at the end of the game the whole ground stayed for half an hour to sing 'Trevor Brooking walks on water!' and demand that he return for a lap of honour. If Trevor ever had doubts about the wisdom of sticking with West Ham, surely the wave of emotion he felt that night removed them. He looked so moved that he might have even muttered something like 'I think the lad Brooking will be quite pleased with that one . . .' as he was carried shoulder-high off the pitch.

Without Devonshire and Brooking, the 1984–85 season was a relegation struggle. Tony Gale, a cultured centre-back, was signed from Fulham and fitted in well at the back, but the side had many other weaknesses. Phil Parkes was suffering from a septic elbow and was replaced by Tom McAlister in goal. He had a reasonably good season, but was no Parksey. Steve Whitton was given another 17 appearances lumbering down the wing before even Lyall despaired of the elephantine winger and dropped him. Paul Goddard looked like he was playing in trainers and began to fall over more than he would score.

A 3–2 home defeat to Southampton just before Christmas was typical. Tony Cottee scored two good goals, the second after a marvellous dash down the right from Paul Allen, but it was all undone by terrible defending. West Ham scored a classic own goal, sublime in its awfulness. Steve Walford, 30 yards from goal and under no pressure, turned round to lob a back pass towards McAlister, only the ball went over his head, on to the bar and bounced in off the hapless keeper's posterior. I stood in the Chicken Run, stunned.

When West Ham played Wimbledon in the third round of the FA Cup Alan Devonshire played in the away game and the replay. *Hammer* then announced that he had flu and he wasn't seen again for the rest of the season. A home game against Manchester United on a Friday night – admittedly on live TV – attracted just 16,674 fans to Upton Park. Cottee had a good season, scoring 17 goals in a struggling side, but that was the only plus. We lost 5–0 at Watford and 5–1 at West Brom. With three games to go, West Ham beat an already relegated Stoke 5–1 at Upton Park with even Diego Hilton scoring, but it wasn't until the penultimate game at Ipswich, when Cottee scored the winner, that West Ham were safe, finishing 16th in the league.

When Paul Allen signed for Spurs for £400,000 the 1985–86 season looked like another struggle. John Lyall signed a couple of hopeless unknowns called Mark Ward and Frank McAvennie, but this was West Ham, and you could never afford to look away or dare not to go to a game. The side went on to have its greatest ever league season.

Admittedly, the kit that season was rubbish – a burgundy shirt with a white pinstripe effect and the sponsor's logo Avco on the front – but everything else was perfect. Alan Devonshire had finally returned from his 18-month bout of 'Devonshire flu'. He was no longer able to completely bend his knee and had lost the speed to go round the outside of full-backs, but he still had all the old skill and adapted himself to a game based more on passing and turning inside defenders. With Dev on the left, the side had shape once more.

The side started with a 1–0 defeat at Birmingham, with Goddard and Cottee as stikers and McAvennie in midfield, but when Goddard was injured, McAvennie moved up front. In the next home game against QPR, you could tell the boy was, as they say, 'a bit special'. Not only did Frank have a distinctive haircut – his peroxide locks being short at the sides and long at the back, just like Shane and every other man in *Neighbours* – but he worked tremendously hard and was full of hunger. He seemed to enjoy playing football much more than most professionals; he played with the relish of a one-time road sweeper suddenly taken from the crowd and given a game. He tackled defenders back and had a roguish grin. That night he scored two crisply taken goals before a crowd of just 15,530. That season he was one of the best strikers West Ham have ever had.

The team lost the next two games at home to Luton and away to Man United, but in the home match against Liverpool, McAvennie again showed his class. His exuberance and determination had forced the normally reliable Grobbelaar, Hansen and Lawrenson into making some terrible errors. First he nipped between a dithering Brucie and Hansen to stroke in the opener, and in the second half, he reached Mark Ward's lofted ball just before the Liverpool keeper to chip it in.

West Ham then went on an 18-match unbeaten run, with McAvennie and Cottee making bets with each other on who would score the best goal in each match. In that sequence of results, Brian Clough's Nottingham Forest were beaten 4–2 at Upton Park with Frank scoring twice and Tony once, the other coming from Alan Dickens.

Suddenly, the whole side looked solid. With two small strikers we were playing the ball to feet rather than lofting in crosses, and Martin and Gale were both footballing centre-backs able to play their way out of trouble. Behind them Phil Parkes had forgotten all about arthritic knees and septic elbows and was back to his England-class form of the early '80s.

Alan Dickens, normally an introverted character, had added aggression to his game and was regularly supplying the forwards with good chances. Little Mark Ward was up and down the right flank every match. He got stuck in and must have been a real pest to play against. And unlike Paul Allen he never got injured. In fact, no one got injured that season.

At the time I'd been made redundant from my job at the National Dairy Council, so I took an October trip to the Scottish Highlands to think about the future. Results were difficult to get when travelling, and it wasn't until a Monday morning in Inverness station that I managed to find a copy of *The Guardian*. There on one of the sports pages was an account of West Ham beating Aston Villa 4–1. Cottee had scored twice, as had McAvennie, and all after Villa had taken the lead. The paper said that McAvennie's chip over the keeper for the final goal was one of the goals of the season.

Returning to London for the Everton home match, it became clear that we were in for a good season. Everton were the champions and under Howard Kendall usually ground out a 1–0 win at the Hammers with Kevin Ratcliffe passing the ball back to Neville Southall at least 50,000 times per half. Trevor Steven scored on the hour, and it looked like another routine defeat, but then came the irrepressible McAvennie. Like a Scouse nemesis from Ramsay Street, the mullet-headed genius latched on to a pass from substitute George Parris to equalise in the 74th minute. Then nine minutes from the end, McAvennie showed phenomenal speed to round Southall and tap the ball into the net before running to the South Bank fans with upraised arms. West Ham just didn't come back in games like that.

The disappointing aspect of that season was that only the fans in the ground saw West Ham's goals. There was a dispute between the Football League and the TV companies which meant that there was no football coverage on TV until January 1986. It seems incredible in the age of Sky that half a season should have been completely lost to the cameras. It's a bit like the BBC wiping all those old black-and-white episodes of *Doctor Who* because they never envisaged the video age. No doubt there are West Ham anoraks that still insist that McAvennie's goals will turn up on old film in a basement in New Zealand one day, but they won't. They have been lost for ever.

It was a different football universe in 1985. The nation was still shocked by the Bradford fire and the Heysel stadium disaster; crowds were dwindling (West Ham had 19,000 for the home match with Liverpool) and being a football fan was something you would never mention on a hot date. Middle-class fans were much rarer than today. Indeed, after the Heysel deaths I remember one person at work saying, 'I hope you're happy now,' as if being a football fan meant that I was in some way personally responsible for the tragedy.

It was in this climate that West Ham kept on winning, ignored by the cameras and intelligentsia. For once, an injury-free West Ham fielded a settled side all season. After the Villa game, the lads won nine in a row: Villa, Ipswich away, Everton, Oxford away, Watford, Coventry away, WBA, QPR away and Birmingham were all beaten. Frank even returned jet-lagged from Scotland's trip to Australia to score the winner at QPR, claiming that the long journey didn't really matter as he'd had half an hour's sleep the night before.

By January, the cameras were back, and Frank had been on *Wogan*. Suddenly, McAvennie was all over the tabloids, thanks to his *Footballers' Wives* lifestyle. He was a regular at Stringfellow's, where he and Peter exchanged tips on tasteful barnets, was dating page-three model Jenny Blyth and about to move in to a mock-Tudor love nest with her. Their new home was in Hornchurch next door to fellow page-three stunner Maria Whittaker. Jenny even appeared on page three of *The Sun* wearing a Hammers scarf with the caption 'Frank and his lads could do with a couple of extra points!' It must have caused a few dropped sugar lumps as the West Ham board took their tea.

Finally, the *Big Match* cameras were there as West Ham beat Manchester United 2–1 at Upton Park thanks to a Mark Ward rocket ('A tremendous goal!' exclaimed Brian Moore, proving that he'd not lost one of his trademark phrases during his absence) and Tony Cottee, who beat both a United defender and Gary Bailey, United's keeper, to the ball on the edge of the box to score the winner.

The cameras were there again as West Ham demolished Chelsea 4–0 at Stamford Bridge. Devonshire shot into the top corner from the edge of the box for the first. Then George Parris raced the length of the left wing, played a one–two and crossed for Cottee to score a marvellous counter-attacking goal. McAvennie unselfishly passed to Cottee for the third, and Frank produced a glorious half-volley for the fourth. It's probably not a match that they included in Roman Abramovich's Chelsea prospectus.

By then, I was working for a free listings magazine with an editor who had all the subtlety of Ian Paisley on a visit to the Vatican. I was unhappy there, but West Ham games still provided a release. My mum and dad had moved to Norfolk, and for the rest of the season I used my dad's season ticket in the East Stand.

A mistake by Neil Orr cost West Ham the game in the rearranged fixture against Chelsea at Upton Park, but after that we kept winning, completing six victories in sixteen days. Sometimes it was with a single goal from Alvin Martin; on another night it was an astonishing eight goals against Newcastle. Admittedly, Newcastle had to put Peter Beardsley in goal for some of the game, but West Ham were unstoppable that night, with a penalty completing Alvin Martin's hat-trick from centre-half. Some bloke called Glenn Roeder even scored an own goal. The Newcastle fans were applauded by the West Ham crowd at the end, mainly because when Whitehurst scored their single consolation goal they erupted as if they'd won the cup.

When West Ham beat Ipswich before a tremendously atmospheric Upton Park crowd of 31,000 it seemed we really might win the league. Dickens had chipped a splendid goal from the edge of the box, Ipswich had levelled but then Mark Ward went down in the box. Terry Butcher went mad disputing the spot-kick decision, but Ray Stewart blasted the ball home as reliably as ever, and West Ham were second.

When we beat WBA 3–2 at the Hawthorns, thanks to a Ray Stewart penalty, it looked like the title could be ours – if Liverpool didn't win at Chelsea. The travelling West Ham fans even succumbed to a 'radio rumour' that Chelsea had scored but, Liverpool being Liverpool, they won 1–0 – Kenny Dalglish scoring the goal – and took the title. I felt a great surge of disgust for Chelsea. If I were the Doctor's companion in *Doctor Who*, that is one game that I would go back in time to change, whatever it did to the timeline.

The last game of the season at Everton didn't matter any more, and we went down 3–1, finishing third instead of second. It had still been an incredible season, from relegation prospects to title challengers. Today, West Ham would have been in the Champions League, yet we didn't have even the UEFA Cup to go for then because English clubs were banned from Europe after the Heysel disaster. It didn't matter, though, as we now had a quality top-three side. Frank McAvennie had scored 28 goals in all competitions and Tony Cottee 25. This was it. We were going to strengthen and build the team of the '80s.

7

McKNIGHTMARE ON
GREEN STREET

1986–89
*Stewart Robson is held together by cycling shorts . . . Frankie goes to
Celtic and is replaced by Alan Dickens up front . . . TC goes to Everton
. . . Allen McKnight earns the tabloid moniker of McNit . . . David
Kelly falls over . . . West Ham thrash Liverpool in the Cup . . . and still
get relegated.*
   Price of Hammer *in 1989: £1*

West Ham failed to consolidate on the club's most successful ever season.
Instead of buying from a position of strength, John Lyall insisted that he
was happy with his squad and he would give the players who finished
third another chance. Somehow, a team that had nearly won the title the
season before, finished 15th at the end of the 1986–87 season.

The squad was so small that it couldn't cope with injuries to the likes
of Alvin Martin or Tony Gale, when all we had was 'Diego' Hilton in
reserve. Alan Dickens started to look fragile in both his tackling and
confidence and rapidly earned the nickname 'Sharon' from certain
sections of the Chicken Run. Mark Ward was now running down culs-
de-sac. George Parris suddenly looked vulnerable at left-back. Alan
Devonshire was soon to go missing and not be seen again for 18 months.

Then there was Frankie Mac. He'd started off well and scored in a great win at Old Trafford, but then he lost his irrepressible hunger. The sharpness went from his game, and a long goal famine followed. He was downing copious amounts of champagne, although he claims he was not as yet using cocaine.

At the end of November, West Ham lost 4–0 at Newcastle in a live televised match. I'd just moved into an asbestos-ridden tower block in Westbourne Park with a short-life housing association and had purchased a £5 TV that took ten minutes to warm up, produced Day-Glo colours and made every character look shorter and fatter. Mark Ward had the build of a Spacehopper as he and Ray Stewart tried to contain a rampant Peter Beardsley. Paul Goddard was now playing for the Geordies and enjoyed himself up against Diego Hilton, in for the injured Martin. Even my dodgy telly couldn't disguise the fact that we were looking pretty rubbish.

When Lyall finally acted, he purchased Stewart Robson from Arsenal for £700,000. Robson was a promising midfield player in the style of Bryan Robson; he was also a local Essex lad who had attended Brentwood School. Lyall later revealed that when he signed Robson he was on the treatment table in the Highbury physio's room. Perhaps that should have told him something. Robson would have been great for us if only he'd ever been fully fit. At times it appeared that his body was held together by the Lycra cycling shorts he wore beneath his kit. Robson didn't require the treatment room, he needed an Allen key and puncture repair kit to sort out his troublesome pelvis.

John Lyall also signed Gary Strodder from Lincoln, a Yorkshire centre-back who looked like a squaddie and whose hair was so spiky it threatened to puncture the ball every time he headed it. The other wrong player at the wrong price was Tommy McQueen, a journeyman Scottish left-back from Aberdeen. Liam Brady, the cultured former Arsenal midfielder, arrived from Italy, although he was past his best.

By now I had a season ticket and was standing in the East Terrace Chicken Run, where the humour was sharper than behind the goals, and the plummeting Hammers were subjected to the equivalent of the heckling that occurred at the early stand-up comedy gigs that were becoming popular around that time. One 2–0 home defeat by Sheffield Wednesday in March 1987 was particularly memorable. Some of the comments rivalled a classic cry from the '70s of 'Come on Hammers! Really pep it up and make it mediocre!' As new signing Gary Strodder warmed up he was greeted with, 'You're stupid! Why did you join us?' Within two minutes there was a cry of, 'Come on Hammers, why aren't we losing?' The lads then conceded the softest of goals. Some Chicken Run fans started to chant, 'Here we go, here we go . . .' while another shouted, 'Come on the claret and blue dustbins!'

The Hammers were turning in another listless performance, after which John Lyall came out with something about injuries being part and parcel of the game. Howard Wilkinson's Sheffield Wednesday were a big, strong, direct side, easily able to outmuscle the Hammers' attempts at pretty football.

'Lyall out! Lyall out!' came the chants, a little unfairly just a year after we'd been challenging for the title. Full-back George Parris thumped the ball hopelessly into touch. 'Ball out! Ball out!' came the modified chant. 'What have you got in that bag, Parkes, a respirator?' greeted poor old Phil Parkes and his arthritic knees as he took his place in the North Bank goal for the second half. By now we could all understand the real cause of Arthur Fowler's nervous breakdown in *EastEnders*.

There was also a very angry bald bloke in a leather jacket, making comments in a voice reminiscent of Ade Edmondson in *The Young Ones*. It was Steve Rapport, aka North Bank Norman, later editor of the fanzine *Fortune's Always Hiding*. He's hollering, 'Brilliant, absolutely brilliant!' and 'Dangerous!' as West Ham's attacks end not with a bang at goal but a whimper. Next he turns to West Ham's diminutive forward line. 'Don't worry Cottee, Snow White and the other six will be coming soon,' shouts Rapport.

'Who can we blame now?' asks one fan. 'We've blamed the entire team, we'll have to start shouting at ourselves.'

The ball ricocheted inside West Ham's area. 'Don't clear it West Ham, it's only in the box! Don't clear it!' Wednesday's Shutt gently rolled the ball over the West Ham line. 'Aaaaaaaagh,' exclaimed the fan behind me in a primeval wail, holding his head with his hands.

That year the papers were full of Aids-awareness adverts and the message had not been missed at Upton Park. 'Condoms! Condoms! You're playing like a team of condoms,' shouted another fan.

The frustrated McAvennie was sent off for trying to chin a defender.

'Remember goals West Ham, they were big in the '70s,' hollered Steve Rapport as the game stumbled towards a conclusion.

'Officer, arrest that lot on the pitch for loitering without intent,' came a disembodied voice as the police surrounded the pitch.

The blank-faced fans walked away like Vietnam War veterans, unable to resume their place in civil society. Walking past the bus station through the alleyway to Tudor Road I heard a supporter being consoled by his girlfriend. 'They were terrible last week, too,' she said.

'No, that was just bad,' he sighed. 'This was absolutely dismal.' All confidence had gone, and it left me wondering how a side that finished third the previous year could end the next season like that?

The next year was worse. West Ham sold the underachieving McAvennie and his *Neighbours* mullet to Celtic, and he immediately started scoring again. Lyall came up with the idea of converting Alan Dickens into a deep-lying centre-forward, to play alongside Tony Cottee. Great expectations only resulted in hard times and a bleak house in my tower-block gaff. Dickens was a skilful if diffident midfielder but not the sort of player who could be used in a strong wind. His striking instincts were as speedy as his namesake's plots. Psycho Cross must have been asking his mother just what was going on, as reports of Dickens's conversion reached the Bates Motel.

When McAvennie was sold, *Hammer* issued a marvellously Micawber-esque statement:

> Mr Lyall does not disguise the fact that we are looking for a striker but stresses there is no immediate panic particularly as the team are playing so well, at the moment. He says: 'We simply want the right player at the right price. It's as simple as that . . . the nice thing is that we are not under any pressure as the team are playing well and winning matches.'

There was the odd throwback to the old days, when there would be a superbly entertaining game at Upton Park. In one such match in November 1987, Tony Cottee scored with a stupendous bicycle kick against Nottingham Forest. That match also featured an inspired midfield performance from Billy Bonds. At the age of 41 he had been enticed out of semi-retirement to bolster the Hammers' injury-stricken midfield.

Bonzo looked about 30, still had a permanent tan and he was still class. When Newcastle's teenage star Paul Gascoigne started to give him verbals in one match Billy simply laughed at him. But for all Bonds' enduring skill, it was a sign of our desperation that we were relying on a 41 year old.

For five weary months Dickens toiled up front, mercilessly clattered by lumbering centre-backs. At other times Lyall tried Ince, Dolan and Diego Hilton up front. Each week the Hammers would be linked with a different striker. According to various newspapers West Ham had apparently tried to buy Kerry Dixon, Mick Harford, John Fashanu, Kevin Drinkell, Colin Clarke, Peter Davenport, Nico Clausen, Lee Chapman and quite possibly Eddie 'The Eagle' Edwards.

The Kerry Dixon saga was particularly excruciating. Ken Bates refused to let Dixon rejoin Arsenal for fear he might rediscover his goalscoring touch, but had no such worries about the Chelsea striker joining West Ham, immediately agreeing terms, only for the player himself to reject the deal and Lyall to claim that 'you have to be patient when you are pursuing quality'. The *Daily Mail* duly labelled West Ham 'the lepers of football'.

'Bring on the *Neighbours* video!' shouted one Chicken Run aficionado, referring to the new Aussie soap opera, during a dire draw at home to Portsmouth – we should be so lucky. That was followed by 'Stewart! It's that green thing with lines around it!' as the full-back pumped another ball in the general direction of France.

At home to Oxford there was a stoppage in play and a frustrated fan ran onto the pitch at the South Bank end and curled a lovely shot around West Ham goalkeeper Tom McAlister. There were huge cheers as he was hugged by a steward, but then he was ejected by the Old Bill, who no doubt assumed that seeing goals at Upton Park might contribute to serious public disorder.

Finally, shortly before the transfer deadline, Fulham's Leroy Rosenior agreed to sign for West Ham. Alison O'Brien, one of the old Brentwood Hammers crew, had just returned from several years teaching English in Spain. We went to the home match against Watford, where Leroy was making his debut.

As a returning expatriate, Alison had several questions. Are West Ham still having all the game and failing to score? Is Billy Bonds still playing?

Is John Lyall still saying he's waiting for the right player at the right price? Yes, everything was just the same, I concurred sadly.

'It's just like walking into a room full of really bad-tempered men!' was her immediate impression of the Chicken Run. It was indeed like walking into a room full of really bad-tempered men, but it was difficult for outsiders to understand what we'd suffered that season.

'I feel sorry for Leroy joining us,' remarked a man moving through the Chicken Run gathering signatures for a petition to sack the board. At least Rosenior wanted to play for us, and he was providing more threat than Snow White and the other six. Then late on in the second half the unthinkable happened. Leroy raced through the Watford defence to deposit a firm shot into the net.

'WE'VE SCORED, WE'VE SCORED, WE'VE SCORED!' screamed the fan behind me. It was less celebration, more group catharsis. Grown men gyrated uncontrollably and programmes and scarves were thrown into the air. We had found a forward! West Ham looked like they might win a home game . . .

'It's only one . . .' muttered the man with the petition.

'LEROOOOY! LEROOOOY!' boomed the North Bank.

Somehow West Ham survived that year, finishing 16th. Leroy at last provided an attacking focus up front and a left-back called Julian Dicks, signed from Birmingham, had a great left foot and tackled like a young Billy Bonds. Mark Ward rediscovered the form of two seasons ago to inspire a 4–1 home victory over Chelsea in the final home game of the season.

But it was only the postponement of misery. For the 1988–89 season was finally to bring us a McKnightmare on Green Street. Allen McKnight was signed from Celtic, where he'd played just 12 games, as the replacement for the ageing Phil Parkes. Tony Cottee opted to join Everton. He was replaced by David Kelly, a £500,000 striker who had scored plenty of goals for Third Division Walsall. Soon after he joined, *The Sun* carried a feature on him headlined 'I Had One Leg Four Inches Shorter Than The Other, Says Half Million Pound Hammer'. Kelly had fallen out of a tree when he was a child, broken a leg and discovered that he had Perthes disease – the bone and muscle were not growing in his left thigh. Luckily, he received treatment, and after five years of limping and various treatment that included an iron bar connecting one ankle to another, he made a full recovery.

McKnight had a fine game on his debut at Wimbledon in a 1–0 victory, where a young player called Paul Ince gave a mature performance as sweeper. McKnight also gave a point-saving performance in a draw at Coventry, but they were the only good games he was ever to have as a West Ham goalkeeper.

Former Celtic and Scotland star Bertie Auld certainly appreciated Lyall's astute signing: 'It was the greatest piece of business Billy [McNeil] ever did when he got rid of McKnight for £250,000 . . . McKnight lacks presence in the penalty box and when he was at Celtic you could almost hear the fans holding their breath as the high crosses came in.'

Was McKnight really that bad? Looking at the video evidence, there was a 3–3 draw at home to Notts Forest where McKnight stood inert in goal as a corner drifted over his head for Nigel Clough to head home, and a bemused Stan Laurel scratching-his-head posture as Clough floated a free-kick into the top corner.

Allen McKnight's greatest mistakes began with a 4–1 defeat at Luton. Then he cost West Ham the game at home to Everton, allowing Trevor Steven's toe-poke to pass beneath his body. During a 0–2 home defeat to Spurs he even allowed himself to be lobbed by one Mitchell Thomas.

A national audience became aware of his talents during a 2–1 defeat at Norwich, screened on live TV. Trying to take a Grobbelaar-esque safari out of his goal, the hapless No. 1 was halfway to Great Yarmouth before Dale Gordon realised that he had been presented with an empty net.

McKnight treated the ball as if it were covered with radioactive dust from Chernobyl. He left us many enduring moments: a Dennis Wise free-kick that trickled through the Hammers defence with all the force of a Steve Potts 30-yarder; a Bryan Robson shot rebounding off his body as if he were a rigid Subbuteo keeper and falling to Gordon Strachan, who scored; an Alan Smith shot that went through the invisible goalkeeper; and a memorable Gary Sprake impersonation during a 1–0 FA Cup victory over Swindon.

That season, West Ham reached the semi-finals of the League Cup. It was after the home leg against Luton that McKnight really encountered tabloid malice in blunderland. He hared from his line to cut out a cross, the only problem being that it wasn't the same cross converted by Mick Harford. The keeper was at fault for the third goal, too, a grateful Roy Wegerle finding a gap the size of Canary Wharf between McKnight and his near post. We lost 3–0 at home in that first leg and 2–0 away. The press began to realise Allen's talents and gave him affectionate nicknames such as 'McNit', 'Mr Boob' and 'McKnightmare'.

The Chicken Run were not too happy. 'I'm not sure if I ever want to play at Upton Park again,' McKnightmare complained to the press. The feeling of the fans was fairly mutual. Soon even Lyall had to admit that the inexperienced goalkeeper had proved catastrophic as he coaxed Phil Parkes and his arthritic knees – and one-time septic elbow – into yet more action. Thanks to Cossack natural hair control Phil's hairstyle was much better preserved than his knees, but despite his physical ailments, the old shaggy dog of a goalkeeper immediately had a bolstering effect upon the West Ham defence. McKnight was later to be transferred to Fourth Division Walsall and then ended up playing for Romford.

West Ham also had problems in attack. David Kelly looked far too frail for the top division and could never please a demanding crowd who longed for Tony Cottee. Ned, as he was known, appeared to have inherited Goddard's studless boots; he never scored a goal for West Ham without falling over.

He's still there on my video today, pushing Des Walker aside to swivel, shoot, score and fall over in one match, and then in another he was already on his backside in the six-yard box ready to slide the ball home after Ward's free-kick was headed down by Martin. 'A pretty unorthodox goal; he scored it while he was on the ground,' commented Brian Moore. Only for Kelly at West Ham it was entirely orthodox.

He even managed to score in a win at Derby when Peter Shilton punched the ball onto his head, causing Kelly to fall over and the ball to spin into the net. Two misses in one-on-ones against Man United's Jim Leighton helped destroy Kelly's confidence. It was a full season before Kelly and Rosenior discovered there was such a thing as an offside trap. Typically, he was much better once he left. Eventually 'Grace' was transferred to Leicester where he scored five times in his first three games, and then scored loads for Kevin Keegan's Second Division championship-winning Newcastle side.

West Ham might have been struggling in the league, but they produced some astonishing cup performances. A fine example was a League Cup match against champions Liverpool at Upton Park. Young midfielder Paul Ince scored twice, first with a header and then with an acrobatic flying volley. Here was our next young star, while ageing maestros Devonshire and Liam Brady controlled the game.

Liverpool pulled a goal back, but in the second half, Steve Staunton decided to play a cushioned header back to Grobbelaar, only for the ball to go into the far corner of the net. Tony Gale then completed a stunning 4–1 victory with a delicious curling free-kick. Upton Park was delirious, the mighty 'Red Machine' of Liverpool just didn't lose 4–1. It was the Reds' biggest cup defeat since 1939. In the FA Cup West Ham managed to win 1–0 at Highbury thanks to a goal from Rosenior.

Yet in the league we were floundering and in serious relegation trouble. It took until April for West Ham to win their second home game. Working as a freelance journalist now, I'd been introduced to Steve Rapport, a freelance photographer whom I recognised as the bloke in the leather jacket in the Chicken Run who made all those comments like 'Remember goals, West Ham? They were big in the '70s!' Steve was a perfectionist both at work and home. His house in Clapham was always immaculately tidy, and he read computer manuals from start to finish. It was no wonder, therefore, that the lackadaisical nature of West Ham used to infuriate the lifelong fan so much.

Using his desktop-publishing skills, Steve started to put together the fanzine *Fortune's Always Hiding*. Our crew on the Chicken Run now comprised Steve, his sister Hannah, the then *Time Out* writer Don Peretta, Joe Norris, who was now managing comedians other than those at Upton Park, music journalist Mike Pattenden, sports writer Denis Campbell and Porky, later to be known under his real name of Phill Jupitus. West Ham was fertile ground for our humour, and perhaps the fanzine's use of wit combined with serious comment forced the club to become slightly less complacent. That first issue for February/March 1989 had a cover that featured a cartoon by Phill Jupitus. John Lyall was reading a newspaper headlined 'West Ham crash to the bottom of division three . . . Lyall speaks blah quality blah no panic blah right players at right price blah blah bad supporters blah still in the cup blah East-End tradition blah blah blah'.

John Lyall had been a very successful manager for much of his 14 years, winning the FA Cup twice, reaching the Cup-Winners' Cup and League Cup finals and winning the Second Division championship. He was also, as the press constantly stressed, one of the nicest men in football. But now there had been three successive relegation struggles and the fear was that he had been at the club too long and could no longer motivate the players. As Jonathan Foster wrote in *The Independent* that season:

> Some of the most potent myths in football have enabled those who control West Ham to enjoy a depth of reverence usually reserved for royalty. George VI's favourite team (and King Olaf's) are portrayed as a happy band of artists sustained in their integrity by the warmth of the East End community.
>
> It is doubtful whether those who pay regularly to enter Upton Park ever recognised themselves in this fantasy. If they did when the fine teams of the 1960s were failing to win championships they do not now . . . West Ham for all the Camelot imagery surrounding their Littlewoods Cup defeat of Liverpool are a poor team who are not bottom of the table because the world ignores their art.

The first issue of *Fortune's Always Hiding* contained an impassioned editorial by Steve in which he vented his anger that the team had only won six games out of their last forty:

> All we ever hear is excuses usually along the lines of 'bad luck', 'injury crisis'. An absence of 'the right player at the right price'. Not once have we heard Lyall say that West Ham are a poor side, lacking in self-belief, pride, aggression, ability or determination.

Fortune's was soon selling an astonishing 5,000 copies of each issue. Meanwhile, the team lurched towards relegation, even without Allen McKnight. 'Come on Hammers, there's a hole in our ozone layer!' suggested one fan. But at least there was entertainment to be had in the Chicken Run from a character in a suit whom we christened 'Lino'. He had a tremendously loud voice, and the players must have been terrified of venturing towards the touchline. At each game he would shout the likes of, 'KEEN! KEEN! FOR F***'S SAKE, PUT 'IM UNDER! PUT 'IM F***ING UNDER! Close 'im darn! Close 'im f***ing darn! Lino you ****! He was never f***ing offside! Devonshire put 'im f***ing under! Hold the line! Hold the f***ing line! Dicks! F***ing get over here

Dicks! You play on the wing! PUT 'IM UNDER! PUT 'IM F***ING UNDER!' If only we had put them under. These days Lino can still be found in the lower East Stand, although now he's respectfully referred to as 'Coach'.

Finally, John Lyall replaced Frank McAvennie with . . . Frank McAvennie. Apparently unaware of Frankie's refuelling habits, he bought him back from Celtic for a huge fee of £1.25 million, £400,000 more than the club had sold him for. It was the right player at the wrong price. What was that about no panic signings? In his first match Frank inspired a 1–0 win at Aston Villa thanks to a great Ince run and shot. Frankie received a tremendous reception from the fans when he returned for the home game against Norwich, but we still lost. He tried hard, but didn't score in the run in.

A home defeat to Middlesbrough, watched by just 16,230 fans, seemed to doom West Ham. We were 1–0 up but Middlesbrough scored twice from corners in the last ten minutes. 'Que sera sera, whatever will be will be, we're going to Shrewsbury,' sang the Chicken Run.

The crowd filtered home: 'I didn't think they could shock me any more . . . it's worse when they play well . . . classic West Ham . . . we could never defend a one goal lead . . . I blame Ward and Dickens . . . no, I blame Lyall . . . he should have taken Brady off . . . I blame the defence . . . where do we go from here . . . we're never going to win again.'

Typically, West Ham started winning their remaining games, just like in 1978, prolonging the misery of their supporters. The side won four in a row against Millwall, Newcastle away, Luton and Sheffield Wednesday away, lost at Everton and then won the penultimate game at Nottingham Forest with two goals from the fit-again Leroy Rosenior. If we won the final game of the season at Anfield then we would stay up. Not too much to ask for there, then.

But with West Ham you just never knew, and so Steve and the *Fortune's* crew drove up to Anfield. Liverpool and the rest of the country was still in shock at the Hillsborough disaster. In the tight terraces around the ground you could feel the warmth between club and fans, stoked by tragedy. Liverpool needed to win to keep ahead of Arsenal in the title race. The away section was full.

The Irons fought bravely, and even McKnight, in for the injured Parkes, didn't make any terrible errors. We soon went a goal down but equalised with a great diving header from Leroy Rosenior. Then Paul Ince was crocked by Steve McMahon and what chance we had disappeared, Liverpool ending the match 5–1 winners. West Ham were down, John Lyall was soon to be sacked and Paul Ince would be posing in a Man United shirt even before he signed up at Old Trafford.

TOP TEN YOUNG HAMMERS STARS WHO FADED

- STUART SLATER: Howard Kendall predicted he would be the first £2-million player. But Slater failed at Celtic and ended up injured for most of his time at Ipswich and Watford.
- KEVIN LOCK: Billed as 'the new Bobby Moore', he never quite got to the stage of winning the respect of Pelé. Had a haircut that made Alan Taylor look stylish. Was soon dispatched to Fulham.
- ALAN DICKENS: Billed as 'the new Trevor Brooking', he had a great 1985–86 season but his confidence faded. Made a disastrous move to Chelsea and now drives a cab for a living.
- MERVYN DAY: Ron Greenwood was convinced he would be West Ham's goalkeeper for the next ten years. After a good season when West Ham won the 1975 FA Cup, he lost form and was sold to Orient after being replaced by Phil Parkes.
- ADE COKER: The 'next Clyde Best' scored on his debut at Crystal Palace and against Tottenham in 1972 but then disappeared from view.
- BOBBY BARNES: Scored on his debut as a 17 year old against Watford and looked set for a great career but was ultimately exposed as too lightweight for the top division.
- DANNY WILLIAMSON: Looked set for a glorious England career when introduced to the side by Harry Redknapp in the early 1990s. Ran the length of the field to score at Bolton. After joining Everton, however, his career was ruined by injury.
- BILLY LANSDOWNE: Scored a hat-trick against Southend in the League Cup and the winner against Burnley in the league in 1979 and, erm, that's about it really.
- JOHNNY AYRIS: Tiny right-winger who was 'the next Harry Redknapp' in the 1970s but only ever made sporadic appearances and never won a regular first-team place.

- MANNY OMOYIMNI: Scored twice at Crystal Palace on his fourth substitute appearance and looked set for a fine career until he forgot he was cup-tied against Aston Villa. Scunthorpe and obscurity then beckoned.

8

BILLY BONDS' CLARET AND BLUE ARMY

1989–94
The St Valentine's Day Massacre . . . Lou Macari won't be betting against the Hammers . . . Bonzo takes charge . . . Trevor Morley brings a cutting edge . . . Billy Bonds' Claret and Blue Army take over Villa Park . . . West Ham go up . . . no one gives a monkey for the Bond Scheme . . . Mike Small gets caught offside . . . West Ham go down . . . and then back up . . . Happy Harry gets his Dicks out . . . home boy Joey Beauchamp pines for Oxford . . . and three-for-one brings Premiership survival.
   Price of Hammer *in 1994: £1.50*

Watching your side lose a Littlewoods Cup semi-final 6–0 on a plastic pitch in the rain on an open terrace at Oldham where the bogs are overflowing with muddy lager effluent is not perhaps the best way of spending St Valentine's Day. 'Don't worry, there's always the second leg,' someone quipped as we drove back down the dark rain-swept motorway in Steve Rapport's black VW Golf. Steve was in silent anger mode: the one in which he says he doesn't know why he bothers but always somehow returns the next week. We were not even dry yet. Big Joe was equally aghast. It was not like we could rely on West Ham scoring seven goals to reach the final at Wembley. It was a long journey home to London and my asbestos-ridden tower block in Westbourne Park.

An injury-depleted West Ham side, with several new signings also cup-tied, could never cope with Joe Royle's vibrant Oldham or the artificial surface. Every ball into the box bounced about ten feet in the air. The game was a cross between five-a-side and rollerball. Eventually the league was to ban plastic pitches, but back in 1990, teams like Oldham were used to playing on the surface every week and had an undeniable advantage. And we were down to David Kelly up front.

Adams scored a fine goal from the edge of the box early on, but when Brady lost possession and Ritchie ran from his own half unopposed to score from the edge of the box, we knew it was going to be a horrible evening. Ritchie scored another, and Barrett, Holden and Palmer completed the rout. Nobody lost cup semi-finals 6–0. Except us. Martin, Brady and Parkes showed their age, Robson was still only half-fit and poor Kevin Keen scampered around the pitch like an eager young puppy chasing squirrels up trees.

Years later, I discovered that my fellow season-ticket holder Nigel was dumped by his then girlfriend for choosing to watch the St Valentine's Day Massacre rather than go for a romantic night out. Yes, she was prepared to kick a man when he was 6–0 down.

Surprisingly, the board had failed to renew John Lyall's contract that summer. It was sad that his experience couldn't be used in some capacity by the club and that they alienated a man who was loved by his players and gave West Ham great service. However, in footballing terms, it was clear that he had become stale as a manager.

Lou Macari had succeeded Lyall, and his reign started promisingly, even if the purists were worried by his reputation for direct football. Replacing the nicest man in football, Macari immediately attacked the complacency of his players and criticised them for not accepting the blame for relegation: 'The way some players are reacting you'd think they got West Ham promoted, not relegated.' That was exactly what the team behind *Fortune's Always Hiding* wanted to hear.

A bizarre incident involving Paul Ince illustrated Macari's point. The young midfielder posed in a Manchester United shirt in the close season after relegation even before he moved to Old Trafford. I'm inclined to believe Ince's later explanation that it was a press cock-up more than anything else and that he had naively supplied the picture to go in the paper on the day that he signed. But 'Judas' was never forgiven. In 1989, we still remembered the example of Trevor Brooking's loyalty. Ince was only 19 years old and could have had a team built around him. Surely he could have given us one season in the Second Division? Well, no, in the new world of agents, he couldn't.

Evangelist Billy Graham had been God's goalie at Upton Park in a Christian rally held in the Boleyn Ground the previous summer. Even he had asked his followers to pray for West Ham 'because I hear they need it', although I did wonder how the ICF had allowed their ground to be taken by a bunch of Christians.

Billy Graham's prayers seemed to have worked. West Ham were top after three games and unbeaten in their first five matches, despite Frank McAvennie breaking his ankle in the opening-day draw at Stoke. However, a 3–0 defeat by Brighton suggested a more troubled future for Macari's inconsistent men. He then signed Foster and Allen. Not the Irish folk duo, but an average centre-back from Forest called Colin Foster and the legendary Martin 'Mad Dog' Allen, a midfielder from QPR who played like a ravenous and possibly rabid canine. The fanzine's Mad Dog moniker was taken up by the fans, and in future seasons, any Mad Dog goal would be greeted by mass howling.

He looked a decent player in the Second Division, and he was hard working with a great shot. (His volley against Barnsley that season was one of the best strikes ever scored by a West Ham player.) Mad Dog became a bit of a cult hero against a very nasty Wimbledon side in a Littlewoods Cup tie. Dicksy had been sent off, but with nine minutes to go Allen raced into the penalty area to take Mark Ward's cross on the full volley and hammer home a memorable goal.

At that time, we were a team that could lose 1–0 at home to Leeds – the winner being scored by Vinnie Jones – but then thrash Sunderland 5–0. Stuart Slater, in his first full season, scored goals and looked a great prospect. In the game against Sunderland he scored a fantastic goal, controlling Eamonn Dolan's header on his chest and scoring with a sumptuous volley from the edge of the box.

Young Dolan, whose career was sadly curtailed by injury and cancer, scored twice in the same game and inspired the most bizarre goal celebrations ever seen at Upton Park. After beating a defender and shooting into the roof of the North Bank goal he ran to the North Bank, jumped up and down from leg to leg while alternately pumping his arms up and down and followed this all up with an Irish jig. When he scored his second, a great first-time shot from the edge of the box, Dolan ran to the Chicken Run with his arms out doing a Dambusters impersonation before descending into yet more arm pumping. It inspired Phill 'Porky' Jupitus to create a full-page 'Donkey Dancing' cartoon in *Fortune's Always Hiding*.

Unfortunately, West Ham were looking increasingly brittle, losing away to teams like Wolves, Bradford and, embarrassingly, 5–4 at Blackburn. Injuries multiplied, Macari tried to play Alvin Martin up front against Oldham, Foster scored an own goal and we lost 2–0 at home. Yet, as ever with the Irons, we went on a good cup run. Macari made 20-year-old Julian Dicks captain, and he responded with several long-range stunning goals in the Littlewoods Cup, including a first-time effort that beat First Division Aston Villa and a rocket that left Peter Shilton floundering in a home draw with Derby. Biffer Dicks, as we liked to call him then, had the sides of his head shaved and a short spiky section on top that resembled a doormat. Although you wouldn't dare tell him that. He always gave us maximum effort, and therefore the crowd loved him.

After a second replay, we beat Derby at Upton Park and were in the semis of the Littlewoods Cup, having beaten three sides from Division One, but our league form was rubbish. Macari realised that the side needed rebuilding. He swapped Mark Ward for Manchester City's Trevor Morley and Ian Bishop. Bish at least looked to be a proper West Ham passing player, if lacking in pace. He also purchased Jimmy Quinn, a proven scorer in the lower leagues.

But Macari's world was rapidly imploding: he was caught up in an FA inquiry over allegations that he placed a bet on his Swindon side losing, just before they lost a cup game 5–0 at Newcastle (it was against football regulations to bet on your own side); commercial manager Brian Blower was demanding an apology from Frank McAvennie after being punched at a club party; and there were tabloid rumours of the team being involved in hotel high jinks before the New Year's Day game against Barnsley. Morley soon scored his first goal, but we still lost 2–1 at home to Hull, having conceded two easy headers.

West Ham surprised no one by going out of the FA Cup to a lower division team, losing 1–0 at Torquay. We'd suffered seven successive away defeats. And then came the humiliation at Oldham. Macari had also been found guilty of betting against his Swindon side. He was missing for a 2–2 draw at his old club Swindon, and we then learned that he had resigned. Macari has since said that quitting was the biggest mistake of his career. The betting controversy would surely have been forgotten in time, and it had occurred with a different club. Although, in a pre-bung era, it seemed pretty scandalous stuff to the tabloids.

Lou had only just begun to forge his own side. His last act was to sign Czech goalkeeper Ludek Miklosko, who played in the match at Swindon. His signings of Mad Dog, Ludo, Bishop, Morley and Jimmy 'the Tree' Quinn were to prove influential over the next few years, and had he stayed, results would surely have improved.

As it was, West Ham turned to an insider to take over. Billy Bonds was appointed, and the move instantly united the club. A full stadium gave him a rousing reception before his first home match against Blackburn. Jimmy Quinn scored with a typical header, West Ham hit the woodwork three times, but, somehow, Blackburn equalised late on.

Bonzo did well to stabilise the club. We started to win away matches again, and Quinn and Morley soon formed an effective goalscoring partnership. Jimmy the Tree was improbably tall and thin, but had good feet on the ground and was great at placing headers. He never seemed to panic when given a chance and was a much-underrated player who should have been given a chance in the top division.

Late in the season, West Ham destroyed Sheffield United 5–0 with Quinn scoring a hat-trick and Stuart Slater mesmerising their right-back Chris Wilder. Ian 'the Bish' Bishop scored a great curling goal at home to Bournemouth, and we were close to the play-offs again, but defeats in away games at Leeds, Newcastle and Sunderland were to end our hopes. West Ham finished eighth, despite a 4–0 demolition of Wolves in the final game, which included Liam Brady scoring in the last minute of his last game to spark a joyous pitch invasion.

The next season, West Ham were much more consistent, and under Bonds set a club record of 21 games without defeat, not losing until a 1–0 defeat at Barnsley on 22 December. Ludek Miklosko was proving to be a fantastic goalkeeper and Bonds' first signing, right-back Tim Breacker from Luton, had improved the defence. Meanwhile, Steve Potts had moved to central defence and despite his lack of height, was proving to be a centre-back with pace and the ability to read the game. Even Colin Foster was looking competent. It seemed a little strange that the Hammers should break a club record without ever looking entirely convincing, but, that season, the club had mastered the art of getting points even when not playing well.

After each home game, the *Fortune's* team would meet in Ken's Café for tea and toasted cheese sandwiches, wondering what we could moan about next. Admittedly, Don did try to argue that we had played unconvincingly in a 7–1 win over Hull City, but, personally, I'd take 7–1 most weeks. Dicksy scored two goals, rampaging down the left and rounding the keeper for one of them, and we also witnessed Steve Potts's only goal for the club – a not very good shot that went straight through the Hull goalkeeper. Whenever Steve Potts scored West Ham always scored seven. Fact.

Trevor Morley had a great season. He was an automatic choice under Bonds, who clearly preferred his work ethic to the fit-again Frank McAvennie's champagne and cocaine lifestyle, although Frank and Jimmy the Tree both scored important goals alongside Tricky Trev. Morley used to irritate Steve Rapport no end with his ability to turn away from goal, but he controlled the ball well and produced moments of skill, such as a great half-volley to win a game at Watford and a lovely chipped free-kick in a 5–0 FA Cup demolition of Luton at Upton Park. Morley's old Man City teammate Ian Bishop was now playing well, too, although we did wonder how he got the time to perform as Ricky in *EastEnders*. His long hair inspired several chants of 'Where's your caravan?' from opposition supporters.

The season was going really well, and the Irons looked certain to go up until the most bizarre injury ever to befall a West Ham striker occurred. Trevor Morley had been stabbed with a kitchen knife and was found lying in a pool of blood on the driveway of his Waltham Abbey house. His wife Monica was present and so was Ian Bishop. Morley declined to press charges after what was described as a domestic dispute. The rest of the story is probably a matter for the scriptwriters of *Footballers' Wives* to ponder.

While poor Billy Bonds pondered losing his top striker to a knife wound, telling the press 'It's very sad, I've lost a striker. But my main concern is for his family', West Ham went on an FA Cup run. After years of being knocked out by the likes of Torquay, the Irons romped to the semi-finals, beating Everton at Upton Park in the cup quarters. Colin Foster scored with a flying volley, and Stuart Slater weaved inside the Everton defence to score with a fine low drive. Slater had been outstanding all night, and Everton boss Howard Kendall said after the match that in Slater he had perhaps seen Britain's first £2 million player.

The semi-final against Forest was ruined from the moment referee Keith Hackett sent off Tony Gale for an innocuous challenge on Gary Crosby after 26 minutes. The pair were running away from the West Ham goal and seemed to trip up over each other, but Hackett ruled that it was a goalscoring opportunity and Gale had committed a professional foul. In the second half, Forest scored through Crosby, Keane, Pearce and Charles. Our Wembley dreams were over. It was the third semi-final that we had lost in three years. Despite their disappointment, for that last section of the game the West Ham fans proved that they were the best in the country and celebrated as if they were winning. One half of Villa Park bounced up and down singing 'BILLY BONDS' CLARET AND BLUE ARMY!' for the final 15 minutes of the match.

Steve 'North Bank Norman' Rapport wrote an editorial in *Fortune's Always Hiding*:

> There is one abiding memory of Villa Park that will last forever
> . . . It's the memory of 18,000 West Ham fans jumping up and
> down for the last 15 minutes of another ritual semi-final slaughter
> singing the loudest 'BILLY BONDS' CLARET AND BLUE
> ARMY!' in the history of the world. The single most poignant
> moment came when Gary Charles struck the fourth and final nail
> in our FA Cup coffin; the entire massed choir missed not a single
> beat of their song. This spoke more eloquently of the pure and
> utter devotion of West Ham supporters than anything witnessed
> during 29 years of watching the Hammers.

It was the performance of the West Ham fans that day that helped start the era of celebration over aggro, fanzines at every club, inflatable bananas, *Fantasy Football*, and Nick Hornby making football a subject worthy of literature. Nobody went out fighting; we simply reaffirmed our loyalty to the club in a joyous celebration of failure. It was astonishing to be part of it. After the game, Ian Bishop said, 'Now we've got to go out and win the championship for all our supporters; they were absolutely amazing at Villa Park.'

The fans invented a chant referring to the BAC sponsorship logo on the shirts: 'BAC means back as champions!' However, West Ham blew the Second Division championship in the final minute of the final game of the season. Bonds had signed a big striker from Luton called Iain Dowie, who scored in the game that sealed promotion. With First Division football guaranteed we could push on for the title. West Ham had to beat or draw with Notts County at Upton Park to be champions; the players would have then received medals rather than simply being promoted. However, Notts County scored twice early in the match, and a tense Hammers side chased the game from then on. George Parris pulled a goal back in the second half, but County defended resolutely, and it was one of those games when time seems to contract exponentially: forty-five minutes appeared to be played out in about ten.

We had a lifeline: as long as Oldham didn't win at home to Sheffield Wednesday we would still be champions. The final whistle went. The PA announcer said that Oldham had drawn 2–2, and the fans invaded the pitch to celebrate. Only a minute later he announced that 2–2 was not in fact the final score and that Oldham had scored an injury-time winner. Promotion was a great achievement for Billy Bonds and the team, but after the astonishing display from the fans at Villa Park we had become fixated on the championship. Somehow we had dropped a five-point lead and been distracted by a cup run. And now we couldn't even relay results correctly. It was so very like West Ham to snatch disappointment from triumph.

To prepare for Division One, Iain Dowie was sold after scoring a respectable 4 goals in 12 games (which made you wonder why Bonds had bothered to buy him) and was replaced by Mike Small from Brighton for £400,000. The other big signing was Mitchell Thomas, who cost £500,000 from Spurs. Thomas was certainly hard working, although a Spurs-supporting mate did warn me that at White Hart Lane it sometimes seemed like he had constructed a series of tunnels under the pitch, because he would suddenly pop up in the most unexpected positions. In fact, anywhere except where he was supposed to be playing.

Despite a long-term injury to Julian Dicks, West Ham started the season reasonably well, even if they were wearing a strange new kit of claret shirts with three white and blue stripes on the shoulders and cuffs. Early on we beat Aston Villa 3–1 at Upton Park, with goals from Mike Small, Leroy Rosenior and full-back Kenny Brown, who raced down the right-hand side to fire an unstoppable shot into the top corner. Steve Rapport and I also travelled to Selhurst Park for a 3–2 away win over Palace. Trevor Morley scored a comical goal, when Ludek Miklosko's goalkick caught him on the foot and trickled home. Small scored with a great diving header from Tim Breacker's cross and looked a bargain at that stage of the season.

But Steve, a demanding spectator, was never convinced by Small, and ultimately he was to be proved right. Nor did he rate Morley and Thomas. And as for every referee . . . as Steve's sister Hannah was later to remark, it was funny how all the referees seemed much better when you weren't standing next to Steve shouting 'Oi, ref, have a word!'

We even beat Spurs 2–1 at Upton Park, Mitchell Thomas popping up into the box from one of his *Great Escape* tunnels and scrambling home the winner. Predictably unpredictable, the side also managed to beat Arsenal 1–0 at Highbury with a well-taken Mike Small goal. During a goalless draw with Liverpool, which left the side in 14th position in the league, commentator Brian Moore revealed that Mike Small had a clause in his contract that would give him a pay rise if he was selected for England. He had scored 10 goals so far that season, but as soon as people started talking about England, his form plummeted.

Then came the calamitous Hammers Bond Scheme. The board was faced with a hefty bill for redeveloping the ground into an all-seater stadium in line with the post-Hillsborough Taylor Report. They mistook the passion at Villa Park for blind loyalty, and decided that the fans could pay for the £15 million redevelopment. The idea was that the supporters would pay between £500 and £975 simply for the right to buy a season ticket. In return, they would be guaranteed their name on a seat and some limited dialogue with the board through the Hammers Bond Company. Selling the fans something they already had in the middle of a recession went down about as well as a Steve Whitton dribble into the advertising hoardings.

The three West Ham fanzines, *Over Land and Sea*, *On the Terraces* and

Fortune's Always Hiding, and the newly formed Hammers Independent Supporters Association, organised a red-card protest at the home match with Liverpool and suggested a private share offer as an alternative. Steve Rapport wrote in a *Fortune's Always Hiding* editorial, 'It would give us a genuine financial interest in West Ham and a real say in the running of the club. The board want to take our money but still keep the club private, which is surely the real reason they have rejected this option out of hand.'

Julian Dicks won yet more respect from the fans, when he said: 'The Bond scheme is wrong. You can't ask ordinary people to pay out £975 to watch their team before they have even bought a ticket.'

The team plummeted as the Bond furore grew. A 7,500-name petition was presented to the board, and there were huge protests against the scheme after a dire 0–0 draw at home to non-league Farnborough in the FA Cup and then after a 1–1 draw with Wimbledon. Thousands of angry fans gathered in front of the West Stand chanting 'Where's the money gone?' and 'We won't take this shit no more!' and unfurled a banner reading 'Lying, thieving cheats'.

When a chant of 'Let's all storm the boardroom!' went up it felt like the storming of the Winter Palace. Billy Bonds then proved that he still had as much bottle as he had when he was a player by appearing in the directors' box and announcing that he loved the club as much as the supporters. He was given a microphone, but to quote *On the Terraces,* 'Like everything else at the club at this present time, it didn't work.' The demonstration ended with an emotional chorus of 'Bubbles'. It was sad to see the club reduced to this; the board had managed to throw away years of goodwill.

Our league form crumbled, and the side went on a terrible run. Stuart Slater lost confidence and the ability to beat players, Mike Small managed to lose all comprehension of the offside rule and Billy Bonds didn't appear to have the nous to turn things round.

Towards the end of the season I went travelling in Australia and wondered if the Bungle Bungle National Park was named after our defence. In pre-Internet days I had to wait for a magazine called *British Soccer Week* to be published for news of West Ham's latest home defeats. Clive Allen was signed on deadline day, but arrived too late to make a difference. However, he did score on his debut in a 2–1 defeat at

Chelsea. After beating Oldham 1–0 on 1 February the side took just 2 points from the next 27, going 9 games without a win. There were aberrations: West Ham beat Norwich 4–0 at Upton Park with Matthew Rush scoring twice.

We were already relegated when we played title-chasing Man United at Upton Park. Suddenly there was a full crowd behind the team and thanks to Kenny Brown's goal the Irons won 1–0, ruining Man United's title bid. Alex Ferguson was to refer to West Ham's effort as 'obscene' and in a way he was right. Why had we not played like that before we were relegated?

In *Hammer* Billy Bonds confessed, 'There is no in-between – we've either been good or bloody awful. People ask me to explain how we can play so well to beat a side of United's quality and then lose to the likes of Coventry and Notts County, and I'm not sure of the answer.'

There was one last fans' party to see Frank McAvennie score his final goals for the club, a hat-trick against Nottingham Forest in a meaningless last game. *Fortune's Always Hiding* folded as Steve Rapport emigrated to the United States. West Ham finished bottom of the division, and the bond between club and supporters appeared shattered.

During the summer of 1992 the board did make one good decision. They brought in Harry Redknapp from Bournemouth to be assistant manager. Redknapp had done well at Bournemouth and had an eye for buying and selling players. He was happier dealing with the media than Bonzo and would give his old mate the support he needed.

West Ham had lost an astonishing 9,000 fans when the new season started. Crowds were down from an average of 21,342 the previous season to just 12,698 by November 1992, at which point the board reduced season-ticket and seat prices by up to 25 per cent. Fewer than 1,000 Hammers Bonds had been sold, when the club had hoped to sell 19,000, and the scheme was quietly forgotten about.

Under the influence of Redknapp the club had sold Slater to Celtic for £1.5 million and purchased Peter Butler, a tenacious midfielder, from Southend for £170,000, Matt Holmes from Bournemouth for just £40,000 and Mark Robson, a skilful if lightweight winger from Spurs, on a free. Alvin 'he's got no hair but we don't care' Martin returned yet again and had a fine season, despite being around 57 years old. Terminator Dicks was back too, fortified by his habit of drinking a litre of Coca-Cola before matches. He managed to get sent off three times that season. One dismissal saw an epic clumping of a Derby player on the halfway line of the Baseball Ground for no apparent reason. Maybe Julian was just a little bored.

The side looked happier under the combined management of Redknapp and Bonds and started to play football again. Clive Allen scored a superb volley in a 5–1 win at Bristol City, and Trevor Morley was once again a regular scorer. Robson had a great season and so too did Kevin Keen, who suddenly looked a much more confident player.

We were always chasing second spot that season so at least there was no chance of missing out on the championship again. When the side beat Sunderland 6–0 in a televised game at Upton Park in early November, it was a sign that the confidence was returning. Keen, Morley, Allen, Martin and two goals from Mark Robson completed the roasting.

A 3–1 away win at Swindon was another key moment, and by the end of the season, it was down to the last game in the chase for second spot and automatic promotion. We had to get a better result against Cambridge than Portsmouth could manage against Grimsby. New loan striker David Speedie scored to ease the worries at Upton Park, but nervous fans still had their transistors to their ears. Portsmouth were winning 2–1, but in the final minute Julian Dicks rampaged down the left to set up Clive Allen for a tap-in, sparking a pitch invasion, a lengthy pause before the restoration of order, and then a hasty final whistle from the referee. We were promoted because we had scored one more goal than Portsmouth. Fans often forget how vital that season was; the influence of Redknapp had saved the club from terminal decline. The 'yo-yo' years were hopefully over.

West Ham finished 13th in their first season in the new Premier League. At first, new signing Dale Gordon's stepovers and dodgy moustache were having little effect and they won only one of the first seven matches. After a 4–0 home defeat by QPR, Harry pulled off one of his famous Virgin Megastore-style three-for-one deals, selling crowd hero Julian Dicks to Liverpool in exchange for left-back David Burrows and midfielder Mike Marsh, and using the extra dosh to sign veteran striker Lee Chapman.

It worked, beginning with a 2–0 win at Blackburn in which Chapman and Morley, striking up an immediate partnership, both scored. Morley's great turn and shot beat Chelsea and both Chapman and Burrows scored in the 3–1 defeat of Man City. By the New Year we were 11th in the league. Morley finally proved he was Premiership class, scoring thirteen goals, while Chapman scored seven before suddenly becoming more interested in setting up theatre bars towards the end of the season. A final flourish to the season came with a 4–1 win at White Hart Lane and a 2–0 win at Arsenal.

West Ham being West Ham, there was further close-season turmoil in the summer of 1994. A transfer was conducted that was bizarre even by West Ham's standards. Billy Bonds and Harry Redknapp proudly announced the signing of Joey Beauchamp from Oxford United. Only nobody seemed to have realised that poor Joey had never travelled beyond Oxford and was terrified of London. I could picture the rustic characters back in Oxford warning young Joey, 'London? You don't want to go there, because they have jeans and motor cars and burger bars and pickpockets and nightclubs and all sorts in the East End, boy!'

After just one day at Chadwell Heath, Joey apparently declared that he was homesick. Our own Jude the Obscure was gazing longingly at the spires of Oxford and missing his girlfriend. The club had agreed that Beauchamp could live in Oxford, but as Redknapp told the press, 'He rang us up and said he was tired and stressed because of being in a traffic jam. West Ham are paying him big money, and if the fans behind the goal knew how much they would be staggered.'

Beauchamp was in a jam of his own making according to Harry: 'Joey Beauchamp has been trouble from nine o'clock on his first day at the club. He has caused me and Billy Bonds nothing but grief. He keeps saying he's made a mistake in joining us and he wishes he had joined Swindon instead. We can't do anything for him because he does not talk to me or Billy or even the players. There is no point in picking him because he does not want to play for us.'

Even Bonzo declared, 'We've done everything to help him; a saint couldn't have done more. But he says he is stressed out and is complaining he is getting headaches. I've even had him crying to me.' Only at West Ham . . .

In one of his rare friendly appearances at Southend he was greeted with shouts of 'Mummy's boy! and 'Bumpkin!' from Hammers fans. It was hard to understand his attitude, since I'd met my partner Nicola that year, and was still commuting to see her in her home in Oxford. It was easy to catch the train from Paddington, and a coach service from Victoria called the Oxford Tube ran day and night. We'd signed Private Pike and he hadn't brought his scarf. Joey was sold to Swindon for £700,000 plus Adrian Whitbread without ever playing a competitive game for the Hammers. He has probably never ventured beyond the Oxford/Reading/Swindon triangle again.

Then it emerged that Bournemouth wanted Redknapp back as manager and the board, fearing that they might lose the real power behind the team's revival, offered Billy Bonds a move upstairs. Bonzo knew he was effectively being removed from his job and, already disillusioned by the Joey Beauchamp saga, resigned. Harry threatened to resign too rather than stitch up his old mate – 'If people think that I've stabbed Bill in the back then I can't stay' – but was ultimately talked into staying by Billy. It was now Harry's game at Upton Park.

WEST HAM'S TOP 21 CUP DEFEATS

- STOCKPORT AWAY: West Ham losing to Third Division Stockport in a 1996 Coca-Cola Cup tie was not that shocking in itself, but what made it really memorable was Iain Dowie rising like the great Northern Ireland striker he was to bullet a header past Ludek Miklosko for the own goal of the century.
- GRIMSBY AWAY: West Ham travelled to the not very romantic destination of Grimsby on St Valentine's Night, 1996. The home side might only sing when they're fishing, but a 3–0 home victory left West Ham floundering and the minnows with a plaice in the next round of the FA Cup.
- NOTTINGHAM FOREST: A 1991 FA Cup semi-final on live TV saw Second Division West Ham thrashed 4–0. Add the iniquitous sending-off of Tony Gale for barely touching Gary Crosby and a goal for Gary Charles and you have a wasted trip to Villa Park, only partially redeemed by the fans' marvellous 20-minute rendition of 'Billy Bonds' Claret and Blue Army!'
- LUTON AT HOME: A 1989 Littlewoods Cup semi-final saw Allen McKnightmare at his worst, failing to collect a cross that Mick Harford scored from and leaving a huge gap for Roy

Wegerle to score. We lost the home leg 3–0 and the away leg 2–0.

- WREXHAM AT HOME: Lampard and Ferdinand were in the side as Wrexham visited West Ham in a third-round replay in the 1997 FA Cup. The first game at the Racehorse Ground had ended 1–1. A last-minute screamer from Russell won the replay for Wrexham, sending the Red Army home in ecstasy. West Ham had the terrible Newell and Jones up front. It was so bad Harry Redknapp offered to resign after the game.

- TORQUAY AWAY: Lou Macari's men travelled to the home of Basil Fawlty in January 1990, played like a team of waiters from Barcelona and managed to lose 1–0. Blue Lou was just warming up for the Oldham away game though . . .

- OLDHAM AWAY: Losing the first leg of a Littlewoods Cup semi-final 6–0 at Boundary Park will never be bettered. Oldham looked like Real Madrid on plastic as they whopped the Hammers, whose fans were left singing in the rain on an open terrace with third-world toilets on St Valentine's Night 1990. The fact that there was no hope for the second leg (which we won 3–0) and I'd already paid for the tickets compounded the perfect West Ham cup debacle.

- BLACKPOOL AWAY: All the classic cup defeat ingredients: northern ground, playing underdogs, January weather and an alcoholic up front. This 1971 debacle saw West Ham lose 4–0 at Blackpool and manager Ron Greenwood threaten to sack Bobby Moore, Jimmy Greaves, Brian Dear and teetotal Clyde Best for going out clubbing the night before the game.

- NEWPORT AWAY: We never did like playing Welsh sides. A side with Brooking and Devonshire, Martin and Parkes managed to lose 2–1 at Newport in the third round of the FA Cup in 1979. Even Bryan Robson's goal couldn't prevent us concentrating on not getting promoted.

- HEREFORD AWAY: In 1974 West Ham lost a third round replay to non-league Hereford United. Clyde Best gave the Irons the lead only for Hereford to score twice and inspire a pitch invasion by kids in parkas at the end.

- QPR AWAY: West Ham completed a memorable 1978

relegation and cup defeat double, being thrashed 6–1 at QPR in the fourth round of the FA Cup. Hopefully, Stan Bowles had a bet on the result. We also lost 5–0 away to Forest in the League Cup that season.

- HULL CITY AWAY: When West Ham went to Hull and back they were beaten 1–0 at Boothferry Park in a 1973 FA Cup tie.

- WREXHAM AWAY: In 1981 we might have reached the League Cup final and been Division Two champions, but we still managed to lose 1–0 away to Wrexham in a second replay of an FA Cup third round tie.

- SWANSEA AWAY: A deflected shot beat Shaka Hislop, their keeper somehow saved a Neil Ruddock piledriver at the end and that was it. Cyril the Swan was on the pitch, and we were out of the third round of the FA Cup in 1998.

- TRANMERE AWAY: Predictably, a long throw from Challinor and a fine volley from Henry did for West Ham, Di Canio and all, at Prenton Park in the usual FA Cup third-round defeat in 2000.

- NORTHAMPTON AWAY: The Irons got their Worthington Cup defeat in early against Third Division Northampton in 1998, losing a second-round two-legged tie 2–1 on aggregate, losing 2–0 away and winning only 1–0 at Upton Park.

- ASTON VILLA AT HOME: We managed to lose a 1999 Cup tie against Villa even though we drew 2–2 and won it on penalties. Then we discovered that late substitute Manny Omoyimni 'just hadn't thought' and was cup-tied. West Ham lost the replay 3–1.

- BARNSLEY AT HOME: In the 1987–88 season West Ham drew 0–0 at Barnsley, but then lost 5–2 at home after extra time in the Littlewoods Cup, the game having finished 2–2 after 90 minutes.

- TOTTENHAM AWAY: After a 1–1 draw at home to Spurs in the 1986–87 Littlewoods Cup, the Irons capitulated 5–0 at White Hart Lane. Chas and Dave were rumoured to be among the Spurs scorers.

- CREWE AWAY: We might have been going up under Bonzo and Harry, but the 1992–93 season also saw the inevitable

Coca-Cola Cup defeat to rubbish opposition, this time drawing 0–0 at home to Crewe and losing the second leg 2–0 at Gresty Road.

- BARNSLEY AWAY: It was grim up north the day the Irons lost 4–1 to Barnsley in the third round of the 1993 FA Cup. We were undone by Wayne Biggins, who made two goals for his team. Trevor Morley scored our consolation from the spot.

9

HURRY UP, HARRY

1994–99
Marco Boogers off . . . Two-Bob Florin goes shopping . . . Dowie
scores the own goal of the century . . . Hartson and Kitson save the
Hammers . . . big John tries to play football with Eyal Berkovic's
head in training . . . West Ham sign a genius in white boots called
Di Canio . . . and finish fifth.
   Price of Hammer in 1999: £2

Harry Redknapp was surely born to manage West Ham United. A man who inspired the adoring legions of the North Bank to convert from Hare Krishna to Harry Redknapp. And like generations of East Enders, Harry could almost have copyrighted the phrase 'wheeler-dealer'.

There was none of the cosmopolitan aura of Ruud Gullit at Chelsea; Harry was more Albert Square than Philippe Albert. He made what he referred to as 'rickets' in the transfer market (i.e. he signed a few crap players) and his side was invariably 'down to the bare bones'. Redknapp's sides were frequently so skeletal that he could have opened up a medical school at Chadwell Heath. Chelsea's Gullit could look cool wearing Gucci loafers without socks; a sockless Harry Redknapp in his claret and blue shell suit would just have looked a bit care in the community.

'Arry Boy was a proper manager: constantly stressed, with a battered face and bags under his eyes. Redknapp and his new assistant Frank Lampard Senior were the Regan and Carter of the Premiership. It was all about family on 'Arry's manor, just like on *EastEnders*. 'Arry's assistant Frank was his bruvver-in-law. 'Arry's boy Jamie had legged it to Liverpool but Frank's boy Frank Junior was still at the family firm. Harry called his wife 'the missus', once confessed to *Over Land and Sea* fanzine that he'd never eaten a curry and also revealed, 'The last film I went to see was *Doctor Zhivago*,' which was released in 1965.

When his autobiography was published in 1998, I interviewed him for *Loaded* at Sportspages Bookshop. During a photo shoot he claimed not to recognise Leicester Square. 'What's this place? I've never been here before,' asked the West Ham gaffer as he wandered through the neon heart of one of the most famous spots in the world. Then he stopped to give a busking tramp some money. 'That's the old West Ham manager, that is,' he quipped. 'It could be me next.'

Was Harry ever pursued by the equivalent of Louise and Posh Spice in his day, I enquired: 'No, I got married young. It was very romantic. I met Sandra in the Two Puddings pub in Stratford, there was a dance upstairs every Sunday night. It was dark and I had a result, really. I think she liked my mate better than me, but she got lumbered with me.'

After a long day signing books instead of players, Harry watched the FC Copenhagen v. Chelsea game on the Sportspages TV, waiting for a taxi to take him back to his mum and dad's place in Stepney: 'I told me mum I don't want much to eat but she'll have cooked me a huge meal. And you know what she'll have cooked? Egg and chips!'

After the messy departure of Billy Bonds, 'H' was in sole charge of the Irons for the 1994–95 season. He even gave a fan a game in a friendly at Oxford City. West Ham fan Steve Davies was giving Lee Chapman so much abuse that Redknapp turned to him and said 'You've got all the mouth, you seem to know all the tactics, go and show us what you can do!' Davies borrowed a pair of boots from the subbed Chapman and played 40 minutes in the 4–0 win. The 27 year old had not played for 7 years but set up a chance for Jeroen Boere and even had a goal disallowed. Strangely, Harry declined to sign him.

However, Redknapp did sign John Moncur from Swindon, who was not only skilful, but in later seasons perfected the art of getting booked in the briefest of substitute appearances. Moncur played alongside Bishop and Mad Dog Martin Allen and suddenly the midfield looked stronger. Don Hutchison arrived from Liverpool, having earned the nickname of 'Budweiser' after he hid his wedding tackle underneath a Budweiser label while on holiday. The pictures made the front of the *News of the World*. '£1.5 million Hutch (that's £250,000 an inch)' read the front cover of the fanzine *On a Mission from God*.

After the usual bad start – the team didn't win until the sixth game – Harry went back to Liverpool for Julian Dicks, who had apparently alienated boss Roy Evans by shaving his head and having a Tasmanian Devil tattoo, and also bought back Tony Cottee from Everton. Players were never meant to go back, but Dicks went on to play some of his best football for West Ham, even if he did still train with the aid of litres of Coca-Cola, while Cottee was top scorer with 13 goals that season.

Veteran Alvin Martin had played superbly for most of the season, but a crucial signing towards the end of the season was the big Danish centre-back Marc Rieper. Lee Chapman also left for Ipswich and to run his upmarket Teatro club and Mike Marsh declared himself homesick for Liverpool and therefore signed for Coventry, before then moving to Turkey and finally Southend.

Harry jigged and rejigged the side. He seemed to be forever on *Football Focus* in his crumpled beige suit complaining that he was terrible to be around, what with the worry of relegation, and he could never shut it away and his missus didn't deserve it. By the end of the season Harry's tinkering had worked. Deadly Don Hutchison didn't always look committed but he had a knack of scoring goals – nine in twenty-three games that season. It was a two-minute walk from my new gaff at Nicola's flat in Aubert Park to watch him net the winner at Highbury. Ludek Miklosko also had a great game that day.

When West Ham were 2–0 down at home to Norwich in March, relegation seemed a certainty. But as a rebuke to all those who ever leave early for the Silverlink, TC scored twice in injury time to earn a draw and start a run of eight unbeaten matches. Rieper and Hutchison scored in a fantastic home win against title-chasing Blackburn Rovers before a vibrant crowd of 24,202. A 3–0 home win against Liverpool in the penultimate game of the season made us safe, and in the final match, an inspired performance from Ludek Miklosko and the goalposts earned a 1–1 draw with a Cantona-less Man United, handing the title to Blackburn.

It was Harry's scattergun approach to new signings that was the most entertaining feature of his stewardship. He could pick up fantastic bargains and gain added value from someone everyone else thought was too knackered, old, drunken, ugly, temperamental, or just rubbish. Yet he could also make some right rickets in the transfer market. (It was always a secret hope that Harry would sign Bolton's Michael Ricketts so that he could then remove him from the side and claim 'I dropped a Ricketts'.)

After the Joey Beauchamp saga, Marco Boogers must rank as one of Harry's greatest rickets. Despite paying £800,000 to Sparta Rotterdam for him, Harry wouldn't play him. Signed for the start of the 1995–96 season, he came on as a sub at Old Trafford, attempted to cut Gary Neville in two and was rightly sent off. Then Boogers boogered off. He returned to Holland and declared himself 'mentally unfit' to play football, which must rank with pining for Oxford as one of West Ham's most bizarre reasons for non-availability. *The Sun* then claimed that 'Barmy Boogers' had been spotted in a caravan in Holland.

West Ham MD Peter Storrie flew to Holland to try and retrieve the situation and came out with the marvellous quote, 'We had our meeting at the Hilton in Amsterdam. I didn't see a caravan, or a tent for that matter. He is certainly not mentally unstable.'

Meanwhile, Harry told the press, 'It seems that every player who can tie his own bootlaces is worth £1 million. I've got one who can't even do that.' Redknapp was clearly not happy with a player struggling to settle in England: 'He's coming back on Tuesday, but I wouldn't put money on him still being here Wednesday . . . He doesn't like the way we train and he doesn't liked being tackled in training. The best thing would be for him to go back to Holland . . . Bloody Boogers! I was having a good day until someone mentioned his name!'

Clearly someone was playing silly Boogers. Harry was later to admit in his autobiography that, 'for the first time in my life I signed a player purely on video evidence'. Signing players by video? VIDEO? If you put all my Monday night five-a-side goals at the Sobell Centre together on video then I could look worthy of playing for West Ham. Contestants on *Stars in Their Eyes* can look good on video. Maybe we should just be grateful Harry put the right tape in the video player, otherwise we might have ended up signing Dr Zhivago.

Events at Upton Park were like a soap opera that season. Boogers eventually returned to Groningen in the Dutch league, and West Ham made another floundering start – it took seven games to register a win. David Mellor had been pontificating on Radio 5's *606* about a Julian Dicks stamp on Chelsea's John Spencer (which Dicksy claimed was an accident), and the shaven-headed left-back was facing an FA charge.

Paolo Futre, a still skilful but crocked Portuguese international had arrived from AC Milan, but refused to play in the opening 2–0 defeat at Highbury because he had not been given the No. 10 shirt. Steve 'North Bank Norman' Rapport was over from San Francisco and greeted me with a Californian hug. After watching Futre's replacement Steve Jones miss a couple of great chances, Steve was back to using Chicken Run expletives. When Futre did play he looked class but very soon had to admit that his career was finished.

Don Hutchison didn't track back enough in an away draw at Southampton and Harry's solution was to throw a plate of sandwiches at him: 'I did hit Don Hutchison on the head with a plate of sandwiches. He had the lot – egg and tomato, right across the nut . . . he wouldn't accept what I was saying and it all got a bit naughty.' After not looking interested during a 4–1 home defeat against Aston Villa, Hutch was sold to Sheffield United.

Redknapp's solution to the side's problems was to sign Iain Dowie, the striker we sold to Southampton after just 12 games, and the man whose battered face had inspired a myriad of jibes on Baddiel and Skinner's *Fantasy Football*.

Alan Ball had told Harry that signing Dowie would get him the sack, but Dowie proved an unlikely saviour, scoring eight goals that season. He was, after all, a Northern Ireland international, although as John Moncur was to say, 'We all know that's like playing for your district side. That's what we tell him anyway.' Dowie had been a West Ham supporter as a kid, too. For all his lack of skill, Dowie was difficult to mark, scary to look at and worked his neck bolts off for us. He was our own Jurassic striker. Iain also gave me hope that at 35 I might yet be good enough to play for the Irons.

Redknapp finally made a decent foreign buy, purchasing Croatian centre-back 'Super' Slaven Bilic. Bilic had a law degree, preferred to live in Chelsea rather than Chigwell and had a tasty earring, too. In his debut at Spurs he immediately established a solid centre-back partnership with Rieper, while Portugeezer loan star Dani scored the winning goal.

The Hammers beat championship-chasing Newcastle 2–0 with goals from Danny Williamson and Tony Cottee, and Kevin Keegan did not love it. By the time we beat Manchester City 4–2 at Upton Park we were safe. Dowie scored twice that day (his last ever league goals for the Hammers), Dicks scored a sensational 30-yarder and the skilful Dani weaved his way through for another. Dani looked like a film star and caused Iain Dowie to quip, 'We've got two good-looking blokes up front now!' But Dani's penchant for asking to be put up in the Dorchester instead of the Swallow Hotel in Waltham Abbey, plus a missed training session after a night clubbing, soon resulted in Redknapp sending him home.

By that time, my companions in the Upper East Stand were old Brentwood mates Steve and Jenny (always arriving slightly late from the pub, finishing their bags of chips), Will Finck, veteran of the Shrewsbury away debacle, Joe O'Brien (nephew of Alison O'Brien, who was in the same group of Hammers fans as me in the late '70s), plus *On a Mission from God* fanzine editor Shane Barber and his mate John Green. Shane lived in Norwich and travelled to nearly every match. He had a share in the club and used to turn up at AGMs to ask Terry Brown awkward questions. It's the fanzines that have led to whatever degree of glasnost we now see at Upton Park, and looking back at my old copies of *Mission*, many of the questions asked then seem prescient today.

After drawing at home to Sheffield Wednesday we somehow managed to finish tenth. In the top half of the table! That night Shane took all the *On a Mission* contributors out for the end of season do, as everyone was working for nothing and we had finished in the top half – we deserved to celebrate. Steve and Jenny immediately ordered the most expensive item on the menu, the lobster. Shane's face went the same colour as our cream away kit.

Redknapp went snooker loopy over foreign players the next season. He signed the Romanian international Florin Raducioiu, who had starred in the 1994 World Cup. Florin inspired numerous puns, and his picture appeared on the cover of *On a Mission* with the headline 'West Ham Are A Two-Bob Club (And Here's A Florin To Prove It)'. The man was clearly a class finisher and scored two great goals for the Hammers against Derby (2–0) and Man United in a 2–2 home draw, but he hated the physical side of the English game, and his lack of commitment caused resentment in the dressing-room.

'Don't ask me how a former world-class player can suddenly become a fairy, but something had obviously happened to Raducioiu and he'd completely lost it. He'd been used to queuing for three hours in Bucharest for a loaf of bread and suddenly he was wearing a £28,000 watch. Perhaps the transition was too much for him,' Redknapp admitted in his honest if not very PC autobiography.

The end of the affair came when Raducioiu failed to turn up for a Coca-Cola Cup tie at Stockport in December. He could not be contacted on his mobile, and the next day Redknapp discovered that Two-Bob Florin had decided to visit Harvey Nichols rather than play for West Ham. Harry's first reaction was to try and sign Harvey Nichols on loan, but when he learned it was a shop, Florin was seen as shop-soiled goods. It was a terrible betrayal from Raducioiu. Romford Market would have been quite understandable, but being seen in poncy Harvey Nichols finished Florin at Upton Park, and he was soon bound for the shopping malls of Espanyol.

That Stockport Coca-Cola Cup tie also marked the end of Iain Dowie's goal drought. He'd not scored in 21 league appearances since his brace against Man City on 23 March 1996. The quick-footed Portuguese loan star Hugo Porfirio wore a permanent expression of bemusement as he was somehow expected to forge a partnership with big Iain. Then on 18 December 1996, Dowie rose like a great peroxide tree to meet a throw-in and thump a header of power and precision into the top corner. It was a sensational goal – at least until Dowie realised that it was Ludek Miklosko he had left floundering in the net. Just a minute earlier Julian Dicks had headed us into the lead. He might have been qualified as a rocket scientist, but that night at Stockport every Hammers fan felt thankful that Dowie would never get to fire any real missiles. During the 1980s Dowie might have started the third world war simply by forgetting which superpower he was fighting for. Four minutes later, Angell grabbed the winner for Stockport.

Ilie Dumitrescu, another Romanian World Cup star, signed from Spurs and was a huge disappointment, although that could possibly be explained by his previous sexploits detailed in the *News of the World* and *Sunday Mirror* ('Soccer Ace and the Cop's Wife'). The only good game he had was when the TV cameras were present for the 2–2 home draw with Man United.

In January, West Ham were in the bottom three and then lost a third round FA Cup replay at home to Wrexham. Youngsters Rio Ferdinand and Frank Lampard had come in and done well, but overall the side looked to be heading for relegation. Russell had hit a last-minute winner with a thumping shot, and after the game Redknapp offered to resign. Terry Brown refused to accept his resignation, and we carried on with on-loan Mike Newell and the hard-working but limited Steve Jones up front, possibly West Ham's weakest ever Premiership forward line.

Harry reacted in the only way he knew: a Green Street market-style two strikers for a bargain £5.5 million deal (later paid for through the close-season sale of Slaven Bilic to Everton for £4.5 million). Paul Kitson came from Derby and big John Hartson was signed from Arsenal. The two players immediately developed a great partnership and saved our season. Their home debuts produced a fine 4–3 win over Spurs live on Sky. Andy Gray salivated about Hartson's tremendously brave diving header for his goal. Dicksy scored a penalty and a header, and Kitson got the other in a highly enertaining match. In midfield, Harry also signed Steve Lomas from Manchester City: like Hartson, he was another player with iffy ginger hair, but was someone who put his foot in and made our midfield competitive.

Kitson scored two in a 3–2 home win over Chelsea and Hartson scored another pair in an important 3–1 win at Coventry. Big Joe and I travelled to Leicester to see John Moncur give West Ham another three points. With Hartson and Kitson up front the Hammers lost only three out of their last thirteen matches. Hartson was powerful and Kitson skilful and nimble alongside him. We absolutely demolished Sheffield Wednesday 5–1 (Kitson 3, Hartson 2) in the penultimate home match and the way Hartson terrorised the Wednesday defence reminded me of a young Geoff Hurst.

A season that had encompassed strikers at Harvey Nichols, refuseniks at Highbury, own goals at Stockport and a FA Cup defeat by Wrexham ended with West Ham finishing 14th and Harry's reputation as a used-player salesman restored.

Suddenly we had a decent side. The next season Redknapp made another fine buy in Eyal Berkovic from Southampton. For the first time since Trevor Brooking had retired, we had a player who could thread balls from any angle through a defence. The skilful Israeli must have made most of John Hartson's 24 league and cup goals that season. It was a shock when we won the opening-day fixture 2–1 at Barnsley. Even more so when the lads beat Spurs 2–1 on my birthday, Frank Lampard scoring the winner at Upton Park.

In the first half of the season, Hartson appeared unstoppable, although after Christmas he scored only four goals. Trevor Sinclair was another shrewd signing, the former QPR winger rediscovering his form with West Ham. The only minus to the season was young Rio Ferdinand's drink-driving conviction causing him to be dropped from the England squad.

That season had many highlights: Stan Lazaridis scoring a stunning 30-yarder to win the game at Newcastle; beating Barnsley 6–0 with the Upton Park crowd chanting 'ABOOOOOOO!' after our new French striker Samassi Abou scored twice; beating Leeds 3–0 with Ian Pearce at right-back being described as 'a flying machine' by Harry; and an epic FA Cup struggle with Arsenal. Thanks to Ian Pearce's goal we drew at Highbury. In the replay, Arsenal took a 1–0 lead, Seaman looked unbeatable and Keown was taunted with chants of 'He's got a monkey's head!' However, Hartson weaved past two players to power the ball home with almost no backlift, and the game went to penalties. There was a fantastic atmosphere at Upton Park, but ultimately we lost on penalties when Samassi Abou hit the post.

A highlight of a different kind occurred during a 2–0 away defeat at Derby when the home fans were taunting old star Paul Kitson, singing to the tune of 'My Old Man's a Dustman': 'Oh Kitson is a wanker, he wears a wanker's hat, he'll never play for England, 'cos he is f***ing crap!' Only Kitson wasn't playing as he spent most of that season injured. The player the Derby fans had mistaken for Kitson was in fact substitute Paolo Alves. And I never did find out what a wanker's hat was either.

With four games to go the side was sixth and chasing a UEFA Cup spot. But West Ham being West Ham they inevitably imploded. My pals Bob and Jane were partly to blame: they insisted on getting married in a 90-minute ceremony on the day of the Southampton match, meaning I had to miss the game. Because I wasn't there, we lost 4–2 at home.

The *On a Mission* end-of-season do saw the crew taking over the Adelphi Hotel in Liverpool after watching a 5–0 thrashing at Anfield. Young Michael Owen made David Unsworth resemble a particularly lethargic triceratops and we were 4–0 down at half-time. A young sub called Manny Omoyimni scored twice to save a point at Palace, but even a last game 4–2 win over Leicester couldn't take us above eighth. But it was still a very respectable performance and for the first time in millenniums we had not worried about relegation.

It must have been a little disturbing for deal-junkie Harry to field a settled side and minimise the use of Chadwell Heath's revolving doors. But the following 1998–99 season saw another mini-crisis develop and gave Redknapp a reason to 'shake up the dressing-room'. Ian Wright had been signed from Arsenal and for half a season looked sharp, before suffering a long-term injury. But Hartson was looking less like the predator of old and more like a podgy Welshman. A criminal conviction for using a hanging flower basket as a football while out with his mates in Swansea was worrying evidence of an active social life.

We were unbeaten in our first three games before a home match with Wimbledon. West Ham were 3–0 up after 27 minutes with Hartson scoring once and Ian Wright banging in two more and revealing a vest supporting the striking Essex firemen. Then West Ham conceded a soft goal, but we were still 3–1 ahead at half-time.

In the second half, Joe Kinnear threw on four big strikers for the Dons. Under the aerial bombardment new Chilean centre-back Javier Margas looked a little like a chicken in a coop mesmerised by an urban fox. He was soon to go AWOL and retreat to Chile. Wimbledon suddenly pulled it back to 3–3, inspired by Hammers old boy Michael Hughes. And then Wimbledon scored a fourth. They'd come back from 3–0 down to win 4–3. BSkyB had been trying to buy Man United at the time. The collective opinion among Steve, Jenny, Will, Shane and me, all emotional shareholders in West Ham, was that Radio Essex was our most likely purchaser.

Morale was restored with a fine 2–1 win against the Spice Boys of Liverpool four days later, but was then undermined by the infamous October training-ground incident involving John Hartson and Eyal Berkovic. When Berkovic told the Israeli press of an alleged training-ground bust-up with Hartson and threatened to leave the club, Redknapp tried to dismiss it all as the usual training-ground fracas. 'It was nothing. John caught Eyal with a tackle, it wasn't a good tackle to be fair with you, and Eyal was obviously very upset with it, and quite rightly so. But John apologised to Eyal and Eyal accepted the apology and that was the end of the matter,' Harry told the West Ham Clubcall line.

Hartson himself claimed in the *Daily Mail*: 'I used to like Eyal . . . but I've lost a lot of respect for him over what he's done. If he wants to leave, so be it. What happened was the sort of silly little training-ground incident that happens all the time. I admit I made a bad tackle but I didn't mean to hurt him. I apologised for it and thought that was that . . . It's time he stood up like a man instead of acting like a baby.'

However, the *Daily Mirror* then discovered that a Sky TV crew had been filming training that day and had caught the whole incident. It printed nine pictures in a frame-by-frame analysis of the clash. First Berkovic is felled by a late tackle from Hartson. As he lies on the ground Hartson pulls him up at which point the angry Berkovic slaps Hartson's thigh. Hartson loses control, lines up his target and boots Berkovic full in the face. The shocked Israeli holds his chin as Hartson is led away by Neil Ruddock, Ian Pearce and Harry Redknapp. It was an assault that might have landed Hartson in jail if he'd committed it in the street and was certainly much more than the 'nothing' incident Redknapp had described.

Berkovic told the *Mirror*, 'If my head was a ball it would have been in the top corner of the net . . . He behaved in a way I have never seen before on a football pitch. There must be something wrong with a player who kicks another one in the head and is not upset about it. Hartson called me later to apologise, but I told him it was too late, it had gone too far.'

Perhaps we should just be thankful that big John never trained with Keith Robson. Shane Barber pointed out in his *On a Mission* editorial that: 'If I kicked shit out of a bloke at work, I'd expect to be sacked and sued. And even if there is a bit of argy-bargy on training grounds the only preparation that particular incident would get you ready for would be the receipt of a red card.'

Redknapp sent Hartson to France for treatment to an ankle injury where he could escape the press furore. He was fined two weeks wages, with Redknapp arguing that he couldn't sack Hartson as that would simply give another club a good player for nothing. In the long term though it was likely that one of the players would have to go.

Soon after the Hartson incident, a 4–2 defeat at Charlton confirmed that Julian Dicks' injury-ravaged knees had finally gone. He was destroyed by Danny Mills and subsequently replaced in the side by Stan Lazaridis as a left wing-back. Big Joe and I sat in the partially covered

Charlton stand and were soaked by an autumnal deluge. Hartson looked overweight and missed two good chances. West Ham were winning 2–1 with a minute to go, but somehow we allowed Charlton to score three times after that. Nothing had changed with West Ham since those erratic days of Ron Greenwood. That Charlton defeat was followed by a surprise 3–0 win at Newcastle.

It was still the era of Oasis, Blur and *Loaded* lads, and something of that culture appeared to have spread to the players at their Christmas party in Romford. Tricky Trevor Sinclair was fined £250 for damaging beauty therapist Belinda Knowles' car, after pretending to be hit and rolling over the bonnet. And all while wearing a wig and '70s-themed fancy-dress costume.

January 1999 was a terrible month. We lost 4–1 at Old Trafford, 4–0 at home to Sheffield Wednesday and 4–0 at home to Arsenal. But Harry was never one to wait for the right player at the right price when he could get three for the price of one. Wimbledon's Joe Kinnear offered £7.5 million for John Hartson. Since we'd bought him for only £3.5 million plus add-ons that represented a big profit. He'd scored only four goals that season, was looking unfit and had tried to decapitate a teammate. He was a 'lumbering Welsh lardarse' according to *On a Mission*. Even Trevor Brooking had been controversial enough to highlight Hartson's large-looking posterior on *Match of the Day*. All good reasons for taking the money, although his subsequent success with Celtic suggests that with the right handling and better discipline big John might have developed into a great player for us.

Harry used the Hartson money to buy giant Cameroon midfielder Marc Vivien Foe for £4 million, ex-Chelsea defender Scott Minto from Benfica for £1 million, and the most entertaining player we had ever seen at Upton Park, Paolo Di Canio. True, Di Canio was serving a ten-match suspension for pushing over referee Roger Alcock while with Sheffield Wednesday, but anyone who had seen him play knew that he was worth far more than the £1.5 million Harry had paid for him. He was a Cantona-esque figure. Redknapp immediately worked out that the way to get the best from Paolo was to flatter him, and described him as a 'football genius'.

Shane Barber told *The Sun*, 'All fans love to see a complete lunatic on the pitch and that's what we've got with Di Canio. West Ham have traded a player who kicks teammates in the head for a player who attacks referees. I don't know if that's progress.'

He was also the first striker ever to play for West Ham in what appeared to be white trainers. He came on as a sub for his debut in a game at Wimbledon and immediately showed an easy mastery of the ball, while the Dons' new centre-forward was derided with choruses of 'Big Fat Johnny Hartson!' by the travelling Irons fans.

The good thing about West Ham that season was that they either won or lost with very few draws in between, so despite numerous defeats we were always in the top half of the table. When Di Canio arrived West Ham were still ninth. Paolo scored the first of his four goals that season in a home win against Blackburn in late February. Foe added bulk to our midfield and slowly the Irons climbed the table.

Di Canio and Berkovic liked playing alongside each other and together destroyed Derby in a 5–1 win at Upton Park in mid-April. We were sixth and the following week Harry described Eyal Berkovic as 'unplayable' after he inspired a 2–1 win at Spurs. So we went and lost 5–1 at home to Leeds in the next home game. Jimmy Floyd Hasselbaink was on top form for David O'Leary's Leeds, while the scoreline was affected by some decidedly dodgy refereeing. West Ham had three players sent off: Wright, Hislop and Lomas. Wright's dismissal resulted in a bizarre act of ill-disciplined petulance: he compounded the damage he'd done to the team by smashing up a TV set in the referee's changing-room.

There was still a slight hope of qualifying for Europe. In the penultimate game Big Joe and myself travelled to Goodison Park to see the Irons charge towards European glory. We lost 6–0. Kevin Campbell scored three and Don Hutchison was made to look like a Scouse Pelé. Harry came up with some Lyall-esque excuses afterwards about it being a long hard season and how even in Bobby Moore's day they never finished in the top half two seasons running.

Luckily, we played an uninterested Middlesbrough in the final game of the season and thrashed them 4–0. Aston Villa had lost their last three games and we went above them to fifth spot. Finishing with 57 points we were ten points behind fourth-placed Leeds and had a goal difference of minus seven, but it didn't matter. We were fifth. Unfortunately, UEFA had done their usual goalpost moving and we wouldn't qualify for the UEFA Cup because teams in claret and blue weren't allowed to play in it.

FA Cup semi-finalists Newcastle somehow ranked above West Ham for a UEFA Cup place, so we entered the Inter-Toto Cup instead.

A season that had included forfeiting a 3–0 home lead to lose to Wimbledon, 13 league defeats, a boot wrapped round Eyal Berkovic's head, a drunken Christmas party, and ended with 5–1 and 6–0 defeats, had also ended with the recruitment of a maverick genius and our best league position since John Lyall's men finished third in 1986.

HARRY REDKNAPP'S TOP TEN RICKETS
- GARY CHARLES: Cost £1 million from Benfica. Scored an own goal when unchallenged from two yards out to win a game for Southampton. While at West Ham he made five appearances, plus the front page of the *Standard* when his car was found abandoned after an accident, with a bottle of whisky left on the front seat. Then in 2004, he was jailed for four months for dangerous driving and failing to provide a specimen after being found in a drunken stupor in his crashed car.
- FLORIN RADUCIOIU: Preferred shopping at Harvey Nichols to turning out for West Ham at Stockport, and in contract negotiations with Harry, Two-Bob's main concern was to get a visa for his pet dog. Just two league goals for an outlay of £2.4 million.
- MARCO BOOGERS: The £1 million signing sliced Gary Neville in half, got red-carded, then retreated to Holland, allegedly in a caravan, and declared himself mentally unfit to play for West Ham.
- JOEY BEAUCHAMP: Signed for £1 million, Joey missed Oxford and his girlfriend, seemed to think London was as far away from his home town as Sydney, and on his first day at the club announced he had made a mistake joining.
- DAVOR SUKER: His wages cost the entire season's income from the East Stand. Started only eight games, scored just two goals and rarely moved beyond a trot.
- TITI CAMARA: The aptly named Guinea international arrived from Liverpool for £1.5 million, but soon proved to be an overweight lump. Never scored for West Ham.

Super Tomas celebrates victory over Preston
in the 2005 play-off final. (© Cleva)

Moore's the name, Bobby Moore. (© Cleva)

Billy Bonds, as seen on the back of *Hammer* in 1972.

Graham Paddon, Mervyn Day and Billy Jennings celebrate another afternoon of successful blow-drying in 1975. (© Cleva)

Trevor Brooking gets mildly excited after scoring the winner at Wembley in the 1980 FA Cup final. (© Cleva)

Below: Frank McAvennie and Tony Cottee: a terrible mix-up meant they played wearing the Hammerettes' hot pants. (© Cleva)

Allen McKnight: 'I'll get me coat.' (© Cleva)

Paolo Di Canio and Martin Keown debate the finer
points of home-made tiramisu recipes. (© Cleva)

Above: The author (left) with Matt,
Fraser and Nigel before the 2005 play-off final.

Below: Alan Pardew's Claret and Blue Army in Cardiff. (© Cleva)

- ILIE DUMITRESCU: The Romanian international cost £1.5 million and only ever had one decent game, a televised match against Manchester United.

- JAVIER MARGAS: The Chilean international arrived for £2.2 million, but after suffering an aerial bombardment against Wimbledon, he went AWOL in Chile for a season. He did return the following year to dye his hair claret and blue.

- RAGGY SOMA: Signed as the replacement for Nigel Winterburn for £800,000, Soma starred in the 5–0 and 7–1 defeats at Everton and Blackburn, before being dispatched back to Norway.

- SCOTT MINTO: Signed for £1 million from Benfica, Minto was a youth star at Chelsea, winning an FA Cup-winner's medal. But when, during a 4–0 home defeat to Arsenal, the Gunners' fans started chanting 'Give it to Minto!' it was clear he had lost it. Featured in the legendary 'We want a new back four!' game at Charlton. Found his level at Rotherham.

HARRY REDKNAPP'S TOP TEN NICE LITTLE EARNERS

- PAOLO DI CANIO: The steal of the century at just £1.5 million. Harry signed a flawed genius with a gift for self-substituting melodrama, goals of the season and memorable tantrums for not much more than Scott Minto. Worth the fee for the Bradford game alone.

- JOHN HARTSON: Bought for £3.5 million from Arsenal (plus add-ons which would eventually have taken the fee to around £5 million). Sold for £7.5 million to Wimbledon when out-of-form and overweight.

- TREVOR SINCLAIR: Other managers said he'd gone to fat, but Harry knew Sinclair just needed a new challenge. Paid QPR just £1.6 million for a player who went on to star for England in the 2000 World Cup. Not only that, he also pulled an Arthur Daley-style stroke, shifting the ageing Iain Dowie to QPR as part of the deal.

- MATT HOLMES: Bought from Bournemouth for just £40,000, he was later sold to the champions Blackburn for £1 million.

- STEVE JONES: Signed from Billericay for £25,000. Harry was to sell the one-time soap factory worker to Bournemouth for £150,000, buy him back for £200,000 and then sell him to Charlton for a useful mark-up of £400,000.

- SLAVEN BILIC: Super Slaven Bilic cost just £1.65 million from German side Karlsruhe, but was sold to Everton for £4.5 million, where his career was eventually ended through injury.

- EYAL BERKOVIC: Cost just £1.75 million, had two great seasons, and was then sold to Celtic for £5.75 million.

- STAN LAZARIDIS: Signed for just £300,000, Skippy was sold to Birmingham for £1.9 million.

- DAVID UNSWORTH: Harry managed to get a seasoned Premiership defender in Unsworth and £1 million off Everton for Danny Williamson, who immediately succumbed to injury. Unsworth was sold on for £3 million to Aston Villa (which the directionally challenged Unsworth thought was close to Liverpool) who then sold him on to Everton within a few days.

- STUART PEARCE: When no one else would go near the 37-year-old defender, Harry signed a player on a free from Newcastle who was soon to play his way back into the England squad.

10

WE'VE GOT DI CANIO,
YOU'VE GOT OUR STEREOS!

1999–2001
Paolo pulverises the Premiership . . . and tries to take himself off against Bradford . . . Rio, Joey and Frank promise to make West Ham the team of the new millennium . . . Manny forgets that he's cup-tied . . . West Ham win the Inter-Toto Cup . . . play four games in Europe . . . sell Rio . . . win at Man United . . . Harry makes a ricket with Titi Camara . . . and gets the tin tack.
   Price of Hammer *in 2001: £2.50*

'PAOLO DI CANIO! PAOLO DI CANIO! PAOLO DI CANIO!' The Di Canio aria, sung to the tune of Verdi's 'La Donne è Mobile', could be heard at Upton Park throughout the 1999–2000 season. Paolo was phenomenal that campaign, scoring 16 league goals and making most of the rest.

His first strike of the season saw him pick up a ball in the box, dummy his way past two defenders and power a shot in off the post for the winner against Leicester City. Then the goals just got better. A good example was the goal he scored against Watford. With the defence expecting him to cross, the quick-thinking Italian somehow steered a free-kick in at the near post.

He defeated the Gunners on his own. His first goal saw him beat most of the Arsenal team in a dribble from the halfway line. When he was tackled, the ball bobbled to Sinclair and PDC was alert enough to prod home the resulting cross. The second was sublime. With his first touch Di Canio controlled an airborne ball and hooked it away from Martin Keown, leaving the hulking defender somewhere on the Barking Road, before sending a perfectly cushioned half-volley into the top corner of Seaman's net. It was even better than Neil Ruddock's barge into the red-carded Patrick Vieira, followed by a statuesque nightclub bouncer 'What, me? I'm A Celebrity Get Me Out Of Here!' pose.

When Paolo scored he would run to the crowd with his shirt over his head falling outstretched onto the turf. When decisions went against him he would wave his arms in the air or make his imploring 'I am an innocent man' gesture. He would beat the turf in frustration and was generally a one-man caricature of a brilliant but temperamental Italian striker.

Against Man United at Upton Park, with the Irons losing 3–0, he scored with a clever volley and then waltzed his way past van der Gouw to bring the score back to 3–2. Another great dribble left him with just the keeper to beat to equalise, but he tried to chip the ball rather than pass to the waiting Frank Lampard. Typically, Paolo responded to that error with an operatic head-in-hands mini-drama.

From a corner against Derby he beat a defender and from an acute angle at the edge of the box, flashed a shot into the far corner of the Centenary Stand goal. Two goals at home to Coventry were also sublime: a run from the halfway line saw him beat a player and then produce a perfect shot from the edge of the box that ricocheted in off the post; the second started with a dummy that sent two defenders the wrong way followed by a nonchalant side-foot finish.

The goal everyone remembers was *Match of the Day*'s goal of the season. Against Wimbledon he responded to Sinclair's deep cross from the right by producing a sumptuous volley with both feet off the ground. The ball flew into the net and Paolo ran away wagging his finger at all those who had ever doubted his non-divine status. 'TAKE A BOW SON, TAKE A BOW SON, YOU WILL NOT SEE A BETTER GOAL!' growled Sky's Andy Gray in the deep voice he reserves for truly momentous footballing moments.

Towards the end of the season, Paolo scored at Highbury, but somehow the Gunners managed to win after a handball and deflected shot from Emmanuel Petit, not that I'm bitter. At the end of the game, he ran over to the West Ham fans as if we had won. He grabbed his badge, waved his hands, and gesticulated upon the greatness of the forthcoming Eastern Empire based on strong government emanating from Chadwell Heath. As *On a Mission* put it, every football fan loves a nutter.

But perhaps the most exciting and certainly the barmiest game I have ever seen at Upton Park was the 5–4 home victory against Bradford. The game turned when Shaka Hislop was injured, and substitute Stephen Bywater came on for his debut. The nervous keeper watched a corner come into the box and Dean Windass headed home. Sinclair equalised, then Moncur scored on 43 minutes with a great 30-yard effort, falling over as he shot and then removing his shirt and running in disbelief to the Chicken Run. Two minutes later, West Ham conceded the inevitable soft goal right on half-time, Moncur being adjudged to have fouled a Bradford player in the box. Beagrie converted the penalty before doing a silly somersault in front of the Bobby Moore Stand.

West Ham started disastrously in the second half. Bywater fumbled a long-range effort, only palming the ball into the path of the scarlet-haired Jamie Lawrence, who scored with ease two minutes after the break. The young keeper looked like he was about to cry. Lawrence, full of confidence, then unleashed an unstoppable curling 30-yarder into the top of Bywater's net.

We were 4–2 down after 51 minutes and from then on the game belonged to Di Canio. He had already had two good penalty claims turned down. All season referees had been swayed by Paolo's reputation for diving. A clear penalty at Middlesbrough had been denied him, and the referee had then booked PDC just to stoke the fires of injustice in his mind further. We were sitting in the Upper East Stand towards the Bobby Moore end, right above the spot where Paolo was fouled in the box. It was indeed a penalty. The referee waved play on.

Paolo began to wag his finger and look outraged. That was normal for him. But then he walked over to the dugout, shaking his head, and made revolving gestures with his hands to indicate that he wanted to be substituted. Harry Redknapp remonstrated with him on the touchline, trying to push him back on to the pitch. The Italian would have been brilliant as a melodramatic actor in old silent films. It also looked quite possible that Di Canio would pick up the ball and tell the referee that he was taking it home. Everybody in the East Stand was laughing at the sheer madness of it all.

It's not that Paolo takes himself particularly seriously or anything, but in his autobiography he later revealed his feelings about the incident: 'I felt the anger of a million injustices, a million wrongs that went unpunished, a million vendettas that went unserved . . . The realisation was that the struggle was over, that my enemies had triumphed. I felt it was time for the warrior to go home and rest.'

Harry Redknapp handled the situation perfectly, telling Paolo to go back out there and fight. A more disciplinarian manager might have taken off Di Canio and transfer-listed him for deserting his teammates, but Paolo returned to the field, seeking vengeance for the million injustices that regularly went unpunished at Upton Park.

When Paul Kitson was brought down and the referee finally awarded West Ham a penalty, West Ham's usual penalty taker, Frank Lampard, prepared to take it, but Paolo grabbed the ball from him. For a minute or so there was a bizarre tugging match for the football. Again, a scene from the playground appeared to have been transferred to a Premiership match. Again, we laughed in disbelief. Lampard saw the crazed look in Di Canio's eyes and gave him the ball. Big Joe, Steve, Jenny, Shane and I were sure that Paolo would miss the penalty and perhaps spontaneously combust on the pitch, leaving only a smouldering boot to remember him by. But no, he strode up and confidently stroked the ball into the net. His grand opera of redemption was being played out before 25,417 disbelieving fans. He returned to the centre circle with the triumphant strut of a vindicated Italian dictator.

All of a sudden, the whole stadium was noisily willing West Ham to make an unlikely comeback. On the 70-minute mark, Sinclair broke down the right side of the box and played the ball inside to young Joe Cole, who danced around a defender and scored from close range, before being engulfed by a delirious mass of humanity at the front of the Bobby Moore Stand. What entertainment; what lunacy.

But there was more. Seven minutes from time, Di Canio weaved his way down the left into the Bradford box, cut inside two defenders, then back again, twisting and turning, and played the ball across the face of the area to Frank Lampard. Frank blasted a left-foot shot into the top of the goal, and the stadium erupted with joy and perhaps some relief that Paolo was not now going to ritually disembowel himself in the centre-circle, which was one likely outcome had we failed to win.

What a game. What a man. What a nutter. The next week *On a Mission* awarded Di Canio an honorary centre-page 'certificate of madness', citing his numerous talents in 'theatrics, sulking, gesturing, turf beating, ball wrestling, self-substitution, referee pushing, shorts tailoring and dodgy hair colouring'.

As Big Joe put it – he works in the comedy business and knows about these things – it was all great box office and would add a couple of thousand to the next gate. Di Canio's absolute contempt for Bradford was marvellous to view – he had to beat at least three defenders every time he got the ball, on principle. What would have happened if the ref had turned down another penalty appeal? I suspect Paolo would have performed an unnatural act with a corner flag and the referee, walked down the tunnel and got on the first plane for Italy.

That season was almost as crazy as Di Canio's histrionics. Harry had entered the side in the Inter-Toto Cup, or the 'Inter Two-Bob Cup' as some fans dubbed it. But winning it meant you qualified for the UEFA Cup – it was bizarre that most English clubs had ignored that route into Europe simply because their players wanted a long holiday. This meant starting the season in July, when most players were still perfecting their pulling routines in Ayia Napa.

It was perhaps apt that we found ourselves playing FC Jokerit in what most fans termed a Mickey-Mouse tournament. We won 1–0 at home thanks to a Kitson goal and drew the away leg 1–1. Having just scaled the Langdale Pikes while on holiday, I descended from the Lakeland peaks to find West Ham playing Herenveen live on Sky on the pub TV. John Moncur was strolling around the midfield with his collar turned up in a half-paced game but again we won 1–0 in front of just 7,485 fans. New signing Paolo Wanchope scored the goal when we drew 1–1 away and that was it: West Ham were in the final.

Meanwhile, the Premiership season had begun and all that Inter-Toto malarkey ensured West Ham were sharper than their rivals. Frank Lampard scored the winner in the opening match against Spurs at Upton Park, and we hardly seemed to miss Eyal Berkovic, who had chosen to move to Celtic for a sizeable fee of £5.5 million. Lampard looked much more effective playing just outside the opposition box, where he could utilise his excellent finishing skills.

Paolo Wanchope scored twice in the first four unbeaten games. The geezer in front of us in the East Stand with the spiked blond hair and white shell suit spent much of the season hollering 'Go on the Chop!' as the player tried to untangle the ball from somewhere within his long ungainly legs.

The Chop was an infuriating player, either very good or very bad, with nothing in between. He confused teammates, opposition centre-backs and spectators, but he still scored a respectable 12 league goals in 35 games. Some critics claimed that with Wanchope and Di Canio up front it was more a circus act than a forward line, but they got results. In the second game of the season, the Chop created an injury-time equaliser for Trevor Sinclair, somehow managing to wrap his legs around the ball and backheel it into Trev's path. Against Newcastle that season he managed to miscontrol the ball, dumbfound the centre-backs and somehow score the winner. The Chop even scored against Man United at Old Trafford – although admittedly the Reds did go on to win 7–1.

We lost the first leg of the Inter-Toto Cup final 1–0 at home to Metz, for whom Louis Saha scored, but at least there was a packed crowd of 25,372. I didn't go to the second leg of the final because I'd just paid £600-odd for a season ticket and we were on holiday and it looked likely we would lose and I wasn't sure if it was a proper competition. So we won, of course. Sinclair, Lampard and Wanchope, expertly rounding the goalkeeper and tapping into the net, scored in a 3–1 away win. West Ham were back in Europe for the first time since 1981, admittedly via a competition that was more *Eurotrash* than Eurovision Song Contest. And all after just three games of the league season.

It looked like it could be a fantastic season. Veteran Stuart Pearce was back to England form at the age of 37, before sadly breaking his leg against Watford in his fifth match. A clever signing by Redknapp, Psycho Mark II was a proper West Ham player; the Bobby Moore Stand loved him for his commitment and crunching tackles. Sinclair was playing well as a wing-back, and with Di Canio in inspired form, anything was possible.

Our European tour only lasted four games. West Ham beat NK Osijek

3–0 at home, with Di Canio scoring another of his 'leaving the keeper on his backside and rounding him' goals, and we won the away leg 3–1. The early November tie away to Steaua Bucharest was a much harder game, though. In the Romanian mud, a rare mistake by Steve Potts led the way to a 2–0 defeat. In the second leg, we pulverised them 0–0. Despite a special Upton Park European atmosphere for the return tie and Di Canio creating numerous chances, bad luck, dodgy refereeing and their keeper ensured that the game remained goalless.

Predictably, we lost in the third round of the FA Cup, this time to Tranmere away. But West Ham looked likely to reach the Worthington Cup final. We beat Bournemouth and Birmingham away, with young Joe Cole scoring his first senior goal for the club – the one he scored against Bradford was only his first league goal. And then we beat Aston Villa on penalties to ensure that we were in the semi-finals. Or at least we thought we had beaten them.

At first, the news on Ceefax seemed like it must be a joke. The one thing you used to be able to rely on in football was the result, but, as we poor West Ham fans now realised, even that was no longer a matter of certainty. I could still see the players taking a joyous team dive in front of the Bobby Moore Stand, when I learned that extra-time substitute Manny Omoyimni had just made the most expensive five-minute appearance in football history.

Having returned from a loan spell at Gillingham, the hapless Hammer came on five minutes from the end of our 2–2 draw. He made no difference to the outcome of the game, which West Ham then 'won' on penalties. Only the next day it was discovered that Omoyimni had made two appearances in the Worthington Cup while on loan to Gillingham. He was therefore cup-tied and ineligible for the competition.

West Ham announced that it was an 'administrative error' – football-speak for a cock-up of monumental proportions. 'The player says he didn't think,' rued a distraught West Ham boss Redknapp. Club secretary Graham Mackrell claimed that he'd been told by Gillingham that Omoyimni hadn't played in the Worthington Cup. Mackrell subsequently resigned as a result of the fiasco along with his assistant, football secretary Alison O'Dowd.

The League ordered the game to be replayed and West Ham lost 3–1, of course. The ties were played in 1999 and 2000. Thus the unhappy

Hammers made history by becoming the first club to both win and lose the same cup tie in different millennia – which should at least keep the pub quiz compilers in work if nothing else. And we were not partying like it was 1999. For all Di Canio's brilliance, the season would also be remembered for a ridiculous error.

After the mistake, which surely even a Sunday League club would have spotted, I couldn't be sure that any result would stand. What if the 1980 FA Cup triumph was overturned as the club had forgotten to register Trevor Brooking? Perhaps the 1975 FA Cup win would be erased as Alan Taylor had played for Rochdale in an earlier round. As for England's 1966 World Cup win, I'm scared that I might discover that someone at West Ham had forgotten to tell FIFA that Bobby Moore, Geoff Hurst and Martin Peters were all born in Germany.

What were Harry Redknapp and Frank Lampard doing? Shouldn't they have been tracking the games of on-loan players for future reference? My mate Matt would never have made such a mistake. He could name the collective age of the Oldham midfield and tell you who played for Moor Green, so he would never have missed a substitute appearance by an on-loan player. The whole club had been made to look amateur, while Manny should surely have been left alone in a darkened room with Paolo Di Canio. As it was he was soon loaned to Scunthorpe.

Apart from the Manny debacle, it was a memorable season. Di Canio was sublime. We finished ninth with just two fewer points than the previous season. Again, we were hindered by only taking one point from the last four games, a sign perhaps of fatigue after a long season. But, as Harry told the press whenever he could, even the great side of Moore, Hurst and Peters had never managed three successive top-half finishes.

Season 2000–01 was to be Harry's last at the club. Despite playing some fine football, it took seven games for the side to register a win. The first home win didn't arrive until 28 October, a Kanouté goal beating Newcastle. The ageing Davor Suker, signed from Arsenal, was costing the whole of the season's revenue from the East Stand, and showed the same mobility as Iain Dowie running through treacle whenever he played.

The defining moment of the season was the decision to sell Rio Ferdinand to Leeds. Redknapp did a good job in talking the price up, turning down an initial £15 million bid. Following changes in EU labour regulations, it was uncertain at that time if the transfer system would even be retained the next season, and it was a world record fee for a defender who was still making the odd mistake and didn't relish tackles in the same way as Stuart Pearce. Away from Upton Park, Rio was to develop into a world-class defender and for all Harry's years of saying that West Ham were no longer a selling club, it revealed that we were just that.

Harry had money to spend, but instead of buying quality he couldn't end his habit of gambling on players who might prove to be bargains. He bought or was loaned eight players from around the world: Rigobert Song from Cameroon; Titi Camara from Guinea; Scotsman Christian Dailly; Bulgarian Svetoslav Todorov; Norwegian Ragnvald Soma; Frenchman Sébastien Schemmel; Australian Hayden Foxe; and Hannu Tihinen from Finland. Harry even had an Argentinian whizz-kid and the Japanese captain (good for shirt sales in the East) over for trials. I wondered if West Ham would soon have to field two reserve sides just to accommodate them all. We joked that Harry had sensed a nice little earner: with so many nationalities at West Ham he'd opened a backpackers' hostel at Chadwell Heath. Footballing wannabes from around the world were put up in bunks and offered discounted *Lonely Planet* guides, cheap fried breakfasts and trips to Covent Garden with tourist guide Mr Di Canio.

Only Christian Dailly was to provide anything like long-term value. Titi Camara looked a slow overweight lump. Song only lasted half a season, Todorov was lightweight, Soma not Premiership class. The best players looked to be loan stars Hannu Tihinen and Sébastien Schemmel, but Harry insisted on sending them back once Christmas-party urinator Hayden Foxe's visa came through. Even so, it looked like our name might be on the cup.

Nicola was two weeks from giving birth to our second daughter Nell when we played Man United at Old Trafford in the cup, so I watched the game from home in case she went into early labour. No one expected us to win, until Paolo Di Canio beat the offside trap, ignored the taxi-hailing Barthez and stroked home the winner. He then ran to the corner flag where the 9,000 Hammers fans were celebrating and mouthed, 'I can play away' to the cameras. Even funnier was Alex Ferguson trying to blame United's defeat on the Old Trafford pitch afterwards. I was dancing with my daughter Lola, singing the Di Canio aria at home, and very nearly went into labour myself. You just don't win at Old Trafford.

We won at Sunderland in the cup and then met Spurs in the sixth round. It was surely Di Canio's year, just like it was Alan Taylor's in 1975. At least it was until Sergei Rebrov scored twice in a 3–2 win for Spurs, becoming the latest in a long tradition of players who looked brilliant against us but not for us. The defending was poor and I wondered if Rio Ferdinand might have made the difference.

West Ham then spiralled into a relegation struggle. Form had slumped since a 5–0 Boxing Day thrashing of Charlton, and the club had won just three out of seventeen league matches after that. Kanouté was injured and Di Canio was playing when not fully fit. At least a 3–0 defeat at Liverpool provided the season's best chant of 'We've got Di Canio, you've got our stereos!' When we lost three in a row with just two games left it looked like we could go down.

That season we'd been joined in the East Stand by three of DC's pals, vicar's son Matt George (his mum doesn't know about his bad language at games), and Brentwood lads Nigel Morris and Gavin Hadland. Gavin and I travelled from Euston to Manchester City together for a crucial end-of-season game: City would be relegated if they lost, free-falling West Ham needed a point to be assured of safety.

'Harry really is down to the bare bones today,' I confided on the train.

'He's been down to the bare bones all season,' muttered one of two outed Irons fans sitting opposite. 'How can this squad underachieve like they have?' Put four West Ham fans on a train with four cans of beer each and they will moan. Injury crises, the selling of Rio, the club's lack of ambition, the aptly named Titi Camara – the journey passed pleasantly enough with tales of mutual horror.

Gavin rummaged through his real-ale guide and selected a couple of likely pubs, while I felt sadly satisfied that Maine Road would be the 48th ground that I had visited in the Premiership and Nationwide League. Groundhopping and real-ale drinking: the joy of away travel is that you can combine two or more obsessions at once.

Miraculously, the Virgin train arrived on time, and we took a taxi to the not-bad-at-all Albert pub, where we supped Hyde's bitter in plastic glasses and were jostled by pint-carrying Liam Gallagher soundalikes saying 'excuse me, pal'.

As we queued up outside the away end Gavin said, 'I hope they don't search me, I've got a razor in my bag.' Oh dear, I thought, they'll think we're the ICF. Apparently, Gav liked to have a shave on the train.

Bizarrely, the steward searched his carrier bag and found a plastic bottle of mineral water, which she made him drink on the assumption that it might be used as an offensive weapon, but missed the razor. 'I went to Millwall once, and the police confiscated a pack of four out-of-date yoghurts from my bag,' Gavin added.

Maine Road appeared to have been designed by a partially sighted four year old with a Meccano kit. Nothing was in sync. The away end had a nominal roof, but it was designed so that rain could penetrate just about every area through huge gaps at the sides. Maine Road was as eccentric as City.

Kick-off arrived. West Ham started well, but when City scored a lucky goal, which took a huge deflection, it was too much for the Hammers fans watching their eighth defeat in ten games. Chants of 'Sack the board!' and 'Where's the money gone?' could be heard from the visiting supporters. To make it worse, we were getting soaked by the obligatory Manchester rain.

However, Redknapp's half-time team talk worked. West Ham absolutely annihilated City in the second half. Todorov brought two great saves from City's keeper Carlo Nash and had a goal disallowed. Pearce and Cole had shots cleared off the line, and Diawara missed an easy chance.

As the Hammers fans attempted to rouse their side with a chorus of 'I'm Forever Blowing Bubbles', the Mancunians pointed at us and responded with 'Town full of Munichs, it's just a town full of Munichs', an insulting reference to London being full of Man United fans. I'd heard worse, such as 'Town full of rent boys' from Middlesbrough fans and 'Reggie Kray is a homosexual' from homophobic Forest fans.

At that point, there was a cracking atmosphere in the stadium, with neurotic City fans frantically whistling for full-time. If I had to explain the essence of football, I would use the gloriously surreal moment when 30,000 Man City fans sang a cacophonous 'We are not . . . we're not really here!' to the tune of 'We Shall Not Be Moved' as an example. Yes, existentialist football fans debating the nature of being and the duality of mind and body. The chant was first sung when City were plummeting from the Premiership to Division Two, while Man United won just about everything, and epitomised the dark humour of those of us who follow crap teams.

In injury time Di Canio had a shot on goal that Nash spilled, but

Todorov spooned the rebound past the post from two yards. After a miss like that, I started to wonder if West Ham really were going down.

City hung on to win 1–0 and we retreated into Rusholme Road in a deluge. Luckily, we were in Manchester's 'curry mile' and escaped from the rain for a fortifying Madras followed by a trip to a pub for some cans of Hyde's bitter and then onwards for a taxi to Manchester Piccadilly.

The train compartment was packed with blokes on mobiles all saying, 'We lost 1–0, I think we're going down . . .' Then there was the rumour that Redknapp had resigned. End-of-season football rumours are invariably false, as that one proved to be. 'That would make my day if he has,' said a morose fan from Watford in a Corrs T-shirt sitting opposite us.

Our new friend spent the three-hour return journey going through all Harry's possible permutations for next season. 'If he plays Lomas what about Song . . . will he play Di Canio and Cole . . . and if he buys a left-sided midfielder will he play Carrick and Lampard . . .' He's probably still going now; that man must even go to sleep with his mind locked in a gridlock of formations, every decision to demote Steve Lomas to sub torturing his footballing soul.

By 9.30 p.m. we were back at Euston. 'We could try the Head of Steam for a pint of Oakham JHB,' suggested Gavin. Only the beer wasn't on – a bit like our talented side's recent slump into the relegation mire.

A week later West Ham beat Southampton 3–0 at Upton Park, Cole, Di Canio and Kanouté finally ending our relegation fears, but days later came the news that Harry Redknapp had been sacked. The board had announced that Redknapp had left 'by mutual consent' after a meeting with chairman Terence Brown, but most commentators realised that was football jargon for being given the sack. Redknapp, who had two years left to run on his contract, said that it was down to an argument about funds for new players that had 'gotten out of hand'. He emphasised, 'Leaving the club was the last thing on my mind when I went over this morning. I never dreamed it would happen. After meeting the chairman it all changed and I found myself out of work. Life in the Premiership will be even tougher next season and I wanted three players to get us up to scratch.'

To this day, the club has never revealed the reasons for Redknapp's sacking, although if I had a plate of chips in Ken's Café for every unsubstantiated conspiracy theory, I'd soon resemble Buster Bloodvessel. Harry might have blown much of the Rio cash, but had the chairman forgotten about the thriving youth policy and the bargains – Di Canio, Sinclair, Berkovic, Bilic and Hartson had all escalated in value.

Whatever the truth, Terry Brown and the board at least owed the fans – the real shareholders of West Ham – some sort of statement. It didn't come. Seven years of solo Redknapp management and nine years at the club had ended and Glenn Roeder was destined to be our new boss.

11

DADDY, I KNOW HOW
TO SCORE A GOAL . . .

2002
West Ham appoint '100–1 outsider' Glenn Roeder as manager . . .
finish seventh . . . sign world-class defender Gary Breen . . . but
start the 2002–03 season bottom of the league.
  Price of Hammer *in 2002: £3*

Under Glenn Roeder, West Ham finished a creditable seventh at the end of the 2001–02 season. The much-derided Roeder overcame early 5–0 and 7–1 defeats at Everton and Blackburn to steer the side to a position that would nowadays qualify a side for the UEFA Cup. He'd tackled various histrionics from Di Canio, persuaded Trevor Sinclair to sign a new contract, bought Repka and Hutchison for £10 million, and had brought on three immensely promising youngsters in Carrick, Cole and Defoe. He'd even managed to survive Hayden Foxe peeing into a plant pot at the players' Christmas party at Sugar Reef.

Having chronicled the entire season in my book *West Ham: Irons in the Soul*, also published by Mainstream, I concluded:

> A year ago a disgruntled fan greeted Roeder's appointment by
> emailing the club website with the message, 'If you think small in

144

the Premiership you are small'. Were the board just lucky in their appointment or could they, for once, have been thinking long term and shown great prescience? A season on, with a bright young coach, a superb collection of youngsters and a ground capacity that has increased by nearly 10,000, the club might just be on the Roeder somewhere and some of us might see West Ham win another trophy within our lifetimes. Or we might be relegated – with West Ham you never know.

It was perhaps just as well that I'd added that last qualification, even if we all thought that realistically there was no way a side as talented as West Ham could ever go down.

In the close season, Roeder's major signing was Gary Breen, the out-of-contract Coventry centre-back who'd had a very good World Cup with Ireland and had even scored against Saudi Arabia. He also signed Edouard Cisse on loan and an unknown young French striker called Youssef Sofiane. But despite finishing seventh the previous term, West Ham had not paid a fee for any player. Significantly, it was the first season with a transfer window. The club would not be able to buy any more players until the transfer window reopened in January.

The 2002–03 season began with much optimism. It soon disintegrated with a 0–4 away defeat at Newcastle, shown live on Sky TV while I was on holiday in Yorkshire. Staying in a Skyless home meant watching the game on Ceefax. Di Canio was injured and young Jermain Defoe was played alone up front. It was goalless at half-time, but then came the Geordie deluge, from Lomana LuaLua (61, 72), Alan Shearer (76) and Nolberto Solano (86).

The following Saturday, the Irons were up against Arsenal at Upton Park and played superbly. Cole and Kanouté put the Hammers two goals up before Thierry Henry pulled one back. Then with 15 minutes left West Ham were awarded a penalty which would have made the game 3–1 and surely guaranteed a home victory. A win would also have given the side confidence for another top-half finish; it could have changed the course of West Ham's entire season. But Fredi Kanouté ambled up to the ball like an American GI about to ask an attractive Wren if she would like to dance to a Glenn Miller tune. A casual stroll, an elegant flick of the boot and then he neatly side-footed the ball towards the grateful Seaman, who saved with relative ease. And this being West Ham, Arsenal inevitably equalised, when Wiltord hammered the ball into the top of our net in the 88th minute. A draw was creditable enough, and *The Guardian* made loan-signing Cisse the man of the match, but come May that penalty would seem awfully important.

In the East Stand we reassured ourselves that with a further two home games in succession we would inevitably climb the table. But no, West Ham capitulate too easily at home to an organised Charlton side. One of Charlton's goals is scored by Jon Fortune, who has a fine game and almost inevitably grew up supporting West Ham – is there any player who didn't? After three games, we are bottom of the Premiership. Still, at least Steve Lomas had returned to the side after injuring his shin walking around Walt Disney World in Florida, presumably the result of a late tackle by Mickey Mouse.

It was obvious that we would beat newly promoted West Bromwich Albion the following Tuesday. Paolo was back and for 30 minutes West Ham bombarded the Baggies goal, with Joe Cole in particular perfecting the art of missing the target from all conceivable angles and positions. Carrick and Sinclair also missed great chances. After half an hour, Albion made a break and Jason Roberts, easily running between the new centre-back partnership of Repka and Breen, slotted the ball home. The away fans did their peculiar 'Boing! Boing! Baggies!' song while they bounced up and down in the Centenary Stand.

For the rest of the game, we attacked the Baggies goal, aiming cross after cross at their defenders, making their colossus of a defender Darren 'Big Dave' Moore look like the greatest centre-back to ever grace world football. We wasted 18 corners. Some fans then cheered when Michael Carrick, playing way below form and having missed an easy chance, was substituted. Carrick's problems seemed to epitomise the side's underachievement. Substitute Jermain Defoe made no discernible difference, while super-nutter Tomas Repka had to be dragged away from a confrontation with West Ham fans by MD Paul Aldridge at the end of the game. You have to question the mental health of any fan wanting to confront Tomas. Glenn Roeder said, 'I can't fault the players' effort . . . Football is not an exact science and it can be a cruel game.' Indeed, as all West Ham fans know, football is a very exact science when the Irons are involved. We lose; we stay bottom.

Things nearly change at Tottenham, in a game again watched by the world live and exclusive on Sky TV. Roeder had introduced Ian Pearce at right-back in place of Schemmel, Davies scored for Spurs, but Kanouté prodded home an equaliser. Teddy Sheringham scored a penalty for Tottenham after Pearce manhandled Robbie Keane but then Di Canio took a quick free-kick and Sinclair scored a superb equaliser. We looked set for a well-earned draw at White Hart Lane.

Then Roeder took off Di Canio with minutes remaining. Some of the tabloids claimed that they had lip-read Paolo saying 'F*** you!' to his boss when he ran towards him after Sinclair's goal. Surely this must have been 'Thank you' . . . Later, Paolo explained, 'We were celebrating together, I was saying "Come on, this is for you Glenn", and I wanted to dedicate the draw to him because I know what he is suffering. We have to stay a unit against the sports writers because they hate West Ham.'

Sadly, Paolo didn't get the chance to dedicate the draw to his boss. You can never trust West Ham when they start backing off. In the 89th minute, Spurs centre-back Anthony Gardner picked up the ball on the halfway line, ambled to within 30 yards of the Hammers goal, where there was surely no danger, and had a shot at goal. The ball deflected off the hapless Gary Breen and past David James.

By late September our best hope of getting any kind of win appeared to be new striker Prince Harry. The Prince was at Upton Park visiting a charity project and was photographed blasting a penalty past youngster Anton Ferdinand in goal. Anton revealed, 'He was going on as if he couldn't hit a ball, but then he smashed it into the top corner. I couldn't get near it!' And all this while wearing a suit and brogues. Harry was presented with a No. 18 Hammers shirt with his name on the back, and it appeared that he might be the answer to our attacking problems. ('We've got 'Arry 'Arry Windsor on the wing!') He was more direct than Joe Cole and (to judge from his past dealings in the Rattlebone Inn) already able to drink like a footballer. But sadly Roeder didn't sign him up, preferring to persevere with Titi Camara in the reserves.

With one point from five games it was time to do anything that I could to help us win. So I resolved to take my daughter Lola to the next home match against Manchester City. It is, of course, the question every dad agonises about: when should you first take your child to a football match?

Lola, then aged four, could chant 'Paolo Di Canio' and had already asked to go to a game. During the World Cup, she'd enjoyed the dispensing of red and yellow cards and had asked, with some perception, 'Daddy, if the player picked him up and put him on top of a very tall house and took the ladder away, would that be a yellow card?'

Things were truly desperate. We lived in Highbury, right next to Arsenal's ground. Arsenal won Doubles and played great football, they took coaching classes at the local primary schools and Lola's nursery teacher Tracy was Arsenal's number one fan. Four was perhaps too young to go a game but I reasoned that unless I acted now, Lola would be Thierry Henry's for life, and, anyway, I could tell Nicola it was a form of childcare.

A first game can influence a child for ever. In *Fever Pitch* Nick Hornby recounted how his estranged dad first took him to Arsenal on his child access days. The result was an unhealthy lifelong obsession with both the Gunners and writing bestsellers.

My conscience keeps asking me if I have the right to inflict West Ham, a side that has not won a major trophy for 23 years, on my daughter. Those inevitable cup defeats to lower-division teams, the taunting at school, that maddening inconsistency, the perpetual struggle to hold on to our young players . . .

But maybe there's some value in supporting a team that frustrates you at every free-kick. What better lesson could there be for a child than that success is ephemeral and all the more valuable when you've had to wait for it? That sometimes losing in the right way is just as important as winning. That being a bit crap makes rare moments of victory all the more worthwhile.

So, I resolved to take Lola to West Ham v. Manchester City. There's always a slight risk your child will sympathise with the opposition, so the opponents have to be chosen carefully. Manchester City would do because they were not Man United, they played attacking football and their fans were similarly long suffering.

On the train to Upton Park, I explained to Lola how you get three points for a win, one for a draw and none for a defeat. 'That's not a good deal – everyone should win,' said Lola, a true Islington girl already, causing the two blokes in replica shirts opposite to chuckle.

'I'm afraid football's not like that, although West Ham are good at winning friends and losing matches,' I told her.

At Upton Park I carried her on my shoulders through the throng of fans and bought her a West Ham cap, priced £6. The unofficial kids' replica shirts offered by the street traders are £20, and as I had already paid a pal £20 to use his season ticket for Lola, I began to wonder if it might not be more lucrative just to give up and let her support Arsenal. Yet carrying her down Green Street evoked memories of my own first trips to football with my dad: the mysterious smells, the stalls selling scarves, the shouts of programme sellers, the noise of animated pre-match conversations, the sense of being part of something bigger than yourself.

We made our way to Ken's Café where I had promised Lola food that would horrify her mum. 'I want sloppy egg and chips!' she declared, provoking more laughter from fellow diners. We held on to our number 79 ticket, and after a long wait, the sloppy eggs and chips arrived to which Lola added huge dollops of tomato ketchup. Kick-off was fast approaching so I bundled Lola's unfinished chips into my bag and we made a rush for the turnstiles.

With West Ham bottom of the league, there was an atmosphere of noisy encouragement in the ground. 'I'm Forever Blowing Bubbles' blared out from the PA, but Lola seemed unfazed by all the raucousness, shrewdly offering my friends her jelly babies. The game kicked off, and Lola had many questions. When Cisse was booked, she asked pertinently, 'What if he put the ball in a dustcart and took it away, would that be a yellow card?'

'That would be a straight red . . .' interjected my pal Nigel.

Sadly, there were few chances in the game but Lola appeared to appreciate the illicit frisson of pulling a chip-and-egg butty from Ken's Café out of my plastic bag. Then we went through the popcorn. There was some use of the 'f' word behind us, but it was hopefully too far away to register with Lola.

I felt a certain pride as she joined in the shouting, saying, 'Come on West Ham, you can do it!', instantly grasping that the perpetual fear of the West Ham fan is that they will not do it. 'What if West Ham scored 71 goals and the other side one, would that be a win?' she asked.

'Daddy would be drinking champagne if West Ham scored 71 goals.'

'And eating chillies,' added Lola.

Half-time arrived with no goals, but Lola was impressed by the Hammerettes dancing on the pitch, who in most un-PC fashion whipped off their skirts, Bucks Fizz style. It was certainly more stressful watching a match with a kid as sweet supplies became just as important as the supply to Fredi Kanouté up front. In the second half a food crisis occurred, Lola having eaten everything in our bag. She sat on my knee and wriggled animatedly, demanding mints. Luckily, Gavin, a fellow dad, helpfully provided chewing gum and water. Then he passed over his Walkman and said, 'This will keep her quiet.' It did too and she sat fiddling with the earphones, listening to a tape of the Cosmic Rough Riders.

I turned off the tape when West Ham got a corner and pointed out Paolo Di Canio as the crowd sang his name to the tune of the aria from Verdi's *Rigoletto*. (Who said that football wasn't educational?)

The game descended into mediocrity and I said to Nigel that Lola had probably enjoyed the Hammerettes more than the football. 'They took their skirts off!' enthused Lola.

Paolo Di Canio was substituted, and I explained to Lola that he needed a rest. 'Why has Paolo Di Canio been arrested?' she asked.

'Come on Hammers, I've been supporting you for 30 years and you can't even score a winner for my daughter!' I found myself cursing as the final whistle neared.

'You're useless, West Ham . . . you're useless, Sinclair!' shouted a boy not much older than Lola who was sitting behind us.

'Daddy, why is he saying West Ham are useless?' asked Lola. I explained that he didn't really think that they were useless. 'It's like when you and your sister have rows, but you still really love each other,' I explained, somewhat optimistically.

The final whistle blew and the crowd muttered its collective disapproval. Bizarrely, it was West Ham's first goalless draw in 41 games. Still bottom of the league, no goals, the stoic acceptance of disappointment, frustration, anger . . . Lola couldn't have had a better introduction to the perpetual hopelessness of being a West Ham fan. But there was something profoundly bonding in walking to the Tube in the autumnal sunlight musing over the game with my daughter. Lola was upbeat on the train home, fortified by a promised packet of wine gums.

'Daddy, I know how to score a goal. All you have to do is stand really close to the net and kick the ball.' I promised to pass on the advice to Glenn Roeder immediately.

12

WILL WE EVER WIN AT HOME?

2002–03
West Ham fail to beat Arsenal, Charlton, West Brom, Man City, Birmingham, Everton, Leeds, Man United, Southampton, Bolton, Fulham and Newcastle at home . . . the fans sing 'we want a new back four' . . . Ruud destroys Mr Breen . . . and then on 30 January 2003 the impossible happens.
  Price of Hammer *in 2002: £3*

The 2002–03 season proved to be one long round of footballing schizophrenia. After the draw at home to Manchester City, the Irons travelled to Chelsea and won 3–2. Di Canio scored twice, the first a stupendous volley, after first flicking up the ball with his right foot, and then firing an unstoppable effort past Cudicini with his left. The other goal was scored by substitute Jermain Defoe (Fredi Kanouté had picked up a long-term injury), and it seemed our season might be turning.

Paolo caused controversy by running to the Chelsea fans after scoring his second and winning goal. He told the press, 'I wanted to challenge the Chelsea fans because they had broken my balls the whole game. So I ran to them and began to yell "I'm the man, I'm the man! So, what now? Who is the winner now?" To me it was really a beautiful, beautiful moment.'

Absolutely. Although we all hoped that the West Ham physio had something for those broken balls – preferably not Ralgex.

The following week the team lost to newly promoted Birmingham. In the first minute, Gary Breen, apparently wandering through Wordsworthian fields of daffodils, tried to shepherd the ball away for a goalkick, but was easily dispossessed and Birmingham went ahead. Joe Cole scored with a well-taken goal for the equaliser, but Stern John then bamboozled the lumbering Repka and fired home the winner.

At least there was some relief to be had in the shape of *The Sun*'s story about West Ham fan and right banker Trevor Luxton. City worker Luxton was exposed to national ridicule after his email about illicit oral sex was circulated to millions on the Internet – even though he later claimed that the whole thing was a joke. Luxton's email claimed that while his fiancée, Jo, was away he was watching Chesterfield v. West Ham in the Worthington Cup live on Sky when his mate's ex-girlfriend Laura came over.

He then boasted, 'I find myself sitting in the armchair with a beer in one hand, remote in the other, West Ham on the box and Laura on her knees s**king my piece.' At which point Jo phoned up and Luxton continued to chat to her while Laura carried on her ministrations.

But one of Trevor's mates circulated the email and an outraged female worker decided 'Let's get this two-timing arsehole in trouble.' She forwarded the email and wrote, 'Send this to everyone you know who works in the City, and hopefully it will get back to his bird!'

Of course it wasn't that big a joke. Luxton had been guilty of a staggering lack of loyalty to those he most loved. After all, what kind of West Ham fan would allow himself to be distracted from the game just because Laura came over?

After the abysmal home defeat to Birmingham, West Ham went and won at Sunderland. Di Canio played a visionary through ball and Sinclair thumped the ball in off the woodwork. Then came another away win at Fulham. For Nigel, Matt, Fraser and me that will forever be our 'Where were you when Estelle Morris resigned?' moment. As a political correspondent for a national paper, Nigel was technically on duty that night, and late in the second half his pager informed him that the education secretary had just quit.

He was tempted to go and file some copy, but we persuaded him to wait another ten minutes because football is far more important than political resignations. We dominated the first half, but the match looked like finishing a goalless draw. The game was most notable for Glenn Roeder's new leather jacket bought with that season's pay rise. In injury time, Zat Knight conceded a penalty, and Di Canio calmly stroked the ball home. At the end of the game, PDC came over to the fans, stripped to his white vest, flashed his myriad tattoos at us and shouted 'F***eeen West Ham! F***eeen West Ham!' several times. It must have been a rather strange backdrop to Nigel's phone call to his news desk to discuss possible angles on the departed Estelle Morris story.

Two away wins in a row seemed certain to start a charge up to mid-table in the Premiership. But no, again we failed, this time at home to Everton, which brought a miserable October to an end. It was as if the players couldn't stand the pressure of playing at Upton Park. Bald ball-winners Lee Carsley and Tomas Gravesen swaggered around the pitch like the Mitchell brothers, easily intimidating Cole and Carrick, probably by accusing them of eyeing up Sharon Watts. Without the injured Kanouté we lacked power and height up front.

It was goalless at half-time but in the 70th minute Everton's Lee Carsley exposed our suspect defence and scored. That season no one had any expectation that we would pull it back. We had better players than Everton, but under David Moyes, Everton were playing as a unit. That was why Gravesen, Carsley, Le Tie and Pembridge could outperform the more skilful Carrick, Cole, Sinclair and Di Canio. Everton sub Wayne Rooney was greeted with cries of 'Who are yer?', but it was so bad that even Titi Camara got on as our substitute.

There was a dire mood in Ken's Café afterwards. Big Joe had braved the October floods to sail in a boat across the Thames from his island home at Hampton. 'Was it worth it?' we asked. DC was incensed, 'Why can 30,000 people see it but not Roeder? Minto isn't good enough! It's a disgrace when you see the goal again. Any organised side can muscle us off the ball!'

After the usual defeat at Liverpool we played Oldham, managed by old threepenny-bit head himself, Iain Dowie, in the Worthington Cup. At least an easy win against Division Two opposition would end the Upton Park jinx. But no, it was instantly recognisable that Iain Dowie was a much better manager than player. Oldham were superbly organised at the back, and for the entire game we made Fitz Hall and his two Second Division colleagues look like the sons of Bobby Moore.

When Oldham gained a corner just before half-time, I mumbled, 'Here comes the soft goal' and it duly arrived as Corazzin headed the ball into the net.

In the second half, a streaker ran onto the pitch clad in black boxers. 'He'll be banned for life,' said Matt.

'Maybe we should all do it!' added Fraser.

'There's only one Iain Dowie,' sang the Oldham fans.

'Bet he never thought he'd hear that at Upton Park!' Nigel quipped.

Joe Cole had a great game but couldn't inspire those around him. Titi Camara, finally getting a full game in the absence of the injured Paolo, Fredi and Trevor Sinclair, had a penalty appeal turned down, Defoe fired against the keeper's legs late on and that was about it. We lost to no-hopers at home. 'It would have been classed as an upset if we had won,' suggested Matt.

In the next league game, West Ham faced Leeds, stuttering under Terry Venables. Unfortunately, our defence was the victim of some form of footballing spontaneous combustion in the first half, as we went into the break 4–1 down. Ian Pearce's weak back-header was gathered by Kewell who crossed for Barmby to slot home after 12 minutes. Even though Viduka was beating Tomas Repka to everything, Di Canio equalised on 21 minutes when he slotted home the rebound after Robinson saved a Michael Carrick drive. But then Repka forgot to mark Harry Kewell who headed home from a corner. Kewell then grabbed his second on 40 minutes when he fired home after James parried his initial shot. Sinclair was wearing a bank-robber-style mask to protect a facial injury, although really it was the defenders who should have been seeking anonymity.

To compound a first half of defensive ineptitude, Christian Dailly woefully underhit a back pass, David James rushed from his goal and kicked the ball against Viduka. It ran kindly for the big Aussie striker who only had to stroke the ball into the net. He then proceeded to taunt the fans in the Bobby Moore Stand with his celebrations. The side went in at half-time to chants of 'Sack the board!' During the break, Jeremy Nicholas made one of the club's bizarre security announcements. 'Will the stadium manager please note: Mr Moon has left the stadium!' He was not the only one.

Repka – who was given a three out of ten rating by *The Sun* the next day – was so bad that he was taken off at half-time. Then, just to confound us fans, West Ham came out for the second half and played superbly, suddenly looking like a side chasing the championship. Substitute Sébastien Schemmel later revealed that it was Di Canio who found a means of inspiring the lads, apparently by doing his finest Marlon Brando impersonation.

'Paolo walked up to every player and told them to look him in the eye because West Ham needed men out on the pitch. Paolo said he did not want to be remembered as part of a West Ham team which had the worst home record. He wanted it to be the best. When Paolo speaks like that I love him, and I will do anything for him. He is a world-class player. The whole team went out in a different mood and fought like men,' revealed Schemmel.

Di Canio was absolutely brilliant after the break, almost wresting the game from Leeds on his own. He won a penalty and converted it himself. Sinclair then headed home a Schemmel corner and West Ham threatened an outrageous comeback. In a late chance, Defoe misdirected a header, but Robinson beat the ball away just before Carrick managed to capitalise on it. The game ended in a 4–3 home defeat and West Ham were the only side not to win at home in the four English divisions at that time.

In Ken's Café afterwards I met Steve Rapport, the former editor of *Fortune's Always Hiding*, who was visiting from San Francisco. In those days he would greet me with a Californian hug before a match, but by the end of that game he had forgotten all that new age California-dreaming stuff and was quoting The Clash's 'Working for the Clampdown'. 'Let anger be the power, you know that you can use it!' he recited. Working for the clampdown was something that it appeared our defence would never manage.

Roeder described the defence as diabolical, demoralising, woeful and appalling after the game. 'I am very angry over the non-defending. We gifted Leeds four goals. It's difficult to legislate for such poor work,' he tiraded, sounding like a particularly miffed maths master. 'It was not just Tomas, who admittedly did not play well. Which of them did? Of all the defenders Nigel Winterburn was the pick. But we did not collapse when some teams would have done so . . . When you score three goals against a team like Leeds and do not get anything from the game it is just shocking.'

With the tabloid pressure increasing, Roeder gave his obligatory speech from *Rocky* about not giving up. 'It is not an option for me to walk away. No one out there seems to believe me when I say I do not live in fear.' It was not an option for this fan to walk away either, even though I did live in fear at that time.

After the Leeds game, there was an undignified spat between former Hammers hero Julian Dicks and Paolo Di Canio in *The Sun*. Di Canio had been one of West Ham's better players during a terrible start, but Dicks cited his absence at Liverpool as proof that he missed too many games in the north. In an article headlined 'Paolo's a Part-timer', Dicks wrote:

> Take Paolo Di Canio. Great footballer but how many away games does he play? He was missing again at Liverpool wasn't he? We all get knocks, but the way he always seems to be OK for home games is a bit of a coincidence. Sometimes you need to bite the bullet and get out there even if you are not 100 per cent fit.

The paper printed stats claiming that in games at Liverpool, Leeds, Newcastle, Man United and Middlesbrough the striker had played in just three out of nineteen matches. In his autobiography Di Canio had written, 'Every day I feel myself absorbing more and more of that bulldog spirit. I have a long way to go before I become like, say, Julian Dicks, a true gladiator and a genuine inspiration, but I'm getting there.' However Paolo seemed to forget those words when he responded to Dicksy in his usual phlegmatic style. 'Dicks is a traitor to West Ham,' he told *The Sun*:

> West Ham fans shouldn't forget what he is really like. How much passion did Dicks have for West Ham when he could not wait to run off to Liverpool to sign for them? It's easy to try to be a hero by kicking, fighting, using the elbow and screaming at opponents. But it's a lot harder to be a total professional for every second of the day setting a good example to the young players. Dicks didn't act totally professionally and didn't train properly.
>
> Maybe if he was a real supporter he would give encouragement rather than make negative comments; since I've been at West Ham we have played 34 matches in the north and I have played in 17 of them. Of the 17 I missed I was suspended for 5 and injured for

12. In the 17 I played we picked up a total of 20 points and in the ones I missed we sadly made just 5 points. Why would I deliberately want to miss matches when I have such a big influence on results?

It was another messy media-generated incident that did little to increase the unity at the club. So to then draw at home with Man United, courtesy of a late and probably offside Jermain Defoe equaliser, felt almost like a victory. David James veered between gaffes and making an outstanding double save from Laurent Blanc and Ruud van Nistelrooy at the end. 'We've got a point, we've got one, West Ham's got a point . . .'

However, the following week we collapsed 4–1 at Aston Villa, despite a rare headed goal from Di Canio. James, Dailly and Pearce were all guilty of yet more catastrophic errors, or 'non-defending' as Roeder now termed it. With West Ham bottom of the table, the next home game against Southampton, live on Sky on the first Monday of December, was even more vital.

Before the game Roeder had reiterated his commitment to the club. He said, 'I don't know the meaning of the word quit.' Although some fans in the Bobby Moore Stand were starting to wish that he did.

There was a rumour before the Southampton match that Fredi Kanouté might be playing but he went down with Devonshire flu instead. When DC said that Ian Pearce was playing up front I assumed that it was a joke. But it wasn't. As cunning ploys go it ranked alongside other infamous West Ham conversions, such as playing Tommy Taylor and Alvin Martin up front. Roeder had given up on Camara and for some reason wouldn't use Sinclair in attack. Pearce performed reasonably well in his unfamiliar role, forcing a good save from Antti Niemi, the Saints keeper, but it was the usual story of missed chances from Defoe and Carrick in the first half.

Late in the game, Paolo Di Canio was taken off with damaged knee cartilage that was set to keep him out for several weeks. As the 90-minute mark approached it looked as if West Ham would at least gain a point. It was Nigel's 40th birthday, and he'd spent much of the game shouting things like, 'Scream for me Hammersmith!' By the time the game approached its end, he morbidly reflected, 'I wasn't old enough to vote the last time we won something.'

DC rushed for the Silverlink. 'Don't miss a goal!' we quipped. He did. In injury time it all went a bit *Groundhog Day*. Southampton broke down the left, and James Beattie bundled in the ball at the far post. West Ham lost at home again. The fans chanted 'Sack the board'. Glenn Roeder said that he didn't know the meaning of the word quit and lamented our defending. He added that the poor performances and results were hurting him as much as the fans. We were still bottom.

There was a huge surge of discontent at the final whistle, although most of the anger was directed at Terry Brown rather than Roeder. 'We want Brown out,' chanted sections of the faithful and a 'Brown Out' banner was held up in the Lower Bobby Moore Stand. After the game, a large group of fans protested in front of the main stand.

The team's problems were numerous: we had forgotten how to defend; Schemmel was off form and nothing like the player he was the previous season; Winterburn was still committed but his pace was slowing; Sinclair hadn't performed well since excelling at the World Cup for England; with Di Canio and Kanouté out, Defoe was too inexperienced to play up front on his own; and there was very little we could do to change things until the transfer window reopened in January.

I thought that perhaps we were in a situation similar to *The Matrix* and we were all actually lying down in caskets with software wired into our brains that forced us to lead a virtual existence in which West Ham never won at home again. But no, it was real. 'We are in a big hole but we can turn it round,' said Glenn. Dressed in his new black leather jacket, he might well have been a character from *The Matrix*.

After the game, we retreated to the Black Lion at Plaistow and started to talk seriously about new managers. We all agreed that Roeder did well to face the questions from the media about his position after each game. He was a decent man and handled the difficult situation with dignity, but the fact was that it was December and we hadn't won at home all season. Roeder had enjoyed a great first season, finishing seventh in the league with the same group of players, but now he was floundering. I suspected that Harry Redknapp, sacked by Brown, would have been experienced enough to shake up the players – axe a few, encourage some and threaten others – in order to get that first home win. 'At least Estelle Morris is available,' I suggested.

'A decent person admitting that they are not up to the job. Now why does that sound familiar?' asked Nigel, morosely supping at his birthday lager.

'And Iain Duncan Smith is probably available, too,' I pointed out.

Would we ever win at home again? Or even away? It seemed not. We conceded a late equaliser against Middlesbrough and lost 3–0 to Man United. Then, unfortunately, we had another home game, against Bolton on 21 December. If we didn't win that one we would definitely be bottom of the league at Christmas, and every team that had been bottom of the Premiership at Christmas had always gone down. I was starting to feel like Reggie Perrin.

'Have a nice day at the match, dear.'

'I won't!'

Had I really got where I am today by supporting West Ham? Before the Bolton game I enjoyed a pleasant pre-match chat in the Newham Bookshop in Barking Road. It's one of the best independent bookshops in London, loved by Michael Rosen and Benjamin Zephaniah. Football books merge with heavyweight political tomes and a fine children's section. Vivien and John at the Newham Bookshop had given great support to my book *West Ham: Irons in the Soul,* organising signings and readings and were just generally enthusiastic about writing.

Before games, the Newham Bookshop was one of the unlikeliest literary salons in London, attracting an unusual cross-section of writers and readers. The likes of Cass Pennant (whose autobiography *Cass* is much more than the standard hoolie book and vividly evokes what it was like growing up as a black kid in Kent in the '80s, as well as having a moving ending in which Pennant discovers that his dad in Jamaica was previously living down the road in Plaistow) mingled with author Gilda O'Neill, Mark from the World Service and Iain Dale from Politico's Bookshop. Trouble was, the trip to the bookshop was starting to be more exciting than the match.

The fact that Edouard Cisse had caught chickenpox from his child seemed to amplify the misfortune of our season. The frequently tardy Gavin arrived nine minutes late, prompting someone in our row of seats to grumble, 'That bloke needs an alarm clock for Christmas.' Luckily there was no danger of him missing a home win. Ian Pearce was again up front and put us ahead after 17 minutes, emphasising how much we've needed a target man. But Bolton equalised through Ricketts.

'Is Tofting in prison?' I asked.

'No, he's on the bench,' said Matt.

'No, that was the judge who sentenced him,' quipped Fraser.

In front of nearly 35,000 fans we never really looked like winning. How many more centre-halfs could we make look good? Jon Fortune, West Brom's Moore, the Oldham three, Yobo, and now the Bolton back line was seemingly world class. We had drawn three out of the last nine matches and lost the rest. At the end there were no demos – 'Do you think that three points out of twenty-seven has bought the fans off?' asked Nigel – just Mud's 'It'll Be Lonely This Christmas' playing on the PA. It'll be cold so cold, without the Premiership fixture list to hold.

It felt like a defeat as Big Joe and I walked to the Tube. 'There's none of that back four you'd want in your team. Roeder's made no good signings, only James and he's gone wobbly. You'd welcome George Graham: he wouldn't get us relegated . . .'

But surely on Boxing Day we could beat Fulham? No, we drew 1–1, Sinclair's penalty equalising Sava's earlier strike. We still had a crowd of 35,025 turning up to watch a team that couldn't win at home. Fredi Kanouté played that day, but then disappeared for the next four games. West Ham looked disjointed and were grateful for a fine David James save and a Steve Marlet miss late on. What chance we had of winning the game was destroyed by Repka's needless sending off in the 90th minute. After being booked he continued to show dissent and was correctly dismissed. Repka argued with the referee that West Ham should have had a free-kick for a handball near their own box. The ill-disciplined centre-back was a liability. His sending off for a ridiculous show of petulance made Julian Dicks seem almost phlegmatic. Even Roeder was moved to describe Repka's dismissal as 'unforgivable'.

The non-bouncing Czech had all the attributes to be a fine defender and was a proven international, yet seemed more intent on fouling than defending, conceded numerous free-kicks on the edge of the box and in the defeat against Leeds was more concerned about pursuing a vendetta with Mark Viduka than bothering to mark attackers. It was just not good enough for a £5.5 million centre-back and the club's joint record signing.

At least Roeder would be able to act when the transfer window opened again, but not before playing out a 2–2 draw with Blackburn, in which David James became 'Calamity James' once more, letting an easy chance bobble over the line. Instead of signing a centre-back, Roeder went for midfielder Lee Bowyer from Leeds. It was a hugely controversial signing. Bowyer had more baggage than most holidaymakers returning to Stansted Airport. He had been convicted for attacking Asian staff at a McDonald's in the Isle of Dogs in 1996 and found not guilty of affray (but branded 'a liar' by the judge) after the infamous drunken attack on an Asian student in Leeds that saw teammate Jonathan Woodgate convicted.

As if West Ham hadn't put their supporters through enough that season – agony, ecstasy, nihilism, cynicism and stoicism – they were now inflicting moral dilemmas on us as well. In football terms it could be argued that Lee Bowyer was a good midfielder going cheap. It could also be argued that if West Ham stayed up, a lot of staff at the club would get to keep their jobs rather than face redundancy.

Some fans wondered if Dr Faustus was the new team physio fearing that signing Bowyer was like selling the club's soul. However, every person has done things that they regret. What the Asian community of Newham deserved was some sign of contrition from Bowyer for his previous actions. I hoped that Glenn Roeder, who seemed an eminently decent man, could have persuaded the star to make a public apology for past misdemeanors and offer a commitment to football's 'Kick Racism into Touch' campaign. It would have made West Ham fans happier to give him a second chance.

I also felt that there was a strong footballing argument against signing Bowyer. He had been a decent midfielder two years before, but we already had Cole, Carrick, Sinclair, Lomas and Cisse, and Hutchison was due to return from injury. It had been obvious all season, to even the most tactically illiterate of 'New Arsenal' fans, that what we needed was a new centre-back. Admittedly, there weren't too many quality defenders available, but, significantly, Birmingham managed to recruit Matthew Upson from Arsenal for £2 million, and his solid performances ensured their survival.

When Bowyer made his debut against Newcastle there was a small anti-racism demo outside the main gates of the club in Green Street, which was sadly given a hard time by many West Ham fans. The Bobby Moore Stand quickly voiced their support for the new signing and adopted a chant of, 'Lee Bowyer, Whooooooah! He comes from Canning Town; he'll stop us going down.'

Just to make Bowyer feel at home, West Ham found ever more inventive ways of failing to win at Upton Park. Against Newcastle, the side played really well, Bowyer showed poise and promise on his debut, and we were winning 2–1 at half-time after great strikes from Cole and Defoe. That elusive first home win seemed to be arriving on 11 January until, with nine minutes to go, Jermaine Jenas scored a tremendous goal for the Magpies with an unstoppable effort from the edge of the box. It was a great game, but what we needed were points.

Predictably enough we lost 3–1 against Arsenal in the next match, but only after Jermain Defoe had scored a fine equaliser. Dennis Bergkamp had also elbowed Lee Bowyer aside before crossing for Arsenal's second goal, but the foul went unpunished.

Then came a dire defeat at Charlton on a Wednesday night. Les Ferdinand had been signed from Spurs and was exactly what we needed up front: good in the air, experienced, not always injured like Fredi, and also, according to Glenn, 'a decent human being'.

The game kicked off late, which caused Nigel, Matt, Fraser and me to wonder if they were waiting for the obligatory late arrival from our mate Gavin. Our defensive line-up of Lomas, Dailly, Breen and Minto caused us much concern even before the match began. We reflected that the full-back pairing of the out-of-position Lomas and the declining Minto was surely the worst in the division.

Charlton dominated early on, but it was West Ham who took the lead. Bowyer, Defoe and Carrick combined to set up Cisse, whose shot deflected in off Charlton's Rufus. Charlton simply waited for our pre-half-time wobble. After 42 minutes had elapsed, Charlton were awarded a free-kick on the edge of the box. We all agreed with Fraser's comment that, 'You won't beat England's number one from there!' Cue Jensen, who arrowed the ball into the top corner. Then Scott Parker scored the second right on half-time, steering the ball home after good work by Euell and bad work by our back four. 'We're going down,' commented Matt, matter-of-factly.

After the interval, Parker scored again. The West Ham defence then appeared to think that Tracker was a piece of confectionery, as a weak Breen header fell to the young midfielder, who shot confidently home. It was the sixth time that season that we had lost a lead. Lomas was being hopelessly exposed on the right, Minto was no longer a Premiership player, Breen was timid and tentative, and Dailly's confidence had gone. Our best defender was new striker Les Ferdinand, who made three important clearing headers.

That season Roeder tried more partnerships than *This Morning* post-Richard and Judy. He paired Dailly and Breen, Dailly and Repka, Repka and Breen, Pearce and Repka, Pearce and Dailly, and quite possibly Gilbert and George in an effort to find a solid centre-back partnership. At full-back, Winterburn was 39, Minto wasn't good enough and Schemmel's verve had gone along with his French courtier's haircut. Vladimir Labant (or should that be Trabant?), the £1 million replacement for Winterburn bought at the end of the previous season, had departed on loan after a mysterious bout of homesickness.

The loyal Irons contingent had seen too much. Most of us were pondering an imminent retirement to the jungle, Colonel Kurtz style. Why were we still West Ham fans? Rather like the team, I could offer no defence.

A spontaneous chant of 'BACK FOUR, WE WANT A NEW BACK FOUR', to the tune of 'Blue Moon', was soon being sung by the entire away end. I was impressed. It had to be the most specific, tactically aware football chant ever. It must have been horribly embarrassing for Lomas, Breen, Dailly and Minto, but was surely a sign that in the era of Andy Gray's marker pen, fans had more tactical nous than ever before.

Perhaps we would soon be hearing chants of 'Back three with rampaging wing-backs, we want a back three with rampaging wing-backs' or maybe even 'Christmas tree formation, we want a Christmas tree formation' followed by 'Second phase ball, we want to win the second phase ball'.

There were further chants of 'We want Minto off the pitch!', 'Nigel Winterburn' (the fans wanted him to replace Minto) and 'Roeder out!' Mild-mannered Nigel was as angry as I had ever seen him, and Matt was using some most ungodly expletives, perhaps imagining the Four Horsemen of the Apocalypse riding into the Valley of Death. Fraser wondered what Bobby Moore would make of it all.

'We want Pottsy on the pitch!' chanted Nigel.

'He never let anyone down,' said the bloke in front of us.

'It all went wrong ever since Roeder didn't bring him on against Bolton,' reflected Nigel.

Then we pulled a goal back, Carrick's shot being deflected into the net off Mark Fish. However, the game had gone away from the Irons, and despite two Sinclair efforts, we never really looked like equalising. At least Roeder tried to give us the requested new back four. Minto was hauled off for the ageing Winterburn and young Glen Johnson was sent on to play at right-back. It was his debut, but he immediately looked more confident and assured than anyone else in our defence. Then, in injury time, a Svensson cross was deflected across the West Ham area, and Kishishev arrived at the far post to score his first ever goal for Charlton.

We really were going down. There was a sombre mood amongst the fans in Charlton station. Then, a train arrived, but the doors remained closed. 'Was this train organised by Roeder?' shouted a man in the queue of dispirited Hammers fans.

'If it was, there would be loads of carriages in the middle and none at the back,' suggested Matt.

'We apologise for the formation of this train. Another one will be coming in three minutes,' said the Tannoy announcer. If only the same applied to our defence.

As the new train shuffled back to London, Nigel launched into a monologue, 'I'm sorry West Ham, it's not you, it's me . . . I just need some time alone, a bit of space to work things out, there's not anyone else . . .'

'So we'll see you at the next home game,' suggested Fraser.

We arrived at London Bridge and sought solace in the old coaching inn, The George. 'Did you see that shambles?' said a bloke at the bar as I'm ordering our round. 'We won't go straight back up. Who will there be left? Just Dailly and Minto!'

After the game, Glenn Roeder, as usual, moaned to the press:

> No, I won't be throwing in the towel . . . Poor decision making is costing us . . . They have defensive responsibilities and they are not carrying them out. Take the third Charlton goal. It was a difficult ball to head clear but then we have a player who should have been picking up Scott Parker. Instead he ball watches, is yards away from him and Parker scores . . . It's back to the drawing board with those defenders now. We just have to hope that they can start to pick up the required skills.

It was left to my old pal Mike Pattenden to provide the funniest comment of the season on the *Fortune's Always Hiding* Internet chat group: 'These "required skills" our defenders need to learn. Are they things like basket weaving and stuffing cuddly toys so that they [the players] can be returned gently to the community?'

Knowing West Ham, they might go and beat Man United in the FA Cup in the next match. Or maybe not. I watched the game live on TV at home with DC and his girlfriend Clare. Thankfully, my daughter Lola preferred to play with her face paints. Ryan Giggs slotted the ball home after a poor goal-line clearance in the eighth minute. Then a shot by Giggs was deflected in off Gary Breen's arm on 29 minutes, Ruud van Nistelrooy danced past three West Ham defenders (including the inevitable Breen) to make it three on 49 minutes and Phil Neville scored his team's fourth goal a minute later. When van Nistelrooy made it 5–0 United gave up on humiliating the Hammers, and Sir Alex Ferguson made a triple substitution. But even with the Reds treating it like a practice match, Solskjær made it six on 69 minutes. At 6–0, DC got up to leave and said, 'I wonder who we'll get in the next round?'

Incredibly, United spared us any more goals for the final 21 minutes. If Manchester had kept their full side on it could have been ten. Gary Breen gave the worst performance I had ever seen from a West Ham defender. He was involved in giving away every goal. Trying to keep up with Ruud van Nistelrooy, he looked like one of the boys chasing Brian Glover's games master in *Kes*. 'Does he have an NVQ in woodwork?' DC had wondered, contemplating alternative careers for the hapless Hammer.

The team that lost that day was: James, Lomas, Breen, Pearce, Minto, Bowyer, Cisse, Carrick, Sinclair, Defoe and Cole. Big names with big egos, but not playing for Roeder or the 9,000 West Ham fans who had made the trip to Old Trafford. Alan Hansen sounded like his Alistair McGowan caricature in the post-match analysis of our defence, every other word being 'deplorable', 'shambolic' or 'kamikaze'.

'Worst Ham' read the headline the next day in *The Sun*. The *Mirror* wrote 'No Spirit . . . No Pride . . . No-hopers. Humiliated Hammers Head For Oblivion'. In a big gesture, Sir Alex Ferguson gave Roeder an hour-long counselling session after the game, hopefully offering some tips on anger mismanagement and the hairdryer technique. When Roeder emerged, he at least showed more fight and honesty than his team.

It was very difficult to watch, excruciating at times. We were abysmal and had some players who simply didn't have the stomach for the fight. You can say wonderful things about Manchester United's skill, their passing and their movement, but not much is said about their work-rate, drive and desire. Those are easy things to bring to the table and qualities that should be expected of every player. But we showed hardly any of that.

We let our fans down . . . Sir Alex was very encouraging afterwards but what he said will remain private. I'm a good listener and all I'll say is that he was very supportive . . . Each defeat is not helping my position but I've never been one to give up on anything and I never will be.

Even *The Guardian* agreed that unless West Ham could beat Blackburn at home the following Wednesday, West Ham's procrastinating board would have to act. Roeder was a decent man, a skilled coach, and working as hard as he could, but not winning at home all season was unacceptable in any league. As The Stranglers once sang, 'Something Better Change'. Even if the board pursued its creditable policy of not sacking managers then surely a defensive coach such as George Graham had to be brought in. At that time, we were an embarrassment.

And then it happened: on 29 January 2003 West Ham played Blackburn Rovers at Upton Park. 'I've got a good feeling about tonight,' I told Nicola as I left the house. Just because we had lost 6–0 at Old Trafford, possessed a back four that would struggle in Division Seven of the Essex Sunday League, hadn't won, home or away, for 14 games and were bottom of the Premiership, having not won at home all season in any of the previous 12 games at Upton Park – or indeed since beating Bolton on 11 May 2002 on the final day of the previous season – you couldn't deny a football addict the escape of ridiculous, hopeless optimism.

Despite my positive attitude prior to each match, after every home game I had come home feeling like the Michael Palin character in *Ripping Yarns* – the one who kicks the furniture after every crushing home defeat.

The feng shui of the ground might have been affected, of course. In the summer, the club had moved the pitch some ten yards closer to the new Dr. Martens Stand, and the lads hadn't won since. Chi energy was not circulating correctly around Upton Park. Could a couple of mirrors on the East Stand and wind chimes hung from both goals cure the problem and result in West Ham producing a relentless charge towards the Champions League? Or maybe there was a Gypsy curse on the ground. This had happened at Birmingham City once and former manager Barry Fry had to urinate in all four corners of the pitch to remove it. We could always bring back Hayden Foxe for that particular task.

'Have you got your lucky pants on tonight?' I asked Big Joe, as we walked beneath the East Stand.

'I've run out,' he confessed. 'I don't have 13 pairs of pants.'

We took our seats in the packed stadium. What other side still got a crowd of 34,743 despite not having won at home all season?

'I see there aren't any "Brown Out" banners tonight,' said Nigel, repeating his standard joke. 'Do you think 6 points out of 42 has bought the fans off?'

At least Roeder had made changes after the Old Trafford debacle. Mr Breen, a hapless excuse for a defender and Rowan Atkinson lookalike, had been consigned to auditioning for Barclaycard ads. The mediocre Minto had gone too, along with Cisse, Defoe and Sinclair, from the side that capitulated so feebly to the Mancs. Yes, Trevor Sinclair, the World Cup star of the summer, the man who wanted a £12 million move last year, was out of the side after a period of woeful form and a mediocre game at Old Trafford. Repka returned from suspension, along with the cup-tied Les Ferdinand and the talismanic Paolo Di Canio, who had recovered after two months out with injury.

Roeder also appeared to have heeded the cries of 'We want a new back four' at Charlton. Minto, Dailly, Breen and Lomas had been replaced with Johnson, Pearce, Repka and Winterburn.

Bizarrely, matchday announcer Jeremy Nicholas played 'The Great Escape' just before the kick-off in an attempt to inspire a revival and thereby banish the statistic that no team bottom of the Premiership at Christmas had ever survived. Perhaps he was forgetting that at the end of the film Steve McQueen crashes his motorcycle into barbed wire and everyone else gets shot. Oh, and Glenn Roeder would surely be the one who falls for the 'Your German is very good' line.

West Ham started brightly, but then again we always did. Di Canio was in inspirational form and it was a testament to his superb fitness that he could come back and play with all his old guile. Even Repka and Pearce looked relatively stable at the back while home debutant Glen Johnson was assured at right-back. 'Mind you, Blackburn don't need to attack until the 40th minute,' said Fraser, referring to the legendary West Ham pre-half-time wobble.

Sure enough, after 38 minutes and against the run of play, Blackburn won a free-kick on the right side of the box when the ageing Nigel Winterburn, outpaced by Gillespie, brought down the Rovers winger. Lomas failed to clear David Thompson's free-kick, and Dwight Yorke, criminally unattended in the six-yard box, stroked the ball home.

Upton Park fell into a disbelieving silence. 'Yorke's only won the Treble with Manchester United; he's clearly not worth marking,' I muttered. Confidence escaped from the deflated Hammers like air from a punctured football. Tugay looked imperious in the Rovers midfield. We were lucky to go in at the break just one down.

Another routine home defeat beckoned. Even West Ham's board would surely sack Roeder if we didn't win at home in 13 games. My friends and I retreated to the bowels of the East Stand. We were too drained even to bemoan another soft goal given away before the break. 'Ferguson had Roeder in his office for an hour on Sunday. Maybe he taught Roeder how to throw tea cups,' I suggested, hopefully.

'There's a vacancy at Barcelona. Maybe they'll come in for Roeder. Imagine the white flags then . . .' added Matt.

The second half kicked off and West Ham were immediately on the attack. Maybe Fergie had taught Roeder how to dish out the hairdryer treatment. You never knew, we might snatch a draw, which was almost like a win these days.

Then, 13 minutes into the second half, Di Canio floated into the box on the left, stepped inside Todd and was scythed down right in front of referee Alan Wiley. Penalty shouts such as that would normally not be given to West Ham, of course, but the man in black pointed straight to the spot. The crowd held its breath. The Hammer's season might turn on that moment. 'Please don't let him take another poncy penalty,' I said to Nigel, remembering the Di Canio effort against Aston Villa the season before, when he chipped the ball straight into the keeper's arms.

A moment's hesitation was followed by a measured run up and boom, Di Canio shot home with an uncharacteristic blast of his left foot, picked up the ball from the net and ran to the halfway line with one clenched fist in the air. Immediately after the goal, Fredi Kanouté, whom we thought sometimes played like a man wearing a Walkman and listening to ambient music, returned from a long period out, presumably because his batteries were flat, and replaced Ferdinand. Les had worked hard but had made little impression on the Blackburn rearguard.

Paolo was magnificent that night. He caused huge problems for Blackburn on the left and even enticed senior citizen Nigel Winterburn into overlaps. But still the winning goal would not come, not that we really expected it to. Jermain Defoe replaced Winterburn close to the end, but it was just desperation.

However, Defoe suddenly wriggled into the area past two defenders. He was covered by McEveley and Todd, who would surely block any shot, but he somehow picked the ball out from under his feet, feigned to cut inside and then arrowed the ball inside Friedel's near post. OH, YEEEEEEEESSS! 'A brilliant goal!' as Brian Moore might have put it. It was a fantastic finish.

Defoe ran to the old Chicken Run and removed his shirt. The whole stadium exploded as if we had just won the Champions League, but all I could think of was how long was left. I was convinced that there were ten minutes to go and that we could easily lose the lead just like against Newcastle. But no, Fraser pointed out that as the game kicked off at 7.45 p.m. there could only be a minute or so left. I had given up clock-watching, so sure was I that the game was lapsing towards another draw. One minute! Surely even West Ham could hold out for one minute.

'I'M FOREVER BLOWING BUBBLES . . . PRETTY BUBBLES IN THE AIR' emanated from the swaying Bobby Moore Stand and even the refined Upper East Stand. The whole stadium was on its feet. Even when we beat Ipswich in our final home game of the 1985–86 season and it looked like West Ham might win the league there weren't scenes like those that night against Blackburn. When we won the FA Cup final against Arsenal in 1980 there wasn't that amount of tension at the end of the game.

'There's going to be free tea in Ken's Café all night if we win this. It will be like VE Day . . .' I muttered.

'There will be two minutes added time,' announced Jeremy Nicholas. It was better than the five I had expected. But there was still time for

Blackburn to get a corner. Ian Pearce, who had been solid and dependable all night, whacked the ball clear. And then . . . YEEEEEEEEEEEEEEEEEEES! We might not have beaten Arsenal, Charlton, West Brom, Man City, Birmingham, Everton, Leeds, Man United, Southampton, Bolton, Fulham and Newcastle, but, 'GRAEME SOUNESS, DWIGHT YORKE, JACK WALKER, ALFRED WAINWRIGHT, JACK STRAW! CAN YOU HEAR ME, JACK STRAW? WE GAVE YOUR BOYS ONE HELL OF A BEATING!'

It had only taken around 1,170 minutes and 264 days during 8 long months. I slapped Nigel, Matt and Joe on the back, and we were shaking hands and hugging. We had done it. We had won a game at home. We had obtained THREE POINTS! At Upton Park!

Glenn Roeder forgot himself, raised both arms in the air and jumped a foot off the ground. It was like seeing an undertaker suddenly break into an Irish jig. I couldn't help but feel pleased for the man. It was like the kid who had been bullied all season suddenly hitting someone back or that moment in *About A Boy* when young Marcus suddenly gets a decent haircut. All season long, Glenn had suffered Chinese burns from Gordon Strachan, sly pinches from David Moyes, headlocks from Gary Megson, chalk on his blazer from Alan Curbishley, but now he had metaphorically landed one on Graeme Souness's chin.

Di Canio rushed to the centre-circle and embraced Jermain Defoe. The whole team were on the pitch saluting the delirious Upton Park masses. 'That's what it feels like to win a home game!' hollered Jeremy Nicholas as he played 'Bubbles' and then 'The Great Escape'.

Even in the days of Moore, Hurst and Peters there were never scenes of celebration like that; 29 January 2003 would forever be enshrined in club history. Hell, even if we were going to go down, we couldn't go down having not won a home game all season. My fellow devotees stumbled out of the stand, half waking, half dreaming, and suddenly I was accosted by my old friend from school, Will Finck. I hadn't seen him all season, but whatever I said can't have made much sense. I just kept mouthing, 'We've won at home . . . West Ham have won at home . . .'

'The Great Escape' was still playing: 'Der der der der, der der der der, der der der der, der der der der . . . WEST HAM!'

I imagined Glenn Roeder being interviewed and announcing that he didn't know the meaning of the word quit and that he would be fighting on until the interviewer reminds him that West Ham had actually won at home.

Outside the stand there were what seemed like a million blokes on their mobiles. I rang Nicola, but the phone kept cutting out, the signal possibly disrupted by the eruption of positive kinetic energy in E13. On Barking Road the connection finally held, and I stammered, 'Nicola, Nicola, something incredible has happened . . .'

'I know, you won,' she laughed. 'You kept ringing up, and all I could hear was singing . . .'

Suddenly I realised what an oppressive weight of failure had been bearing down on my cranium all season. We retreated into a heaving Black Lion at Plaistow. Amid all the mayhem, Gavin had remained cool enough to recommend the Adnams Broadside. Gallons of it hopefully. The TV in the bar had on *Sky News*, but, bizarrely, it was all about Liverpool v. Arsenal. Why wasn't West Ham winning the top story above Arsenal, above a likely war with Iraq, above everything? There should have been all-day rolling news bulletins with a big red flash in the corner of the screen announcing 'BREAKING NEWS: WEST HAM WIN AT HOME'.

I never thought it would happen again in my lifetime! Grown men were in tears. Strangers were embracing, and children were probably being fathered. There were rumours of free tea in Ken's Café and special £5-off vouchers at the West Ham United Quality Hotel. Glenn Roeder was almost smiling. The impossible had happened . . .

This is Pete May reporting for *News at Ten* from the coronary unit in the Black Lion, very close to a delirious and disbelieving Upton Park. West Ham have won at home; messages of congratulation have been coming in from around the world. A national holiday has been declared by Tony Blair. Now back to the studio for the secondary news on the achievement of peace in our time and an end to religious intolerance and third world debt . . .

TOP TEN WEST HAM CHANTS

- 'WE WANT A NEW BACK FOUR!' As demanded away to Charlton in 2003 after another inept display at the back.
- 'IS THAT ALL YOU BRING AT HOME?' A swift reply to the Manchester United DJ announcing an attendance at Old Trafford of 67,582.

- 'HE'S GOT BIRDSHIT ON HIS HEAD!' Used to bait QPR's Marc Bircham, who had blue-and-white hair.
- 'WE'VE GOT DI CANIO, YOU'VE GOT OUR STEREOS!' Sung by the away fans during a 3–0 defeat at Liverpool.
- 'YOU'RE SHIT AND YOU SLAP YOUR BIRD!' Sung by the Bobby Moore Stand at Stan Collymore after the infamous incident in which Collymore hit Ulrika Jonsson.
- 'IT'S QUIET IN THE LIBRARY!' Sung whenever West Ham visit Highbury.
- 'HE'S GOT A PINEAPPLE ON HIS HEAD!' Used to bait Leicester's Jamie Lawrence and then adapted for Nottingham Forest's Jason Lee.
- 'SHILTON, SHILTON, WHERE'S YOUR WIFE!' Chanted by the North Bank when Peter Shilton was caught taking an extra-marital drive in a country lane with a girl called Tina.
- 'WE ALL AGREE, DOWIE IS BETTER THAN BERGKAMP!' Chanted at Highbury when West Ham were losing to Arsenal.
- 'BIG FAT, BIG FAT JOHN, BIG FAT JOHNNY HARTSON!' Used to bait former hero John Hartson when West Ham played Wimbledon at Selhurst Park soon after selling the heavy-duty striker to the Dons for £7.5 million.

13

TOO GOOD TO GO DOWN

2002–03
Paolo accuses Glenn of disrespect . . . Brevett arrives . . . Repka and James show fighting spirit (with each other) . . . Glenn Roeder suffers a brain haemorrhage . . . Trevor Brooking takes charge and thumps the dugout . . . Paolo scores as West Ham do the double over Chelsea . . . and still get relegated at Birmingham.
   Price of Hammer *in 2003: £3*

West Ham being West Ham, they followed up the epic first home win of the season against Blackburn by losing 3–0 at home to Liverpool. After nine minutes the Irons were 2–0 down thanks to a goal from Baros, who had risen unchallenged to convert a corner, and one from Gerrard, who had fired the ball home following a weak punch from James. When Heskey made it three from yet another corner after sixty-seven minutes the game was dead. Every goal stemmed from a Liverpool set piece. It was *The Great Escape* all right, only it was the bit where the tunnel collapsed. The only positive point was the appearance of Rufus Brevett as a substitute. Signed from Fulham for a small fee, the combative and committed defender looked like he might solve our problems at left-back.

   Roeder, who had failed to buy a centre-back in the transfer window, seemed to be as mystified as the fans by three goals conceded from set-pieces. 'We do plenty of work on the training ground on set pieces, but it comes down to individuals and their responsibilities and my players didn't fulfil theirs. Fear crept into their game.'

The West Ham boss was an ex-defender, so it was baffling how his back four could be so badly organised. Had Liverpool not had a goal disallowed, they would have scored four from set pieces.

In the next game, West Ham lost 1–0 at Leeds, and Fredi Kanouté was sent off for slapping Seth Johnson. It was a ridiculous act of petulance from someone who had missed most of the season. A three-game suspension could make the difference between survival and relegation.

Terry Brown wasn't too impressed with his team either. The following weekend, with the team due to play at West Brom, an email Brown had sent to a disgruntled fan found its way onto the back pages. The reclusive chairman was surprisingly scathing of his team in print:

> I note your comments regarding our manager's abilities, but I do not believe Glenn could have foreseen that David James and Trevor Sinclair would return from the World Cup with a loss of form. He could not have allowed for the injuries to Paolo Di Canio and Fredi Kanouté, nor would he have expected Christian Dailly and Tomas Repka to turn from one of the best centre-back partnerships to possibly one of the worst.
>
> I am sure there is considerable debate about whether Glenn should have been dismissed prior to Christmas but what never ceases to amaze me is that supporters will blame everyone (myself, the board, the manager) for what has happened and totally excuse the players, who I remind you, are the sixth highest paid in the Premier League.
>
> We now have a difficult task ahead of us and everyone here will do their utmost to ensure the team does remain in the Premier League. I can only apologise for the dismal performance to date.

Brown was not quite correct in claiming that injuries to Paolo Di Canio and Kanouté could not have been anticipated, since a look at the career records of both these players showed many absences because of injury. It was also possible to detect the previous season that, despite a sound defensive record at home, away from Upton Park Repka and Dailly looked vulnerable. However, Brown's point that West Ham's stars had performed like overpaid prima donnas for much of the season would not be disputed by any of the Burberry–clad geezers in the Bobby Moore Stand. If only Billy Bonds could have made yet another comeback to grab some of the miscreants around the neck and threaten them with his stubble. He was a perpetually honest footballer who would have embarrassed some of that season's underperformers with his constant commitment.

West Ham's match at West Brom, third from bottom, was a microcosm of the season so far. Fraser and I arrived in Birmingham to discover that every pub was about to close because 'Birmingham fans might be coming in'. This caveat was announced with the sort of fearful tone that Tubbs and Edward reserve for road builders and strangers in *The League of Gentlemen*.

The game was a nervy relegation battle, with effort compensating for the disjointed football. Darren Moore's header hit the post for Albion after just seven minutes, while Albion's Udeze also had a goal controversially disallowed for offside. At the other end, Trevor Sinclair missed an open goal. Hoult parried Carrick's drive and Sincs somehow managed to direct his header down and onto the bar. However, Sinclair, cited in Brown's email as one of the key underperformers of the season, redeemed himself just before half-time when his effort went in off the far post, following a Lomas cross.

The Hammers went into the dressing-room 1–0 up, although both Fraser and I agreed that Di Canio didn't look fully fit. He had shown some skilful touches and played Lomas in for the cross that made the goal, but PDC didn't appear to be running at full pace and also wasted a good chance when he chose to try to lob Hoult rather than take a direct run on goal.

If Paolo wasn't fit then the time to substitute him was at half-time. But, bizarrely, Roeder started the second half with Di Canio on the pitch only to then substitute him for Defoe three minutes later. Di Canio walked slowly towards his manager, threw his captain's armband down in disgust and shouted something along the lines of, 'I will never give you tips on couture again. See, I will throw off my sunglasses, too. Leaders like Mussolini were never substituted. You disrespect me, you sleep with your koi carp. You will never taste my home-made recipe for tiramisu again!'

It didn't quite seem the best way to handle Di Canio, a man with an ego the size of a house. Fraser immediately recognised that it was a 'loss of face' that was really riling Paolo. Redknapp knew how to get the best out of PDC, with a combination of flattery, love and recognition of his maverick nature; embarrassing public substitutions were only likely to add to Paolo's sense of himself as a brilliant but persecuted outsider. Similarly, whereas Howard Wilkinson failed with Eric Cantona, Sir Alex Ferguson saw Eric arrive at Old Trafford and think to himself, 'This stadium is big enough for me.' Sometimes a flawed genius needs different treatment from the rest.

As soon as Di Canio went off, West Brom scored, Dichio powering a header through James's hands. The whole ground started singing 'Boing! Boing! Baggies!' Clearly *The Magic Roundabout* was still big in those parts. Dichio was winning everything in the air for the Baggies. At one point, he flicked on a ball for Hughes, whose volley was well saved by James. When the offside flag then denied Dichio, it didn't stop Repka from confronting James. What sort of a nutter confronts a man with the physique of David James? Super Tomas, that's who. There was a pushing match before Brevett pulled Tomas away. As the *Daily Mirror* later commented, next to a picture of the shaven-headed Repka confronting the peroxide-barneted James, 'Hammers are putting up a fight – the trouble is it's with each other'.

Then West Ham scored again. Bowyer crossed a ball to the back post, Defoe cushioned a volley to Les Ferdinand, whose header hit the bar, but Sinclair headed home the rebound. The visiting West Ham fans celebrated wildly in the Smethwick End, but for the next 23 minutes, West Ham's defence scaled new lows. It was David James against the rest. Repka miscued, Dobie was clear and James saved brilliantly. Trevor Sinclair then attempted a ludicrous 30-yard back pass and played the ball straight to Hughes again, but James made a superb stop, tipping the striker's effort over the bar.

At one point, there was a scrummage in the mud of West Ham's penalty area that looked like one of those depictions of the game between English and German troops in World War One. Endless swipes at air and scuffed clearances couldn't quite seem to clear the ball. It was the sort of thing that Danny Baker makes a living out of. Shortly after this, the hapless Hughes was through on goal again, one-on-one with James, but, once more, the England custodian saved the Hammers. Mercifully, the final whistle blew. James had won the match for the Irons. We had been lucky, but that win took us up to third from bottom, above WBA. We spent the rest of the season chasing Bolton, one place above the relegation zone.

After the final whistle, Glenn Roeder gave an Alastair Campbell-like spin on the Repka/James shoving match: 'There was a little spat between David and Tomas, but that just shows how much this team wants to win. That sort of thing doesn't worry me at all. It shows they care. That they're ready to fight.' As for the Di Canio tantrum on being subbed, Roeder said, 'I wondered if Paolo was 100 per cent fit. In my opinion, he wasn't moving freely. Football is a team game.'

The following Saturday, West Ham were much better, beating a disappointing Spurs side 2–0 at Upton Park with a goal from Les Ferdinand, against his old club, and one from Michael Carrick. It was Carrick's first of the season – a poor return from such a talented player. Di Canio was absent, presumably still injured. West Ham kept a clean sheet and were starting to look like a team. Johnson was composed at right-back and Lee Bowyer hit the post and made some good attacking runs from midfield. Even Repka looked reasonably solid.

In the following day's *Sunday Mirror*, West Ham's soap opera continued. Paolo Di Canio 'lifts the lid on life at West Ham'. He claimed that 'Too many senior people at the club are ready to accept relegation and if West Ham go down no fewer than seven players will leave [what, only seven?].'

As for that substitution at West Brom, surely Paolo wasn't still sulking? Erm, yes, well, actually, he was. Although what he said did make sense:

> Roeder should remember that he substituted me twice this season against Blackburn and Leeds and nothing happened. But I have principles and morals. I live for them and uphold them thoroughly.
>
> At West Brom we were 1–0 up and the manager asks me if I feel OK. I say sure, I can run and I can play. But just before the start of the second half I can see Jermain Defoe get up from the bench. I'm not stupid. If Roeder had spoken to me in the dressing-room I probably would have felt anger but I would have

accepted it. He could have told me we need to keep the pressure on and Defoe with his pace can do the job. Fair enough.

But to use the trick of calling me off three minutes later smacks of a lack of respect. You don't do that to a 20 year old, you don't do that to your captain. If Roeder treats everyone the same he will never be a great manager. Look at the way Spurs treat Teddy Sheringham and Chelsea Gianfranco Zola, players who are older than me who get the respect they deserve and have earned . . . I will speak out every time people don't grant me the respect I deserve.

As if to annoy their supporters even more, West Ham then went on an unbeaten run. A draw at Everton was followed by a home win over Sunderland. Why couldn't they have done that earlier in the season? Roeder settled on a back line of Johnson, Pearce, Repka and Brevett and the defence improved considerably. Repka looked focused and was at last playing like an international defender.

Di Canio wasn't picked, even when fit, prompting the memorable quote from Roeder of, 'Have we missed him? No comment.' The fit but not selected Di Canio turned up at home games looking like a movie star in shades and big coat and sat in the stands. Having defended Paolo for much of his first season, Roeder was now banking everything on a firm stand against the striker, whose contract would not be renewed at the end of the campaign. Ferdinand and Defoe were playing well together, and a fit-again Fredi Kanouté scored against Sunderland and Aston Villa. But even so, with Paolo's experience and big-game temperament, it seemed perverse not to consider him for the biggest game of all, away to relegation rivals Bolton on 19 April.

We were unbeaten in six games, although Lee Bowyer was trying to play with injury and was sadly out of form. He was soon to disappear to the treatment table. One reason for West Ham's sudden resilience was the recruitment of Aussie Alan 'Big Al' Pearson, a 6 ft 6 in. former second-row rugby forward from Queensland, as motivator or, to use his more poncy title, 'biometric physiologist'. Commenting on Big Al, David James said, 'Something was missing and he got us going.' Although I did wonder why the sixth-highest earners in the Premiership needed motivating.

A 2–2 draw at home to Aston Villa saw West Ham lose another two precious points despite twice taking the lead through Sinclair and Kanouté. Defoe produced a brilliant dribble late on, only to shoot straight at the keeper. One major plus from the game was young Glen Johnson. At times, the perfect timing of his tackles was reminiscent of Bobby Moore.

Then came the vital match at Bolton during the Easter break. To lose that game would mean that West Ham were virtually down. I was at Nicola's mother's for the weekend and heard the result while I was helping my daughters pick up horse manure with a shovel and wheelbarrow in the top paddock. It seemed somehow appropriate.

It was an ill-tempered game, settled by a sublime 30-yard strike from Jay-Jay Okocha. With Bolton moving six points ahead of West Ham, several players lost their discipline. Or maybe they were frustrated at the realisation that they hadn't started to play until the final ten games of the season. Ian Pearce was sent off at the end for chopping down Andre, and after his red card pushed Gudni Bergsson. Joe Cole and Rufus Brevett were also involved in an undignified fracas as they left the pitch. It was an incident that provoked a police report to the FA. So much for the soccer academy. Cole was as angry as anyone had ever seen him. He was wrong to end up in a fight, but he was one player whose commitment couldn't be faulted that season, even if his finishing could. Defeat seemed to genuinely hurt him. We were now six points behind both Bolton and Leeds, with an inferior goal difference and just four games left. David James summed up the mood when he faced the press and explained, 'When it mattered, we didn't do it.'

West Ham retained some hope of survival after beating Middlesbrough 1–0 at Upton Park two days later, Sinclair scoring the goal. Then came the terrible news that Glenn Roeder had collapsed after the game. After giving the usual press interviews he had gone to sit down in his office and collapsed some 90 minutes after the final whistle.

He was flown by air ambulance to the Royal London Hospital in Whitechapel. At first, it was feared that he had suffered a heart attack. Later it was announced that the 47 year old had had a brain haemorrhage. After a spell in intensive care, he later had surgery to remove a small lesion on his brain.

Suddenly, relegation and football didn't seem that important any more. There was shock and a little guilt for most fans. It emerged that a bottle was thrown at Roeder's house in Hornchurch on the eve of his collapse. The boss had usually tried to deflect criticism from the players. After each humiliating defeat he had conducted himself with restraint. Week after week, he had answered questions about his own future. Roeder was later to claim that his brain haemorrhage had nothing to do with stress, but could it be just coincidence that it happened two days after West Ham's relegation became a near certainty?

There had been numerous pressure points all season: the dismal run of not winning at home; being bottom at Christmas; the 6–0 humiliation at Old Trafford; the Bowyer controversy; the Di Canio substitution furore; and the 'six-pointer' at Bolton. Plus there was also the ridiculous iniquity in the English game to take into consideration: relegation from the Premiership meant a reduction in income of at least £20 million. Roeder knew that the jobs of numerous staff depended on him keeping the Hammers up.

Paul Goddard and Roger Cross took charge of training, while the club acted swiftly to appoint director Trevor Brooking as caretaker manager. Could the West Ham legend, who had never managed at any level, win the last three games and achieve the ultimate escape?

The players were buoyed by a visit from Faith Roeder, who sent them Glenn's good wishes, and Brooking relaxed them with his inimitable calmness in the face of all adversity. 'It has been a difficult few days,' said Trev, who would probably have described the start of World War Three in a similar fashion. 'You could say, "Well, it is not going to happen", and you could use it as a weak way of going out with a whimper. But with Glenn and the players having worked so hard for 35 games and getting 15 points in their last 8 games, everyone wants to give it everything in the next two and a half weeks – and that is what we are going to do.'

He also moved to end the feud with Di Canio, whom, a year earlier, he had selected in his all-time top West Ham XI. PDC was out of the game at Man City with a stomach virus, but Trev revealed, 'I've said to Paolo that as soon as he's fit he'll come in. If he can contribute for 10 minutes or 90 minutes at any stage, then Paolo, if focused and fit, will be able to contribute.'

Against Manchester City, Brooking made a brave and innovative decision, deciding to play three strikers – Defoe, Ferdinand and Kanouté

– together up front. We had played 4-4-2 all season, yet now we had three top-quality forwards fit – it made sense. The game was live on Sky, and I watched it in a state of perpetual anxiety at the Famous Cock Tavern in Highbury with Matt and Lisa.

We saw a new Trevor Brooking that day. Gone was the old 'sitting-on-defence' TV pundit. Trev was on his feet throughout the game, whacking the dugout in frustration, and possibly letting an expletive (or at least a 'blooming') pass his lips. Kanouté tapped the ball over the line after substitute Don Hutchison had hit the post to score the only goal of the game, and somehow we held on – suddenly, escape might just be possible.

Before the next game, against Chelsea a week later, Brooking hinted that he might recall Paolo Di Canio. Di Canio was, as ever, incensed: that time by press accusations that he was in some way responsible for Roeder's brain haemorrhage. Just before Roeder's collapse the 'Special One' had pronounced:

> It looks to me as if Glenn Roeder is heading for the third relegation of his career. If that happens, he will discover that all the clever voices who told him to drop me will be the same ones who now turn on him. Glenn's an example of what I find incredible in England. Young managers have control of clubs and don't know how to handle players.

Before the Chelsea game, PDC correctly insisted that Roeder had been under pressure from a number of sources, including a less than harmonious dressing-room:

> I respect Glenn as a human being and mean it when I wish him and his family the best of luck. We should pray for him every day. When I have said things in the past I have been talking about football, which is his job. There is pressure every day, from the supporters and people who, when we lose, say Roeder is not good for West Ham.
>
> There is pressure too in the dressing-room from the young players who, when he says you have to play this way, they say 'F*** off, Glenn!' So I am not the only one; everybody has said

something. Last year, Trevor Sinclair was on the transfer list all season. So did he put Glenn under pressure? Every manager in the world is under pressure from star players. Just being at the bottom puts you under pressure.

Although Paolo being Paolo, he couldn't quite resist portraying himself as the biggest victim of all:

> Whenever I say something people like to blame me. I should be in the psychiatric clinic after what has been said about me. People are entitled to have their opinion about me as a player, but they are wrong to say I have a problem in my brain.

The situation looked impossible for Brooking. But perhaps there were worse things than relegation. In the non-footballing world, US and British forces were invading Iraq in order to remove its supposed weapons of mass destruction. Only like West Ham, it was later proved that the Iraqis could not mount an attack in 45 minutes.

As the invasion was relayed to British TV screens, the tirades of 'Comical Ali', the Iraqi Minister of Information Mohammed Saeed al-Sahaf, became a national cult. He insisted that Iraq was winning the war even as the American tanks were entering Baghdad. I wondered if al-Sahaf could be appointed as West Ham's new spin doctor so that he could claim West Ham were in fact third from top and that Division One did not exist. Imagine the quotes to the *Newham Recorder*:

> As usual we will slaughter them all! Chelsea will burn in their Ferraris as the Irons achieve the mother of all victories! Claudio Ranieri shall not cross beneath the castles of Upton Park without his boots crumbling in the dust of his own broken dreams! The Blue-Flag waving imperialists will reap nothing except disgrace and defeat. I am thinking their graves will be made at Upton Park. Chelsea – our initial assessment is they will all die.
>
> The Savage barbarians of Birmingham will be sent home to be butchered in the Nationwide. We will finish them soon. As our Leader the great Trevor says, 'God is grilling their stomachs

in hell!' These infidels will be committing suicide by the hundreds on the gates of St Andrew's! Victory is already ours!

Strangely, Comical Ali was never invited to apply for a post at Upton Park to work alongside Big Al as our secret motivator.

The Chelsea game was one of those matches that makes me proud to be a West Ham fan. The new statue of Moore, Hurst and Peters winning the World Cup had been unveiled in Barking Road to add to the occasion, and rarely can a game have been so emotionally charged: London rivalry, fear of relegation, concern for Glenn Roeder, affection for Trevor Brooking, the possibility of Paolo Di Canio wearing the claret and blue shirt for his last home game. The crowd were expectant and from the early choruses of 'Come on you Irons!' and 'Stick your blue flag up your arse!' you could sense exactly what the club meant to its extended community.

Brooking recalled Di Canio to the bench, but continued with Kanouté, Defoe and Ferdinand up front. Incredibly and infuriatingly, we played superbly against a side chasing a spot in the Champions League. The Chelsea team included such stars as Cudicini, Gallas, Desailly, Lampard, Petit, Gudjohnsen, Zola and substitute Hasselbaink.

Early on, Kanouté had a powerful header tipped over the bar by Cudicini. The Chelsea keeper saved a Sinclair volley and Lomas scuffed a free header wide. In response, former Hammers star Frank Lampard had a header kept out by David James's knee.

West Ham were a revelation. The Chelsea defence couldn't contain the floating Fredi Kanouté, who often drifted wide to terrorise the Blues defence, made up of top internationals, with his strength, pace and step-overs. Trevor Sinclair was no longer the peripheral, jaded figure of earlier in the season. He was jinking down the wing, feinting and getting in excellent crosses. Brooking had also coaxed a good performance out of Christian Dailly, replacing the suspended Ian Pearce, in his first full game for three months. Repka was solid, Steve Lomas a dynamic presence in midfield. Glen Johnson was having another fine game as an overlapping full-back and so too was the committed Brevett. We were full of desire – ten months too late. But still the goal wouldn't come. Sinclair beat Gallas twice in the same move and crossed for Kanouté, only for the striker to power his header just wide of the post. Then Sincs crossed again for Lomas to head for goal but Cudicini tipped the ball over the crossbar.

On 56 minutes, Brooking replaced Ferdinand with Di Canio. It was the crazy one's last ever game at Upton Park. Would Di Canio's sense of the theatrical change the game? The answer came 15 minutes later. Kanouté held the ball up on the halfway line, played a one–two with Di Canio and passed inside to Joe Cole. The youngster released the ball quickly to Sinclair on the right whose shot deflected off two defenders on the edge of the six-yard box and fell to Di Canio, who reacted first to swivel and shoot the ball high into the net. Cue pandemonium. 'West Ham's goal was scored by PAOLOOO DI CANIOOOOOOO!' hollered announcer Jeremy Nicholas.

Brooking jumped up in the air, red-faced and clenching his fists, appearing to have metamorphosed into Stuart Pearce. Paolo reacted with his usual restraint, pulling off his shirt, swinging it above his head, running towards the corner flag in his vest and sliding down onto his knees with tears running down his face before being engulfed by his teammates.

There was a tremendously nervous last 19 minutes to get through, though, in which Zenden had a volley saved by James, and Lampard produced a great shot that was equally well parried by the West Ham keeper. Despite the Chelsea chances, I somehow knew that it was Di Canio's day. The final whistle blew and the Italian ace collapsed in tears onto the turf. He was then hugged by caretaker boss Brooking, and there were triumphant scenes and more choruses of 'Stick your blue flag up your arse!' We had done the double over Chelsea. 'The Great Escape' played over the PA system. Paolo threw his shirt into the crowd. It was as if we had avoided relegation already. If any performance deserved to keep a team up, it was that one against Chelsea.

In just two games Brooking had tried a new formation and reintegrated Di Canio. We were out of the bottom three. We had 41 points and no team had ever been relegated with more than 40. If Bolton lost at Southampton in a five o'clock kick-off, West Ham would stay one point ahead of them. Managers may have hated Di Canio, and his tantrums might have been bad for team morale, but as a fan you couldn't argue with his class or his entertainment value.

PDC, the most vociferous player on the planet, confounded everyone further by declaring himself 'lost for words'. However, he did manage to mutter towards the cameras from *The Premiership* that, 'This shirt is in my heart for the rest of my life.'

Certainly his teammates seemed to appreciate his contribution. Joe Cole said:

> Paolo is a very special kind of player. He's the kind of geezer who will come on and do a thing like that. It was written in the script. I don't care what happens off the pitch. I'm only interested in what happens on it. And in those circumstances you can't have a better player around.

David James added:

> He gave all the players confidence that we have been lacking for most of the season. He is a special player, and he proved it again today. To be honest, I couldn't see Chelsea scoring . . . But I thought it was funny when after the game he could barely speak and he didn't do interviews. Who would have expected that? But that's typical of him. You never know what to expect.

Trevor Brooking explained, in his usual understated manner, how he had inspired the player who had so confounded Glenn Roeder: 'You have to take the rough with the smooth with Paolo and today it was the smooth. But to be fair, he wouldn't be the same player if he didn't have that bit of edge.'

Joe Cole declared that the fans were 'different class, as always', and when asked to sum up Trevor Brooking he came across more like a Dickensian urchin than ever, simply by saying the word 'Gentleman', while quite possibly doffing his cap.

We then watch the Southampton v. Bolton game in a Plaistow pub: the Saints fail to win. Brett Ormerod somehow contrived to miss a chance from two feet out and Bolton went above West Ham in the league on goal difference: theirs was minus 11 and ours was minus 17. It all depended on the final Saturday of the season. West Ham needed to win at Birmingham and Bolton had to lose or draw at home to nothing-to-play-for Middlesbrough. Meanwhile, Harry Rednapp's Portsmouth had already been promoted to the Premiership and now threatened to bypass West Ham.

The next Sunday I was sitting in the away end at Birmingham with DC, Matt, Gavin and Fraser, full of terrified anticipation. West Ham, playing in their white away strip, started purposefully. Defoe had a shot smothered while trying to round Birmingham keeper Bennett. Jermain also had a free-kick headed off the line. Then came the news that Bolton were 2–0 up after just 21 minutes. 'Two-nil to the Wanderers!' chanted the gloating Birmingham fans. Why did Bolton have to be playing Middlesbrough with their rubbish away record? The news dampened the emotion among the West Ham contingent and at half-time it was still goalless.

In the second half, the news emerged from the numerous Walkmans around the away end that Ricketts had scored for Middlesbrough. The Hammers almost scored when Defoe put in a cross that Matthew Upson headed against his own crossbar. However, Cole then crossed from the left, and Les Ferdinand stooped to head the Hammers ahead. There was an outpouring of celebration and desperate hope among the travelling Irons contingent. But we were still in the hands of sodding Middlesbrough, who were practically on their sun loungers already. Later in the match, Cole crossed and Fredi Kanouté hit one of the best volleys I had ever seen, only for the ball to thump against the far post. There was no news from the Reebok.

Then, ten minutes from time, Hughes jinked the ball in to Horsfield, whose shot deflected over James as Brevett tried to intervene. At least it produced a double entendre, as on the TV highlights the commentator declared 'and Horsfield squeezes it in off Brevett's tackle!' Robbie Savage taunted Brevett as the goal went in, and, for a moment, I wished Sir Trevor would shed his gentleman-of-football image and run onto the pitch to chin the blond merchant of menace.

Brooking replaced a tearful Brevett with Di Canio, but things got worse. After 88 minutes, West Ham were caught by a counter-attack, Savage crossed and Stern John shot home off the crossbar. 'We are Premier League! I said, we are Premier League!' chanted the Brummie hordes.

A minute later, Defoe put in another cross and Paolo Di Canio stooped to head home, making it 2–2. It was a bizarre moment: a West Ham goal greeted in near silence. The team pressed for a late winner, but the score was unchanged from the Reebok Stadium, and, as the final whistle blew at St Andrew's, West Ham were relegated. This is the end, my friend, the end.

Trevor Brooking walked onto the pitch to try and console the players. Di Canio shrugged his shoulders. Some fans were in tears. The papers the next day focused on a sobbing young boy in a claret and blue Afro wig. One set of fans paraded a defiant 'We'll be back' banner. 'I'm West Ham till I die,' chanted the Irons fans and, bizarrely, this earned applause from the previously horrible Birmingham supporters.

One player who didn't appear to be suffering too much was Jermain Defoe. Less than 24 hours after relegation, he submitted a transfer request. Perhaps he wrote it on the coach back to London to save on postage. There was no sense of personal responsibility for the team's relegation or any sense of obligation to try and get the club back. And what were his advisers doing letting him act so crassly?

Defoe's attitude was a sad contrast to that of his boss Trevor Brooking who spent three years with West Ham in Division Two. 'There were no regrets. I had an allegiance to the club, and it worked out well in the end. By the time we were back in the First Division we had won the FA Cup and competed in Europe,' Brooking had told the *Standard* a few days earlier.

We had only lost one of the last ten games, but relegation was the result of a catastrophic first half of the season. Later that night on *The Premiership*, Di Canio said, 'You can't wait and say 15 games to go, it's OK, we have plenty of points to make.'

Admittedly, West Ham had been tremendously unlucky going down with 42 points, but we should never have been relegated with a team full of internationals. Carrick, Cole, Sinclair, James, Bowyer, Ferdinand and Winterburn had all played for England, while Defoe and Johnson had starred for the England Under-21s. Dailly and Hutchison were Scottish internationals, Repka a Czech international and Di Canio and Kanouté should have been internationals. I couldn't help but think of the dismal dropped points at home to WBA, Everton, Southampton, Fulham and Bolton, and that Kanouté penalty miss against Arsenal back in August.

At last the hope was over, and we West Ham fans could get on with the despair. The players trudged off the field and we left the ground to walk back towards Birmingham New Street station. Only shouldn't someone tell the Brummies that football violence is passé? Gangs of feral individuals were hunting for aggro. I pulled up the collar of my Levi's jacket to try and conceal my West Ham away shirt. There could be few worse places than Birmingham on a Sunday afternoon when you've just been relegated and the locals are attempting to ambush you at every corner.

We travelled back to London and it took three pints of Hopback Summer Lightning in the Head of Steam at Euston before Gavin, Matt and I regained a little optimism. 'In Division One our season tickets go down £30 and we get four more home games,' announced Matt. And for groundhoppers there would be the chance to visit Rotherham, Wigan, Grimsby, Crewe and Wimbledon's new ground in Milton Keynes. And who really needed Di Canio, Defoe, Cole, Carrick, Kanouté and Sinclair when we had Repka and Dailly?

That night I arrived home to find a card from my daughters Lola and Nell that declared, 'Well done West Ham' in a salute to the Irons' brave struggle for survival. It was a fine gesture from the children towards their sad dad. The next morning, four-year-old Lola asked a poignant question: 'Daddy, will you be sold, too?' she asked. If only I could be. Sadly, I'm stuck with the Hammers for life.

THE TOP TEN THOUGHTS OF PAOLO DI CANIO

- 'I have seen women and children crying in the street and I find it difficult to contain my own emotions so I cried with them. My heart dies at the thought of it all. I pray West Ham will still be a Premiership club at the end of the day.'
  On West Ham's impending relegation, May 2003
- 'I'm sorry but I'm a bit lost for words.'
  After scoring the winning goal at home to Chelsea, May 2003
- 'Whenever I say something people like to blame me. I should be in the psychiatric clinic after what has been said about me. People are entitled to have their opinion about me as a player, but they are wrong to say I have a problem in my brain.'
  On being accused of adding to the pressure on Glenn Roeder, April 2003

- 'To use the trick of calling me off three minutes [after half-time] later smacks of a lack of respect. You don't do that to a 20 year old, you don't do that to your captain. If Roeder treats everyone the same he will never be a great manager . . . I will speak out every time people don't grant me the respect I deserve.'
  On being substituted at West Brom, February 2003

- 'Glenn's an example of what I find incredible in England. Young managers have control of clubs and don't know how to handle players.'
  On being dropped by Glenn Roeder, March 2003

- 'I wanted to challenge the Chelsea fans because they had broken my balls the whole game. So I ran to them and began to yell, "I'm the man, I'm the man! So, what now? Who is the winner now?" To me it was really a beautiful, beautiful moment.'
  On scoring the winning goal at Stamford Bridge, September 2002

- 'How much passion did Dicks have for West Ham when he could not wait to run off to Liverpool to sign for them? It's easy to try to be a hero by kicking, fighting, using the elbow and screaming at opponents. But it's a lot harder to be a total professional for every second of the day setting a good example to the young players. Dicks didn't act totally professionally and didn't train properly.'
  After being criticised by Julian Dicks, November 2002

- 'Crazy with joy I ran towards Roeder and shouted at him "It's for you, Glenn!" Four minutes later Roeder substituted me and I left amid applause and I embraced him. And what do I read the day after in the newspaper: "Di Canio argues with Roeder because he substitutes him." In England they massacre you with a headline then apologise in small type.'
  On tabloid allegations that he shouted 'F*** you!' to his boss when he ran towards him after Trevor Sinclair's goal at Tottenham, September, 2002

- 'The man who comes to my house and feeds my piranha fish said he would kill them if I left West Ham to join Manchester

United. So I told him I would not go. And I begged him don't kill them, they are like my children. And now the fish are happy.'

On not joining Manchester United, February 2002

- 'The club [West Ham] is falling apart. After Harry Redknapp was sacked and Roeder, a man with no personality, replaced him, I predicted this would happen.'

On joining Chalrton, August 2003

14

FEELING BAD ALL OVER

2003–04
*Roeder returns only to be sacked after defeat at Rotherham . . .
Trev is back . . . Pards takes over . . . we lose 4–3 to WBA after being
3–0 up . . . Hayden Mullins is our saviour . . . Jermain scarpers . . .
Marlon is the wild one . . . on comes the man with a horn . . .
Mattie Etherington destroys Ipswich . . . and Iain Dowie's Palace
cause gloom at the Millennium Stadium.*
   Price of Hammer *in 2004: £3*

West Ham were playing away at Preston on a sweltering afternoon in
early August. After ten years we were back in the old Second Division or,
as it became known, Nationwide League Division One. The Division
One season kicked off a week earlier than the Premiership. It all felt too
soon.

It had been a dispiriting summer. Chairman Terry Brown began by
saying that we were not going to have to sell most of our best young
players. After all, we had already saved a huge amount per season on Paolo
Di Canio's wages when he joined Charlton. Glenn Roeder might have
dropped Paolo, but Alan Curbishley, one of the best managers in the
game, clearly felt he could cope with his eccentricities. Other players out
of contract who had left included Lee Bowyer, Gary Breen, Edouard

Cisse, Nigel Winterburn, Scott Minto, John Moncur, Raymond van der Gouw and Les Ferdinand – representing a big saving on Premiership wages. Sébastien Schemmel was escorted from the training ground by security men after an altercation with Roeder and soon left, too.

In fact, everyone left except Jermain Defoe, the one who had asked for a transfer within 24 hours of relegation. Which was very funny indeed. Over the summer, Trevor Brooking had a series of chats with Jermain, and deflected the blame for the transfer request onto Defoe's agents at SFX: 'I told Jermain at his age he needs good people around him. I don't know who suggested taking the course of action he did but they have done him a total disservice. He has been completely let down. He is not the insensitive, greedy young footballer that has been portrayed . . . The whole thing was handled very badly by SFX.'

Terry Brown and the other directors announced that in view of the new financial hardships being endured by the club they were halving their earnings following relegation. Instead of the reported £492,000 p.a. Brown received in the Premiership he would now have to scrape by on around £246,000. He wouldn't be relying on Nectar points and Lotto tickets just yet, but at least it was a gesture.

For several weeks it looked like we might retain most of our squad. Johnson and Kanouté both said they were happy to stay, and Christian Dailly said that he wanted to play for West Ham in any division. (Give it a few years, we joked, and it might be the Vauxhall Conference, Christian.) There were rumours that Sinclair and Kanouté might go, but there was no sign of youngsters Cole, Defoe or Carrick leaving. Glenn Roeder had thankfully recovered from his brain haemorrhage and was ready to lead the season's promotion campaign.

Everything changed in early July. Glen Johnson was sold to Chelsea for £6 million. The Stamford Bridge club had just been purchased by Russian billionaire Roman Abramovich and he appeared to be buying just about every player in the league with his huge wad. It was undoubtedly good money for an 18 year old who had played only 12 games for West Ham, but even so, it was a hugely dispiriting sale. With such a promising youngster as Johnson at right-back there was hope for the future, even if older players like Cole and Defoe went.

The press started talking of a 'fire sale', and it seemed that there was something of a financial inferno at the Boleyn Ground. Terry Brown was standing in his dressing gown trying to dial 999, while Paul Aldridge was throwing buckets of lager from the Bubbles Bar over the burning West Ham United Quality Hotel and the soon-to-be-closed excess merchandising stores.

Kanouté went to Spurs for £3.5 million, but at least we got young winger Matthew Etherington in exchange. Then Joe Cole was hoovered up by Chelsea for a further £6 million, and Sinclair went to Manchester City for just over £2 million. We had sold £18 million worth of talent over the summer.

Would there be anybody left to play? Roeder did at least sign David Connolly from Wimbledon (the only club in the league more skint than us) and pointed out that Connolly was a proven scorer in Division One, netting 24 goals in 28 starts for Wimbledon the previous season. We also signed lifelong West Ham fan Robert Lee, now aged 37, from Derby County on a free transfer. Although, had the club displayed more ambition, we could have got him from Charlton before Kevin Keegan's Newcastle moved in some ten years earlier. Finally, we recruited Liverpool's young striker Neil Mellor on loan for the season.

Even with these three signings it was a scratch side that took on Preston at Deepdale. Rio Ferdinand's younger brother Anton was given his debut at right-back but looked out of position and not yet ready for first-team football. Richard Garcia was played in midfield but didn't look up to the standard either. Deadly Don Hutchison returned to midfield and with his talent should have excelled at that level but only had an average game. Neil Mellor was up front but having hardly met his new colleagues, achieved little. The untried Youssef Sofiane came on as a sub for Garcia. After Di Canio, Cole, Kanouté and Sinclair we were now watching Garcia, Mellor and Sofiane. Steve Lomas had undergone an operation to remove 'a piece of bone floating about in his ankle' and Carrick was out, too. We were, as Harry Redknapp might put it, down to the bare bones.

There were 3,000 loyal West Ham fans at Preston, despite the misery of Birmingham and having lost 18 players. Many were wearing 'Brown Out' T-shirts. Glenn Roeder was back in the dugout, sweating in the heat, his hair still cropped after an operation on his brain. We still had David James, the England No. 1, in goal and Defoe up front. But the relegation depression was exacerbated after just 90 seconds when the Repka/Dailly pairing was again breached, and Preston's Eddie Lewis headed past James.

I watched the game live on Sky with Matt and Lisa in the Famous Cock Tavern on a humid afternoon. London seemed more like Mississippi, and after another famous cock-up, we needed more cold lager. Only suddenly there was hope: Defoe showed his international class, reacting quickest to reach Hutchison's cushioned header and instantly stabbing the ball past Preston goalkeeper Jonathan Gould after five minutes. Phew. Only 22 more days left till the transfer window deadline of 31 August.

The game slowed in the near-100 degree heat. Preston were denied a good penalty claim after Repka brought down Ricardo Fuller. North End were looking the more likely to score when Roeder substituted the labouring Mellor for Connolly after 60 minutes. Nine minutes later West Ham broke quickly, Connolly cut inside a defender and finished sharply, running arms outstretched to the travelling fans.

West Ham held on to win on the opening day, and everything looked a little better. But during the post-match interview, Connolly celebrated his winning goal by, erm, lambasting Glenn Roeder for playing Neil Mellor ahead of him. Mellor had only signed after being picked up in a service station the night before. Connolly raged:

> I felt it was terrible the way I was treated. Apparently, the only reason Neil Mellor came here was because Glenn promised Gérard Houllier that he was going to start him today. Neil could've gone to Sunderland, but they wouldn't promise he'd start, so he came to West Ham. The rest of the players were surprised; it's not Neil's fault. I have to sit down and see where we go from here. What if I hadn't come on today and scored?

Blimey, another player wanted to leave, and after just half an hour on the pitch. I wondered if he'd have reacted the same had his boss been Sir Alex Ferguson. 'I've known David since he was 16, and he's an angry ant,' Roeder responded.

'That's just the sort of thing your uncle would say, "Oooh, you're an angry ant, you are,"' muttered my fellow season-ticket holder Dan, incredulously, at our first home game of the season – a not very inspiring match against Rushden and Diamonds in the Carling Cup.

'It's great the way he really grasped what being at West Ham was all about. Join and then immediately start slagging off the manager,' commented Matt.

Our numbers had been reduced that season. Gavin had childcare commitments; Big Joe refused to give Brown and Co. any more of his dosh. It was down to me, Matt, Nigel, Dan and Fraser. That was if we were not sold, too.

The Carling Cup tie was on 13 August 2003, which was also my 44th birthday. Nicola said I could do whatever I wanted to, but, sadly, that was watch West Ham play Rushden and Diamonds in front of just 13,150 people while trying to asses if young debutant David Noble was the next Joe Cole (the answer was no).

It took ages to get a ticket from the ticket office before the game. (Early cup ties were no longer included in the price of a season ticket.) Ironically, one of the ticket-office windows was closed 'due to staff shortages'. Meanwhile, our shirts were emblazoned with the logo of our new sponsor Jobserve, the Internet recruitment agency. At least we beat Rushden 3–1 with Angry Ant scoring twice and Defoe once. After the game, there were more 'Sack the Board' demonstrations outside the main stand.

Four days later, there were many more fans at Upton Park: nearly 29,000 turned up to see the first home game in the Nationwide against Sheffield United. Terry Brown used *Hammer* to print a two-page statement defending the board. Brown revealed that the bank had asked for £8 million in loans to be returned and that with a drop in income of £20 million he was obliged to raise £28 million over the summer, which had been done via player sales and the reduction of the wage bill.

Brown wrote:

> Those who say we should have shown more ambition and kept the whole squad together [with £30m at stake if we are promoted] need to understand that by November we would have run out of cash and any cheques drawn by the club after that time would have bounced [including wage cheques].

He went on to say that had he revealed the club's plight:

> . . . my former colleagues in the Premier League would have smelt 'blood in the water' . . . Prior to the sale of Glen Johnson I

received several calls offering, for example, £500,000 for Trevor Sinclair, £1.5 million for Jermain Defoe and Glen Johnson respectively, and even £2 million for Joe Cole on the basis that we would then 'save the wages'. I was sorry to see Glen leave, but the £6 million we received from Chelsea was the turning point in our current financial fortunes, and I received no further frivolous phone calls after Glen signed for Chelsea.

He was probably correct in saying that he could not own up to West Ham being brassic when he was trying to flog as many players as possible. Brown also said that Joey Cole would have had to leave at the end of the season regardless of relegation, because he had refused to sign a contract extension beyond the summer of 2004. He argued that going into administration would have put many local suppliers of West Ham out of business, and now that the club was 'in a sound financial position' it could still afford a wage bill of £17 million p.a., compared with £3–4 million for many Division One competitors. What was more, Brown continued, 'We have no need to sell any more players for financial reasons and that includes Jermain.'

The questions Brown didn't answer were what was the true level of the club's debt (that summer it was rumoured to be around £30 million), how had we managed to get into so much debt, why were the directors paying themselves so much, why were clauses not inserted into players' contracts reducing wages in the event of relegation, why was Roeder not either sacked or offered an experienced assistant for the second half of last season, and why had the club no contingency plan for relegation beyond thinking 'it couldn't happen to us'?

As for the 0–0 game against Sheffield United, Jermain hit the post early on, and the rest of the match deteriorated into a dour struggle with West Ham failing to break down the big, resolute, well-organised Sheffield defence. Another new signing, Kevin Horlock, who had started his career at the Hammers and cost £300,000 from Manchester City, looked tidy and hard working in midfield but too similar to Robert Lee. Then, Rufus Brevett broke an ankle, which was likely to keep him out for several months.

Throughout the summer, Nicola had insisted that being in the Nationwide would be a marvellous opportunity to do some groundhopping, so there was an element of excitement when we took a break at our friends Fleur and Richard's house in North Yorkshire: West Ham were playing at Rotherham. To get to the stadium I had to take a bus from Bedale to Northallerton, and trains from Northallerton to York and then York to Rotherham, but, hell, it was a new ground.

Rotherham was a land of scrap-metal mountains, wasteland, pubs with bouncers outside, blokes with Freddie Mercury moustaches who weren't gay and classy venues such as the Blue Minx Gentlemen's Club and Lady Diana's Cellar Bar, but the locals were unfailingly friendly. The man selling the Rotherham lottery tickets was happy to explain how the extra income 'means everything to a club like us'.

A bar called The Tivoli, with gold curtains and a cheap chandelier, fronted the main wooden stand. It could easily have doubled as Rotherham's version of the Phoenix Club. Inside the dated stands, the bogs were old-style urinals: a small groove in a black floor awash with overflowing urine. An advert on the stand read 'L. F. Booth – buyers of all kinds of scrap'.

West Ham arrived late in their plush coach. Bizarrely, the team had refused to use Rotherham's tiny changing-rooms and had gone back to their hotel instead. Ronnie Moore's team talk had been made for him. Soft southern 'Fancy Dans' and all that. Roeder should have pointed out to the players that it was the relegation that they contributed to that had led them to having to perform in humble surroundings.

Ian Pearce returned to the centre of defence after suspension, and Repka was used as an emergency left-back. Ferdinand again looked uncomfortable at right-back as Rotherham bamboozled West Ham in the first half. 'WHO ARE YER?' asked the Rotherham fans among the 8,739 crowd, creating a cup-tie atmosphere. Byfield scored, and Rotherham had several more good chances.

Roeder took off Ferdinand, moved Repka to right-back and tried Horlock at left-back. We improved a little when Carrick came on for the lackadaisical Hutchison. Christian Dailly proved his bravery by playing on even though he'd had a tooth knocked out. Jermain Defoe then hit the post with a free-kick that bounced out rather than in. The home crowd were enjoying themselves. 'Pollitt for England!' they chanted every time their unknown custodian made a save, mocking poor David James who had gone from being England's No. 1 to losing at Millmoor.

The terrace full of Hammers fans was left to chant, 'Are you watching, Terry Brown?' As I left the ground I was consoled by a Rotherham fan – yes, a Rotherham fan. We had fallen that low.

One thing no one expected was Glenn Roeder to be sacked. It was certainly an embarrassing defeat, but we had only played three league matches, winning one, drawing one and losing one. Yet suddenly Terry Brown acted: Roeder was out. As Kevin McCarra wrote in *The Guardian*, 'West Ham's sacking of their manager was as ill-timed as one of Tomas Repka's less decorous challenges.'

Why stand by him throughout the relegation season and then sack him? Why allow him to buy players only to disrupt the side at the start of the new season? Was it all a plot to prevent a new manager complaining too much about the sale of players? Perhaps it was hard for the chairman to sack a man who'd just come out of hospital, but there was never going to be a good time to do it. And what other managers were available? Still, after an afternoon of being humiliated in Rotherham by a team with tiny dressing-rooms and a stand that looks like the Phoenix Club, I'd take Brian Potter as our new gaffer.

Trevor Brooking was once again appointed as caretaker manager. Again he made it clear that he didn't want to take the job on full-time. However, it was clear how much he is loved in east London from the warmth of the reception he received at the start of the next home game against Bradford. West Ham won 1–0 thanks to a magnificent Defoe solo effort, and Trev took the team on another fine run. Brooking's side won against Ipswich away, Reading at home (Christian Dailly scoring his first ever goal for the Hammers) and Crewe away. Realising we needed a left-back Brooking signed Wayne Quinn from Newcastle and Nicolas Alexandersson from Everton, both on loan. Defoe and Connolly had scored ten goals between them at that point and were looking like a promotion-winning partnership, even if they didn't ever pass to each other.

Just before we played Reading, it was revealed that the Royals boss Alan Pardew was the man that the West Ham board wanted to replace Roeder. He had taken Reading from the Second to the First Division and to the play-off final for a Premiership place the previous season. Iain Dowie, the other outstanding candidate, appeared to be considered too inexperienced and later became the Crystal Palace manager. An official approach for Pardew was rebuffed by Reading's chairman John Madejski. The Royals manager then resigned, which was a brave step. He was a hero at Reading and not expected to win automatic promotion; at West Ham, where a team of internationals had been sold, the pressure would be huge.

Reading took the matter to the High Court where they sought an injunction to prevent Pardew from moving. Eventually, West Ham agreed to pay compensation of £380,000 plus costs, and the court ruled that Pardew must take 'gardening leave' until the game against Nottingham Forest on 22 October. Trevor Brooking, who in a sitcom would surely be played by Richard Briers, declared in his inimitable English way that he intended to 'jog along' as Hammers manager until Pardew took over.

Brooking's first setback was at Gillingham. It was another ground to be ticked off my groundhopper's list, and Tony Mayer, my mate Vicky's dad and Gillingham's number one fan, was happy to get me tickets. We sat in the open Brian Moore (temporary) Stand. You would have thought that a stand named after Gillingham's most famous fan might have had scratch-and-sniff Sunday roast smells attached to the seat or 'Oh, what a great goal!' soundbites in the gents. It was indeed temporary, being constructed with the sort of scaffolding that builders erect around Victorian houses that need subsidence work.

In the first half, Repka, Dailly, Pearce and Quinn looked solid at the back and an uninspiring draw seemed likely. West Ham passed the ball around a lot but with little penetration. Then, two moments of petulance cost us the game. Repka gave a free-kick away, then argued about the decision, resulting in the referee advancing the free-kick a further ten yards forward. It was still 30 yards from West Ham's goal, and I was confident that they wouldn't beat England's No. 1 from there. Except Marlon King did, arrowing the best goal of his career into the top corner. We still had a chance of getting a draw, though. That was until Jermain Defoe argued about a throw-in with a linesman and was sent off. Even Trevor Brooking looked a little cross. An act of stupid indiscipline had wrecked any chance of a comeback. Gillingham then scored a second, the ball deflecting in off Repka.

'Go on, fatty!' cheered Vicky as Gillingham's rotund goalkeeper Jason Brown cleared all West Ham's efforts.

'I can't believe it. We've beaten West Ham. We've beaten West Ham!' exclaimed Tony. Yes, another team had beaten us in their 'cup final'.

While most Hammers fans were berating Defoe for getting sent off,

Brooking just 'had a chat with Little J and told him to look upon it as part of the learning process and to ensure he bounced back in the next game to prove his commitment to the club'. Defoe did just that, scoring a hat-trick as the Irons came back from 2–0 down to win 3–2 in a Carling Cup tie in Cardiff. Whatever the problems with his attitude, it was clear that Defoe was too good for the First Division.

Brooking's second stint as caretaker continued with a home draw against Millwall and a 3–0 demolition of Crystal Palace. Palace were so bad that even the lumbering Neil 'Gerd' Mellor scored twice. We could easily have had five. A last-minute volley from sub Don Hutchison won the next game at Derby, and it looked like Trevor Brooking really did walk on water.

However, as Brooking's reign came to an end with home draws against Norwich and Burnley, the overachieving team started to falter. After the patchy 1–1 draw at home to Norwich, Trev was moved to use the word 'blessed', when he said, 'We had two or three chances to cross the blessed ball and we don't and they get possession and score!' Yet with just one defeat in 14 games as a caretaker manager Brooking must have been one of the most successful West Ham managers ever – although, admittedly, he had never been tested working the transfer market. Just imagine how good he might have been if he had ever got angry with his blessed players.

Before the Forest game, I read Alan Pardew's programme notes in Ken's Café. You can imagine my surprise when I saw that my name was mentioned. It seemed that instead of making raised permaculture beds to grow organic vegetables in, Pards has used his gardening leave to read my book *West Ham: Irons in the Soul.* Pardew wrote:

> During my sabbatical from football one of the books I read was *Irons in the Soul.* Without doubt it is a true fan's view of recent events at the club. I'd like to thank Pete May for writing the book because it's given me an honest insight into West Ham, and if results go extremely well, I might even try a pre-match breakfast in Ken's Café.

Top man. I was so chuffed that I ordered an extra cup of Rosie Lea. As for the match, Andy Reid scored a great goal for Forest, with Defoe getting one for us in a 1–1 draw. Pards' first three league games ended in draws, while we lost against Spurs in the Carling Cup to a Bobby Zamora goal. Pardew started to make his mark on the team by signing Brian Deane. Not one for the purists, but Deano had scored goals wherever he had played and a big centre-forward was an essential option in the First Division. Pardew also signed Hayden Mullins, who was the greatest player alive, judging by the manager's initial enthusiasm:

> He is 24 and has played 250-odd First Division or Premier League games – and in my opinion this boy is a Premier League player . . . I think ultimately he is a central-midfield player for us . . . He is very much a destroyer, and I think we are desperate for one of those.
>
> I think, to be fair, Premier League clubs have looked at him for a long time and not gone for him; I feel that is as much his fault as them not taking the gamble, and he needs to get another 20% out of his game – I see that is in there, and it is up to me to get that out of him . . .
>
> He is so quick and so good defensively that you could actually give him a job to do on somebody in the Premier League, and I don't think you would see them.
>
> I think that tool would be important to us in our armoury, but let's not start thinking about the Premiership yet because we have to remember where we are – this player has got to help us get out of this division.

Mullins played in a number of positions over the season, switching from right-back to centre-back, centre midfield and left-back but, for all Pardew's faith, never wholly impressed the Upton Park faithful.

Pardew was still seeking his first win as West Ham boss after five games in charge when West Ham played West Bromwich Albion at Upton Park. After the game he must have been pining for a return to gardening leave.

West Ham were brilliant for eighteen minutes, running up a three-goal lead thanks to two Brian Deane goals and a great run and goal from Jermain. In the East Stand we joked that the match was never safe with West Ham unless we scored four. A few doubts where raised when Rob Hulse outpaced Dailly to pull one back. Then, on the 40-minute mark, Hulse fired a beauty into the top corner and there were serious jitters amongst the West Ham fans. To make it worse, right on half-time,

Jermain Defoe, who had already been booked, was shown a straight red card for a late and high lunge on Sean Gregan.

West Ham were still 3–2 up at half-time, even if we were down to ten men, but, in the second half, all belief seemed to have gone from our game. Brian Deane sliced at a Koumas corner and scored an embarrassing own goal after 77 minutes, and James produced a feeble punch to clear the ball, only to see it fall to Lee Hughes, who shot home off Tomas Repka.

Pardew, realising just how fragile his new side was, sounded like he needed a pint in the Black Lion. 'I'm not going to forget this day, and I won't let the players forget it either,' he said. 'It's something I will make sure they live with for the rest of the season. They were terrific to start with but did not roll up their sleeves and dig in when that was called for.'

Earlier that week, Terry Brown had declared in a letter to shareholders that, 'I genuinely do struggle to understand why some people seem to have suffered a mini-emotional collapse following our relegation.' Maybe after that result he would understand. Nurse Ratched, the screens.

Pardew took action by signing Marlon Harewood from Nottingham Forest. A further two draws followed before I decided to help Pards gain his first win by taking my daughter Lola to West Ham v. Wigan, which was a kids-for-a-quid game. We thrashed them 4–0, and Lola immediately adopted Marlon as her favourite player. He scored two and made the others with his speed on the right. She told Miss Denton (another Hammers supporter) at her school that Marlon Harewood was her favourite player. She didn't remember the old stars. Seeing her youthful enthusiasm reminded me that one day there might be new heroes.

For the rest of the season we were consistently inconsistent. We lost 1–0 at home to Stoke in a dire Tuesday night performance, but followed that by beating Sunderland 3–2 at home after being 2–0 down. The Bobby Moore Stand ended the game chanting 'Super Tomas Repka!' as he threw his shirt to the crowd. Playing at right-back he had been steadier and had even been seen overlapping in the opposition half. Repka had also grown his hair, which made him look less psychotic and must have improved his image in the eyes of the referees.

When we were two goals down he suddenly turned into a combination of Julian Dicks and Stuart Pearce, making crunching tackles and a number of clenched fist gestures to the Bobby Moore Stand. He looked like he wanted to play for us. Although, being Tomas, he did nearly get sent off as well.

We lost at home to Ipswich on Boxing Day against a team that had no shots on goal in open play, their strikes coming from a penalty and a deflection. Yet still the fans remained fantastically loyal. We got 34,483 for a home game against Rotherham. Could Chelsea beat that if they were relegated to Division One?

Jermain Defoe was sent off for the third time that season in an away draw at Walsall. At the end of January, with the transfer window about to close, Defoe moved to Tottenham. As Terry Brown had said that we didn't have to sell any players for financial reasons, it was presumably Pardew's choice. It was horrible to lose anyone to Spurs, but Jermain had been sent off three times and had just served a massive suspension. Clearly he was frustrated to still be playing for us.

Ironically, in the January issue of *Hammers News* Defoe was quoted as saying:

> I love the fans and everyone at this club. The club means so much to people. I remember once we were up at Blackburn and staying in a hotel. There was this girl of about 14 standing with her parents . . . Her dad came over to me and said that his daughter wanted to meet me but she was too shy. I told him to tell her not to worry and he should send her over. I started to walk towards her and she burst out crying. I couldn't believe it. She was really emotional. She said she loved West Ham, and I was her favourite player. I will never forget that day and tell that story now. It shows our impact on the fans.

She must have been really happy when he left.

As part of the £7 million Defoe deal we got Bobby Zamora, a West Ham supporter. Zamora had only been given a few games at Spurs, although he was already a proven scorer in Division One, having notched 14 for Brighton the previous season. His potential was apparent when he scored on his debut in a win against Bradford.

David James was sold to Manchester City and replaced by young Stephen Bywater. James might have been England's goalkeeper, but, for all his brilliant saves, he had also made a number of errors in Division One. Pardew swapped Ian Pearce for Fulham's Andy Melville and signed Wimbledon youngsters Jobi McAnuff, Adam Nowland and Nigel Reo-Coker.

Yet still we lacked consistency. Our success seemed to depend on the form of Matthew Etherington, who with regular football had become a winger of pace and skill. We then lost at home to Preston in January and were down to eighth place. West Ham were 3–1 up at Sheffield United, but ended up drawing 3–3 after an injury-time equaliser. We beat skint Wimbledon 5–0 and were 4–0 up at half-time against Crewe but struggled to win the game 4–2. Marlon scored a fantastic long-range goal as we drew with leaders Norwich, and then we were thrashed 4–1 at Millwall. At home, the crowd would turn easily, and other teams waited for it to happen. We couldn't hold on to a lead, and some of the younger players seemed intimidated to be playing for a club with big expectations.

Some relief from league football was provided by the FA Cup when we drew 0–0 at Premier League Fulham. One of Lola's teachers, Stuart Houliston, was the Fulham mascot. He got hold of some tickets, and we watched him run around the pitch, his long legs sticking out from beneath a giant Dabs keyboard. He was taunted by the West Ham fans who alleged that the mascot needed a good feed. In the replay we lost 3–0, Marlon Harewood missing five chances and having one of those games when he seemed to be aiming at Plaistow station.

During April we seemed to have blown our play-off chances, losing at Reading (where the gleeful home fans chanted 'Pardew out!' and greeted him with 'Judas' banners), drawing at home to lowly Derby and then losing at Crystal Palace. Jon Harley, on loan at left-back, returned to Fulham. Since Brevett's injury earlier in the season, the position had been a problem.

One fan who was simply glad to see West Ham whether they won, lost or drew was Gary Teeley. It took a lot of courage to survive a week-long ordeal as a hostage in Iraq – and then to emerge to meet the TV cameras wearing a West Ham shirt. Teeley, 37, had been kidnapped by Shia militants in Nassiriya. He was released unharmed and, being a true fan, was desperate for news of the Irons. Presumably his captors had decided that although they had suffered Saddam Hussein, genocide, invasion, insurrection and near civil war, it wasn't really fair to hold a man who'd been through relegation and the sale of his entire team.

Wearing his Hammers shirt, Teeley told reporters, 'There were instances when I thought, "This was the time, this is no more and this is where it all stops."' But then, like the rest of us, he decided to carry on visiting Upton Park and received a deserved ovation when introduced to the crowd before the Coventry game.

West Ham then confounded us all again. In the final four games, the side were unbeaten – defeating Coventry, Stoke and Watford – and then travelled to Wigan, who were challenging for the final play-off place. It was torture for poor Matt who had travelled up the night before: the vegetarian broth up north had bacon in it, and he also failed to get a programme. Some 7,000 West Ham fans took up an entire side of the ground. In the first half, Anton Ferdinand was exposed as a makeshift left-back and only Bywater kept us in the game. The Hammers improved in the second half but still seemed to be heading for a 1–0 defeat when substitute Brian Deane rose over the Wigan defence to head home a Michael Carrick free-kick in the 90th minute.

It was cruel for Wigan, because that Deane goal denied them sixth place and let Crystal Palace, who had enjoyed a tremendous revival under Iain Dowie, into the play-offs. We didn't care, Palace were rubbish, and we were not worried about them.

We had finished fourth, and perhaps that was reasonable when you considered the turnover of staff. In just one season we had lost Di Canio, Bowyer, Breen, Cisse, Winterburn, Minto, Moncur, van der Gouw, Les Ferdinand, Johnson, Sinclair, Kanouté, Cole, Schemmel, Pearce, Defoe and James. In that same season we had signed, or taken on loan, Connolly, Etherington, Lee, Mellor, Horlock, Kilgallon, Quinn, Alexandersson, Mullins, Stockdale, Deane, Harewood, Melville, Harley, Shabaan, Reo-Coker, Nowland, Zamora, McAnuff, Carole and Sirnicek. Oh, and there had been three managers, too.

West Ham played Ipswich at Portman Road in the first leg of the play-off semi-final. It was a 12.15 p.m. kick-off and Matt, Fraser, Nigel and I found ourselves in the foyer of the Ipswich Theatre, drinking cappuccino and eating baked potatoes with vegetable korma topping: irrefutable proof that football was now a middle-class sport. Before the game, we were taunted by the Ipswich mascot – a black horse. Then with Hayden Mullins at left-back and Tomas Repka at right-back, and after Zamora missed a good early chance, we were taunted by the Ipswich attack. Bent scored in the second half, and it was advantage Ipswich.

The second leg at home was one of those Upton Park nights that I'll never forget. In an attempt at unnerving the Ipswich players, Alan Pardew had warned that the place would be 'jumping'. It was, too. The TVs had been turned off in the stands because Pards wanted people in their seats early. Just before the kick-off, Pardew resurrected an old tradition from the '60s and '70s. 'And now we're going to bring on a man with a horn!' declared Jeremy Nicholas. A huntsman in red coat and riding hat came onto the pitch and played 'The Post Horn Gallop'. Coach Roger Cross had told Pards that when it used to be played before games 'it made the hairs on the back of your head stand up'. The famous hunting clarion call helped create the best atmosphere at an Upton Park match in years. With the government set to ban hunting, it seemed that all those Countryside Alliance types might soon find alternative employment winding up football fans. As for Tomas Repka, no fox in the E13 region would be safe that night.

There was a phenomenal atmosphere in the ground. The fans in every part of the stadium were in song, even in the normally sedate East Stand. A new-ish staccato chant of 'Irons!' echoed across Upton Park. 'It's just like the old days,' mused Fraser, fondly remembering beating Preston in the 1964 FA Cup final. Stupid home defeats were forgotten. What other club would get such a response after being relegated and selling half the England team?

In a letter to season-ticket holders, Alan Pardew later wrote, 'In all my years in the game, I have never experienced a night quite like Tuesday 18 May . . . The pride and passion for the Claret and Blue is legendary. I can't think of any other club that enjoys such a close relationship with its fans.'

Following on from 'The Post Horn Gallop' the players hounded the opposition for the whole game. Ipswich's Bent missed their best chance when put through after just two minutes. Then Town resisted the Claret and Blues' surge until the 50th minute. Etherington received a corner on the right-hand side of the pitch, cut inside and unleashed a thunderous curling shot into the top corner of the goal at the Bobby Moore end. His goal provoked the biggest celebrations since Jermain Defoe's winner against Blackburn, and the ground was alive with expectation.

With the aggregate scores level, the breakthrough finally came from football genius Christian Dailly, who had been a consistent figure all season at the back for West Ham. Etherington's 71st minute corner rebounded off Richard Naylor to Christian, and the West Ham captain shinned the ball gently into the corner of the net. Upton Park erupted. In the final minutes, Westlake hit the bar for Ipswich but somehow we held on. Down the Barking Road and all the way to the Black Lion the streets were full of fans in claret and blue singing 'We're all going to Cardiff, we're all going to Cardiff, la la la la!'

Our opponents in the final were Crystal Palace, who had beaten Sunderland with an injury-time goal from defender Darryl Powell. Iain Dowie, the Palace manager, was a West Ham supporter. It was also the club where Alan Pardew enjoyed his best years as a player and where Hayden Mullins grew up. Palace, who only qualified for the play-offs because Brian Deane had scored a last-minute equaliser at Wigan. Palace, who under Dowie had risen from near the relegation zone to the top six. They would be grateful to just have got to the final, I thought. We would surely beat them and at least keep Michael Carrick and wipe £20 million off the debt. We were just 90 minutes away from the Premiership.

Trying to get a ticket in such a short space of time was chaotic. Nigel had joined the automatic tickets for home cup ties scheme and was guaranteed one. I faxed over a cup-tie application form, others applied online, there were various confusing windows of opportunity to apply for extra tickets from Ticketmaster and nothing arrived in the post until a worrying three days before the final. It was almost as difficult as booking an Apex train ticket to Cardiff, but that feat was eventually achieved, too.

My plan was to stay the Sunday night with my old pals Sean and Julia in the Llandaff district of Cardiff. After a night in their absent daughter's bed, I took a leisurely walk alongside the River Taff through Pontcanna Fields and on to the Millennium Stadium. The city had been divided into two halves, and the West Ham area around the station was a mass of flag-waving, drinking fans singing 'Bubbles'.

The team that meets in Ken's Café were all there: Matt, Lisa, Nigel, Fraser, Big Joe and DC. After a pre-match pint we headed into the Millennium Stadium and the feeling of nervousness was overpowering. It was hugely impressive to see the West Ham contingent spread over three levels and the numerous banners draped from the stands that said things like 'United We Stand' and 'Thurrock Boys'. Due to the vagaries of the ticketing arrangements, I was sitting next to Nigel, but the rest of us were in different parts of the ground.

Nigel, not tempting providence or a south London-based God at all, sent a text message to his Palace-supporting mate that read, '3–0 against a pub team.' Some bloke called Mr Woo did lots of juggling skills before the game, the PA played 'Bubbles' and Palace's 'Glad All Over', there was a huge fanfare, and on came the teams. Early on it was apparent that Hayden Mullins was being played out of position at left-back, and Routledge was causing him problems. There was little rhythm to either sides' game.

Repka managed to clear off the line when Michael Hughes lobbed over Bywater, then the Hammers came close to opening the scoring. Etherington cut inside from the wing but shot over. Carrick then found a rare moment of time in the midfield mêlée and played a great pass through to Zamora, who was running goalwards. Bobby's shot hit the target, but the ball rebounded off the keeper's feet. The side wasn't gelling, though. Harewood couldn't get into the game at all on the right wing.

After half-time, Lomas hit a fantastic dipping volley that Vaesen tipped over. Palace didn't have stars but were playing as a team. After 60 minutes, Andy Johnson ran across the Hammers defence and just beat Repka to the ball. He then had a shot that rebounded from Bywater's hands, and the lumbering Neil Shipperley – a veteran who was now so rotund that he resembled a Sunday League centre-forward – was there to tap the ball in. The Palace end erupted; Nigel and I felt the colour drain from our faces. Would David James have held that one?

Never have 30 minutes of a football match seemed to pass so quickly. Pardew made a series of baffling substitutions, taking off anyone with pace who might score. First Zamora, then Harewood and Connolly. We ended the game with Brian Deane and Don Hutchison up front and Nigel Reo-Coker on the right wing.

Late on, Michael Carrick made a run into the edge of the Palace box and was hacked down. It was a certain penalty, but the referee had seen nothing illegal. It was our last chance. The final whistle blew, and the Palace players jumped on top of each other. Rocket man Iain Dowie sprinted onto the pitch. The PA played 'Glad All Over'. And I was feeling bad all over.

We met Matt and Lisa outside the stadium, and we could hardly talk. The Hammers fans filed past looking like extras from *Shaun of the Dead*. I picked up a dusty claret and blue flag from the floor and claimed it for my daughter Lola. It seemed to sum up our day. Whoever was selling the flags saying 'Goodbye Nationwide. Hammers are Back' had wisely retreated.

I walked back by the Taff through Pontcanna Fields. Noisy Palace fans were celebrating in the pubs on Cathedral Road. I sat on the grass for an hour, unable to move, then walked back to Sean's house and had a couple of thirst-relieving pints in a Llandaff pub on the way.

'I'm so sorry,' said Sean, in the manner of a man consoling the bereaved. Carrick would go now. And for the next decade we would be watching Rio Ferdinand, Frank Lampard, Jermain Defoe, Joe Cole, Michael Carrick and Glen Johnson in the England team, while West Ham faced another 46-game slog against the likes of Crewe. We had planned to drive down to Westward Ho! to see Sean's mum, only I thought that it would be a celebratory trip. The drive to Devon entailed trying to escape Cardiff on roads packed with thousands of cars full of celebrating Palace fans, horns blaring, scarves out of windows: Palace in Wonderland. A West Ham fans' limousine with blacked-out windows drove past, and a disembodied hand emerged to give a one-fingered salute.

The next day Sean and I walked along the coastal path from Westward Ho! to the village of Clovelly. The sea was calm, the sky clear and spring flowers were emerging all along the path. Could nature soothe a befuddled and distraught football fan? No it couldn't. Had Wordsworth supported West Ham he would never have written another word. We had been 90 minutes away from the Premiership and the possible rebirth of our club. And we lost.

THE DREAM TEAM WEST HAM SOLD
- DAVID JAMES: Calamity might have been England's No. 1, but he could never really replace Allen McKnight in the fans' affections. West Ham soon sent him to take art classes and study Friends Reunited websites at Manchester City.
- GLEN JOHNSON: Not half as good as Gary Charles, Johnson was sold to Chelsea after just 12 games, for £6 million.

Currently struggling to get a game with the London Globetrotters.

- **RIO FERDINAND:** Forgetful centre-back with no pace, aerial power or ability to read the game. Was sold to Leeds United for £18 million as we cunningly lured the Yorkshire club towards financial disaster. Then sold by Leeds to Manchester United for £30 million, even though Neil Ruddock was really much better.

- **PAUL ALLEN:** Young crybaby who was soon sent to boarding school at White Hart Lane to toughen up. He was replaced by Mark Ward.

- **PAUL INCE:** No tackling ability at all. Couldn't shoot. Terrible engine. But always very loyal to West Ham and still receives a great reception at Upton Park. The Governor achieved nothing at all at Manchester United, bar the odd cup and championship.

- **MARTIN PETERS:** Was ten years ahead of his time so we cunningly sold him to Spurs ten years before his time. Couldn't drink half as well as Jimmy Greaves.

- **FRANK LAMPARD:** Average podgy midfielder with no goalscoring ability, sold to Chelsea for £11 million. What can José Mourinho see in him?

- **MICHAEL CARRICK:** No close control, no passing ability, Carrick was sold to Spurs for £3 million where he is now studying advanced mullet growing.

- **JOE COLE:** Schoolboy footballer who could dribble a bit, sold to Chelsea for £6 million. Steve Whitton was much better at close control.

- **JERMAIN DEFOE:** As a finisher he was never in the same class as David Kelly or Mike Small. Fetched £7 million when Tottenham surprisingly bid for him.

- **TONY COTTEE:** Far too small to be a striker. Diminutive goal-hanger who was bought by Everton for £3 million in 1987 and easily replaced by the club, with Alan Dickens being converted into an ace goal poacher.

SUBS

- JOHN HARTSON: Provided no physical presence up front, terrible in the air, was bought by Wimbledon for £7 million even though John Radford was a much better target man.
- FREDI KANOUTÉ: Another player sold to Spurs for £3.5 million. Prone to playing while wearing a Walkman playing ambient music.
- EYAL BERKOVIC: For some reason objected to having teammates attempt to kick his head off in training. Sold to Celtic for £5.5 million.

15

OH TEDDY, TEDDY, TEDDY, WENT TO WEST HAM AND HE WON SIXTH PLACE!

2004–05

Teddy Sheringham signs . . . Sergei comes home . . . Carrick transfers his mullet to Tottenham . . . stuttering in the league . . . Tomas goes barmy . . . the kids are united . . . and Bobby came from White Hart Lane and at Portman Road he really is better than Jermain.

  Price of Hammer *in 2005: £3*

'Mark Noble, whoooah! Mark Noble, whoooah! He's only seventeen. He's better than Brian Deane!' Something changed in the match against Leicester. We only drew 2–2. Marlon Harewood had a penalty saved late on that should have proved the winner. But at last West Ham were playing with a little style. We had seen an entertaining match, and I had enjoyed going to a game again.

Young Noble had been dipping his shoulder and beating people, showing an arrogance and class way beyond his years. He gestured to the Bobby Moore Stand like it meant something to him. Anton Ferdinand was composed at the back, and alongside him, Elliott Ward was winning headers and looking like the love child of Billy Bonds with his '70s hairstyle. Nigel Reo-Coker was starting to produce something like his true form in midfield, Marlon Harewood looked like he could become a Premiership-quality player. As the whistle went there were the usual mutterings about another two points dropped at home, but there was something there. A spark. We had a bunch of kids who wanted to play for our great club. And the crowd responded. We just might have a team.

It had been a long, long season. The summer of 2004 was one of footballing despair. What could Pards do after the play-off-final trauma? What could we supporters do? For a few weeks, I couldn't talk about football, but then the addiction kicked in again: that strange urge to log on to the official club website or search for West Ham snippets on page 412 of Teletext. At least Pards would have a whole season to work with and it would be his team. Once Carrick had left, every player who could be sold had been sold, and with the season not ending until 30 May, it was a mere six weeks before we kicked off again.

Pards made some brave decisions that summer. He sold David Connolly to Leicester for £500,000. Angry Ant scored a total of 14 goals the previous season, although his scoring rate had declined after Christmas, mainly because he was being played in midfield. He worked hard and was popular with the fans. We immediately envisaged a Connolly-inspired Leicester romping to promotion.

Angry Ant's replacement was Teddy Sheringham, signed on a free from Portsmouth. It was not often that a European Cup winner joined West Ham, even if he was 38. Teddy had still scored regularly for Pompey in the Premiership the season before, and as he had never been reliant on pace he surely had another year left in the Championship. Sheringham told the club website that he had always supported West Ham: 'I was a Hammers fan as a youngster and stood on the old North Bank with my big brother watching the likes of Alan Devonshire, Ray Stewart, Billy Jennings and Graham Paddon. So, to get the opportunity of playing for this great club after all these years is an honour.'

This was slightly contradicted by his 1988 book *Teddy: My Autobiography*, which revealed, 'At first we went to West Ham and I enjoyed that, but I didn't discover what being a true fan was all about until I went to Tottenham for the first time when I was a little bit older. I was hooked.' But still, at least he had been to West Ham and knew something of the club's traditions.

Teddy was soon joined by keeper Jimmy Walker, who played superbly at Upton Park the previous season when Walsall drew 0–0. Luke Chadwick, once spoken of as the successor to David Beckham at Manchester United, was signed on a free, and Sergei Rebrov, another supposed Hammers fan, also joined the club. The one-time £11 million star was available on a free transfer from Spurs and was therefore worth a gamble, despite the fact that the old Spurs manager Glenn Hoddle always insisted that he couldn't play Sheringham and Rebrov in the same side.

Sergei revealed that, 'When I looked into Alan's eyes when he said he wanted me, I knew there wouldn't be a problem.' All very Mills and Boon. He also claimed, 'Whenever I got the chance I watched West Ham on TV at Upton Park. It was a tremendous moment for me when Alan Pardew invited me to join the squad for pre-season training.' Nigel, Matt and I imagined the young radio ham Sergei sitting at home in the Ukraine, ignoring Dynamo Kiev and desperately trying to tune in to the World Service for news of his beloved West Ham.

We knew Michael Carrick would go even before he did. He wanted Premiership football, although just one goal and a failure to dominate crucial games the season before made me wonder if he would ever fulfil his promise. There were rumours he would go to Arsenal. Yet he was still at Upton Park for the pre-season friendlies. Pards thought that he would stay and so sold Jobi McAnuff for £500,000 to Cardiff, one of the young prospects we were supposed to be building a side around. And then Carrick went anyway. A firm bid from Spurs of around £3 million finally arrived. It had to be Spurs. Carrick joined Defoe and Kanouté, and it seemed that we were now a feeder club for Spurs and Chelsea. Several Premiership clubs were also said to have enquired about Marlon Harewood, but he stayed with us, and so too did Matthew Etherington.

Pards said that 'we want to win this league' and if you based results on wages, then we should have. The season began on 7 August with a 0–0 draw at Leicester. It was a respectable result, particularly as the returning Rufus Brevett was red carded and we ended the match with ten men. Nicola, the girls and I were house sitting in North Yorkshire again, and so I watched the home match against Reading on Ceefax. Teddy Sheringham scored a late winner, and it seemed we were over the play-off-final defeat. But, crucially, Christian 'Football Genius' Dailly suffered another injury and would miss nearly the whole of the season.

I was sitting outside a delightful pub in the Yorkshire Dales village of Redmire, drinking a pint of Black Sheep in the sun, when I received a text from Nigel. We had lost 3–1 at home to Wigan. The verdict from the lads was that Wigan had taught us how to pass and completely outplayed Pardew's men. Nigel predicted, with some confidence, that, 'Sergei Rebrov will never score a goal for us in open play.'

Teddy Sheringham scored twice in a 3–2 win at Crewe, and I returned to Upton Park for my first game of the season, a 1–0 home victory against Burnley. It was a struggle. Adam Nowland, a young player signed from Wimbledon, who for much of last season had looked nowhere near good enough for West Ham, had improved his game and fired home the winner with a deflected long-range shot.

In the East Stand the season-ticket holders were down to Nigel, Matt, Fraser and me, Dan having departed to spend more time with the son whom he fathered after we had beaten Chelsea 1–0 and looked likely to stay up. We lost at Coventry after Sheringham gave us the lead and then won at Sheffield United with a late Teddy free-kick.

In my next home game, we defeated Rotherham 1–0, too, with Mattie Etherington scoring a great free-kick. It seemed that for most of the season we would be trying to work hard and beat teams by the odd goal; the old flair had gone and we were now an average to good side in the renamed Coca-Cola Championship. Although, a home draw against Ipswich produced a much better game and Kelvin Davis made some superb saves to prevent a home win.

When Pardew signed both Fletcher and Mackay, I wondered if Godber would soon be joining, too. It was not actually an attempt to compile an entire side named after the stars of the '70s sitcom *Porridge*: Malky Mackay, captain of Norwich's Division One championship-winning side the previous season, had been signed to fill the gap left by Dailly's injury, while Carl Fletcher was a hard-working Welsh international signed from Bournemouth for just £250,000.

Pardew, a man who had worked as a glazier, liked the fact there was no transfer window in the Championship that season and carried on rebuilding the side. Brevett looked to have lost pace after his year-long lay-off and was replaced by Chris Powell from Charlton, who was to consistently occupy the left-back position. He also signed centre-half Calum Davenport on loan from Spurs. Described as 'a head on a stick' by

Stephen Bywater, Davenport looked cool and classy and far too good for the division.

Despite the influx of new players, for the rest of the season every good result was seemingly followed by a bad one. When we played at Nottingham Forest it was an emotional day because it was their first game since the death of Brian Clough. But Harewood tapped home, and we were in control with seven minutes to go. Suddenly, Forest equalised with a 30-yard shot. Then, in injury time, Marlon King made a run at the West Ham defence, Mackay backed off and King curled a great goal into the corner to seal the victory for Forest.

West Ham beat Wolves 1–0 at Upton Park, with Teddy Sheringham jinking the ball over a defender and sweeping home to score a lovely winning goal. But then we lost 1–0 at QPR. The home side were fired up after several successive victories, and the blue-and-white-haired Mark Bircham was a severe aggravation to the Hammers in midfield – even if the away fans did taunt him with 'He's got birdshit on his head!'

We had several injured players, but it was proof that our squad wasn't good enough. The one positive from the game was that Anton Ferdinand looked like he was developing into a quality centre-back. On the other hand, Zamora looked flat, Lomas was a fading force, Reo-Coker underachieving and Mullins had never looked a natural right-back. Sergei Rebrov had been given another chance but the Ukrainian was more enigmatic than the last episode of *The Prisoner*. He stood out in the Championship because he could control the ball and flight in a good corner or free-kick, but he just didn't seem to achieve very much in games. Sergei seemed a diffident character, lacking the determination of his one-time Ukraine strike partner Andriy Shevchenko. A sort of Stuart Slater of Ukrainian football.

Reserve keeper Jimmy Walker played brilliantly and saved a Frank Lampard penalty during the 1–0 Carling Cup defeat at Chelsea. Trying to make the Coca-Cola Championship more interesting by groundhopping, I travelled away to Plymouth. Unfortunately, my Argyle-supporting mate Adam had to withdraw from the trip due to family commitments, and I travelled to the game at Home Park on my own.

The Plymouth constabulary had clearly been buying too many books by retired hooligans. They seemed to regard every West Ham supporter as a member of the ICF. Because of storms and floods, a special bus service operated from Tiverton Parkway station to Plymouth. All football fans were separated from the other travellers and put on special coaches. During the 90-minute journey to Home Park there was a constant police escort, presumably in case some irate Devonians came at the coaches with strategically placed dairy-farming equipment. So much for low-profile policing, you'd have thought Osama bin Laden was coming to the West Country. At the ground a cordon of 100 police made a ring around the coach. A policeman even removed the plastic top from my bottle of mineral water as I entered the stadium.

Steve Lomas scored with a header, and Marlon had a good goal, scored from an Etherington cross, wrongly disallowed for offside. But you could never trust West Ham with a single-goal lead, and Wooton equalised from outside the area with an effort that Bywater might have done better with. Harewood had looked hungry and motivated during the game, but Zamora was again a disappointment.

After the game, a three-hour rail journey was transformed into a six-hour Palin-esque epic. There was another 90-minute police escort back to Tiverton and an inept decision not to hold the London train that departed just as we arrived, meant an hour-plus wait with no food surrounded by hundreds of Old Bill. The expense of all the police attention must have been huge, yet the amount of aggro I witnessed was nil.

We followed a draw at Plymouth by getting thrashed 4–1 at Cardiff. Predictably, Jobi McAnuff was among their scorers. The Cardiff DJ got into trouble for playing the *Steptoe and Son* theme and dedicating it to the few travelling Hammers fans. Quite right, too: he should have played the *Fawlty Towers* theme instead.

West Ham beat QPR 2–1 at Upton Park with Marlon scoring a thunderous winner, but then in the next home game we had eighteen shots at goal compared to Brighton's one, but managed to lose 1–0. Pardew signed yet another ex-Spurs player in Maurice Taricco. He played 20 minutes of a 1–0 defeat at Millwall, suffered an injury that would keep him out until January, and then, in a commendably honest act, ripped up his contract rather than have West Ham pay him for not playing. Either that or he just thought we were rubbish. In that game, Marlon Harewood was sent off when he received a second yellow card for diving (he wasn't), and Pardew was booed by the West Ham fans when he took off the in-form Luke Chadwick for Bobby Zamora.

We went two goals down at home to Watford, but goals from the on-loan giant Daryl Powell and Reo-Coker brought us level. Sergei Rebrov played in an orange armband to show his support for the revolution in Ukraine and ended up scoring the winner by tapping home Etherington's cross. Nigel was immediately taunted about his prediction that 'Sergei Rebrov will never score a goal for us in open play'. It was to prove to be his only one.

That result was followed by a fine 2–0 win at Sunderland, and we were 1–0 up at home to Leeds in the last minute and had nearly won three in a row, but, of course, Leeds got a very dodgy penalty and we only drew. We then lost the next game at Preston. We just never get a run going. West Ham were two goals down at bottom-of-the-table Rotherham, but drew 2–2 thanks to two penalties. We then beat top-of-the-table Ipswich four days later. We followed this by playing absolutely dreadfully in a dire 2–0 home defeat to Sheffield United. Malky Mackay must have passed to the opposition on 327 separate occasions.

We lost 4–2 at Wolves: the defence and new keeper Jimmy Walker played like ageing members of Slade. Then the lads lost at home to Derby – it was kids-for-a-quid and my daughter Lola's first ever Hammers defeat – and all the press talk was about the pressure on Pardew. He was brave, faced the press and deflected all questions about his position after each defeat. He also said that Bobby Zamora was out of form because there was such huge pressure on him being a West Ham fan. In response, we argued that we were West Ham fans, too, and somehow coped with the pressure. And it didn't seem to affect Teddy Sheringham.

We almost lost at home to Cardiff, but Carl Fletcher, who had adapted to the Championship well and never stopped running, scored an injury-time winner. Our season was a bit like one of those first generation *Star Trek* episodes where good and bad parallel universes exist in different dimensions. In the bad universe, Spock has a beard and West Ham lose to the likes of Brighton; in the good universe, Spock doesn't have a beard and West Ham win away at the top three clubs in the division. If only we had a Scotty to mix matter with antimatter in a controlled implosion to somehow propel us through warp space back to the Premiership.

Having struggled for four matches we then thrashed Plymouth 5–0. My Argyle-supporting mate Adam did make it to that match, and I had never seen a more morose football fan on the Tube home. Plymouth gifted West Ham three first-half goals: scoring an own goal from Rebrov's inswinging corner, conceding a penalty from another Sergei corner and then allowing Mackay to score while unmarked.

We followed this up by winning 1–0 at Gillingham, before losing three in a row. A late effort finished West Ham at Leeds, while an injury to Anton Ferdinand disrupted the defence. Against Preston we lost to our nearest play-off challengers in depressing fashion. Stephen Bywater miscontrolled the ball into the path of Preston's Nugent and presented him with a tap-in for the first goal. Then Tomas Repka was sent off. Brian O'Neill caught him with an arm as he ran past, but there was no excuse for then running ten yards to head-butt the Preston player in front of the referee. I told the others that he was a liability and should never play for the club again. Pardew took off Mackay, leaving tiny Carl Fletcher as our main centre-back, and Preston's Agyemang dribbled through the defence to make it two. Despite sub Zamóra's late consolation goal, we lost 2–1.

Repka was fined two weeks' wages by Pardew and told the club's website, 'I apologise to all our fans for my behaviour during the match against Preston. I will do my best to repay our supporters' faith in me when I have served my three-match suspension and promise to do my best to help the team in its bid for promotion.'

In his next programme notes, Pardew explained, 'We all love him here, but his gung-ho, win-at-all costs attitude sometimes gets him into trouble.' Which was probably what he'd say about Grant Mitchell, too.

There was also uncertainty off the pitch. The press speculated on possible takeover bids from millionaire Michael Tabor, David Sullivan and a consortium fronted by Tony Cottee. (Would TC make a scrapbook of his greatest board meetings?)

Meanwhile, the club had settled a court case against Barrie Abrahams, one of the members of a group called Whistle that was seeking to install a new board and had published an open letter to Terry Brown in May 2004. The club sued for defamation, claiming that Whistle had overstated its level of debt. Brown explained the club's reasons for suing:

> The decision to take legal action was not made lightly . . . We fully accept that football is now a very high-profile industry and that our roles will attract scrutiny and, on occasion, robust criticism.

However, we do not accept that legitimate criticism extends to gross misrepresentation of the company's financial position.

To some fans the decision to spend the club's money suing three people who were West Ham supporters seemed unnecessarily heavy-handed and was another PR own goal.

Away to Reading was probably not the ideal game for Pardew to face next. 'No pride, no passion' read my text from Nigel, as we went down 3–1. Some West Ham fans chanted 'Are you Roeder in disguise?' at Pards. They sang, 'We are West Ham's claret and blue army' rather than 'Alan Pardew's claret and blue army'. The under-pressure boss had played Hayden Mullins rather than young Elliott Ward at centre-back and a lack of height at the back had been exposed by Reading at set pieces. Sometimes Pards' team selection seemed to be designed around any possible formation that kept Mullins in the side. I had never known a manager to have such faith in one player. When I mentioned this to Hillsy, a Palace-supporting mate, his email reply was interesting:

> I think everyone who's ever been connected with Palace is haunted by the knowledge that somewhere inside Hayden is a fantastic player. We all saw it – he had a great season once and looked like a future England player. Since then, well who knows . . . Pardew must wake up in the night with new ideas about how to make him rediscover that form . . . I don't know. Just try persisting with him until he's too old to run any more.

Pardew's position was further undermined by the next game against Crewe. Winning 1–0 thanks to an excellent Sheringham free-kick, West Ham conceded an injury-time header to allow a Crewe side that hadn't won since selling Dean Ashton to gain an unlikely point. Young Elliott Ward had come in for his first full league game at centre-half and looked composed alongside Anton, but all the talk afterwards was of the beleaguered West Ham boss. *The Guardian* even claimed that West Ham had offered Pardew's job to Gordon Strachan.

Then came the game against Leicester and a little bit of hope as a result of the way we played, despite the scoreline. We were down to eighth in the table, and in the East Stand we had taken to chanting 'Oh,

Teddy, Teddy, Teddy, went to West Ham and he won eighth place!'

I thought that we would never win at Wigan. Pardew had dropped Fletcher so that Hayden Mullins could play in central midfield and dropped Bywater for Jimmy Walker. Repka returned to be gung-ho at right-back. However, West Ham being West Ham we did win. Ferdinand and Ward stifled the prolific Wigan strikers Ellington and Roberts. Matt, who was at the game, said that Mullins had a good game in midfield and Shaun Newton, a bargain ten-grand signing from Wolves, looked lively on the right of midfield. Matt got a programme too, even if the vegetarian broth was still full of ham. Harewood and Sheringham scored the crucial goals. The squad then stayed in Lancashire for a Tuesday night game at Burnley, and another Teddy goal sealed victory there, too.

West Ham were now seventh, and suddenly there was optimism as we chased Reading for a play-off spot. We beat relegation-threatened Coventry 3–0 and for once the result wasn't in doubt at the final whistle. Bobby Zamora scored the third with a diving header, and I wondered if his confidence might just be returning. A home draw with Millwall was scrappy, but we had stopped losing.

Ferdinand and Ward were looking a solid partnership at the back. The pair were both only 20 years old but had an understanding from playing alongside each other in the junior sides. Ward did simple things well, while some of Anton's interceptions and runs from defence were reminiscent of some bloke at Old Trafford. The pair were terrific in a 1–0 win at Stoke – Zamora touched home the winner.

The doubts returned with a 2–2 draw at Brighton when West Ham had twice led and with the news that Teddy Sheringham was injured and out of any play-off semi-final. Then a Friday night home defeat to Sunderland in front of 33,482 fans seemed to have destroyed our chances. We'd performed well – Marlon had even poked us ahead – but Sunderland played like champions in the second half. Stephen Elliott ran at Ward for the winner: the young centre-back gave him too much space, and the ball was in the net.

However, the next day the results went in our favour: no one expected Reading to lose at home to Wolves. We were level on points with Pardew's old team with one game to go. West Ham secured a comfortable 2–1 win at Vicarage Road, with Anton Ferdinand scoring his first goal for the club. To celebrate he ran to our end to perform some sort of David Brent dance routine. Reading lost 3–1 and we were secure in sixth place. The most difficult part of the day was trying to find DC's car in two identical multi-storey car parks after the match.

We were back in the play-offs and faced Ipswich again. The man with the horn was back as well. Matthew Etherington started the home leg in exhilarating fashion, roasting the Ipswich full-back and setting up early goals for Harewood and Zamora. Bobby missed a good chance soon after but was looking a formidable striking presence once more. However, just before half-time, we conceded the obligatory soft goal; perhaps it was written into every player's contract that they must remember to let a goal in right on half-time. The referee gave a free-kick against Repka, who appeared to have won a good header. Tomas argued, the referee moved the free-kick ten yards across the box because of his dissent and Miller's free-kick deflected in off the post and Walker. Suddenly, Ipswich were buoyed up for the second half.

Kelvin Davis produced a Gordon Banks-like save from Ferdinand's header in the second half, but Ipswich equalised when Walker and Ferdinand bumped into each other in the box and Kuqi fired home the loose ball. So the game ended 2–2, and Ipswich were surely on their way to Cardiff.

Fraser and I travelled from Liverpool Street to Ipswich for the second leg. I was not optimistic, but as soon as we were outside the stadium there was an astonishing sense of belief from the Hammers fans. They were singing before the kick-off and didn't stop for the rest of the game. A classic chant had been revived: 'We all follow the West Ham over land and sea (and Millwall). We all follow the West Ham on to victory!' With support like that I suddenly thought, hey, this might be possible.

Pardew had got his tactics right. Fletcher came in for Newton and did a good harrying job in midfield, while Harewood was utilised wide on the right. Ipswich's Currie worried Jimmy Walker with one shot that he deflected over, but, otherwise, we were in control. Somewhere amid all the traumas of the season the team had bonded into a unit. Ward was making rugged interceptions at the back, and Hayden Mullins was finally justifying Pardew's immense faith in him. He was a midfield colossus, winning crucial tackles and allowing Reo-Coker to play freely. Zamora was also eager up front, taking on men, crossing and providing a mobile target to aim at.

Unbelievably, Tomas Repka was also repeatedly rampaging down the right wing. Suddenly he had metamorphosed into an attacking full-back of genius and, just before half-time, knocked out Kelvin Davis with a cross-shot. Scotty's controlled implosion appeared to have happened.

Etherington had an opportunity to score but he shot against the keeper, and it was still goalless at half-time. We dominated the second half against the jaded Ipswich side. Still we sang. Then, Marlon broke down the right, played the ball across goal and Zamora, who had read the pass, stroked the ball into an unguarded net. Could we hold on? Harewood played a good one–two down the right and crossed to Zamora, who met the ball waist high to cushion a Di Canio-esque volley into the corner of the net. 'ZAMORA, WHOOOOOOAH! ZAMORA, WHOOOOOOAH! HE CAME FROM WHITE HART LANE, HE'S BETTER THAN JERMAIN!' sang 4,000 voices with Irons in their souls.

The final whistle blew. We were going back to Cardiff. We celebrated on a train that didn't arrive back at Liverpool Street until gone midnight. But not too much, because this time there was a job to be completed.

TOP TEN MOMENTS OF TOMAS REPKA MADNESS
- Rampaging down the length of the pitch and nearly scoring his only ever goal for the Hammers in the play-off final against Preston at the Millennium Stadium. However, he hit the post.
- Conceding a penalty at Chelsea in the Carling Cup and then grabbing the fallen Arjen Robben by the shirt collar and shouting scary Czech things at him from a distance of two inches, just as the commentator was saying how much he had improved his disciplinary record.
- Turning into a combination of Julian Dicks and Stuart Pearce in the home game against Sunderland in December 2003 and making a number of clenched-fist 'Come on!' gestures to the Bobby Moore Stand.
- Being sent off in the 90th minute against Fulham in December 2003. Disputing the non-award of a free-kick for handball near West Ham's box, Super Tom was first booked for dissent, continued to argue and was then sent off. Glenn Roeder described Repka's dismissal as 'unforgivable'.
- Being restrained from confronting his own fans by West Ham

MD Paul Aldridge after West Ham lost at home to WBA in September 2002.

- Giving a needless free-kick away at Gillingham. Then arguing with the referee, who advanced the free-kick ten yards, allowing Marlon King to rocket the ball into the top corner of the net.
- Suddenly metamorphosing into an attacking full-back of genius at Portman Road and knocking Kelvin Davis out with a cross-shot in the play-off semi-final against Ipswich.
- Getting sent off against promotion rivals Preston in March 2005. Having been caught by Brian O'Neill, he then ran ten yards to head-butt him right in front of the referee.
- Being sent off for two bookable offences on his West Ham debut away to Middlesbrough in September 2001.
- Being sent off in his third game for West Ham, for a second bookable offence after bringing down Blackburn striker Grabbi in the 7–1 defeat at Ewood Park.

16

PARDS' TIMES

AUGUST 2005
Alan Pardew on why West Ham can be as big as Arsenal . . . how Pards sold Terry Brown a new car . . . why Defoe had to go . . . the new serene Tomas Repka . . . the pressure on Zamora . . . Hayden's strength . . . and how West Ham reached its tipping point.

West Ham have reached their tipping point. Alan Pardew is the sort of modern football manager who reads books on business management. He's a big fan of *The Tipping Point: How Little Things Can Make a Big Difference* by Malcolm Gladwell. When he first mentions *The Tipping Point* I envisage new signing Yossi Benayoun on one end of a see-saw, with Neil Ruddock on the other. But this is serious stuff. 'It's an excellent book and really relevant to us,' enthuses Pards. 'It's about how if you're doing enough right things then suddenly you can tip into success. Like your book? What's going to tip your book from being a normal book into being a million seller?

'It talks about the New York crime wave and "broken window syndrome". The tipping point wasn't chasing murderers, it was making sure the windows on the trains were fixed and the ticket machines were working. People's behaviour improved and crime went down 60 per cent.

'That's true in any environment. If you walked in here as a new player you'd think not the best buildings, but, yeah, they're having a go here trying to make it look right, be positive. The training's proper. It's done right. I've tried to take the club forward. When I arrived here the walls at this training ground were mauve. It was a dark, dingy Portakabin place. Look at it now! It's still Portakabins but it's bright, it's positive.

'We put the menu up, what time's kick-off, what time lunch is, who's doing what warm-up with what sports scientist. I believe if you're doing enough things right you'll get success. We're moving forward. We've got to take some massive steps. We're years behind Man United and Arsenal. We've got to bridge that gap quick.'

We're sitting in the meeting room at Chadwell Heath, four days before the start of the Premiership season. The room has a tactics board with the names of players like Bellamy and Dickov and the odd mysterious arrow. On the walls are motivational posters featuring words from the likes of boxer Muhammad Ali, athlete Kelly Holmes, basketball star Michael Jordan and cyclist Lance Armstrong. The quote from Ali reads, 'The fight is won or lost far away from witnesses, behind the lines, in the gym, and out there on the road, long before I dance under those lights.' These are something the tracksuited Pards is proud of: 'Again it's little things, but we made sure the West Ham logo was on them, too. It really irritates me that the tactical board hasn't got a West Ham badge on it, but the makers in Indonesia won't do it. It's not a massive cost, it's detail. Get the details right, then the players will follow your guidelines to the letter.'

Pardew reads anything that might help him, because he feels psychology is a big part of the modern game: 'You've only got to see the debates between Mourinho, Wenger and Ferguson to know that. We've got players on huge salaries, with the best computer, the best car, model girlfriends, so what's going to motivate them now? It has to be the psychology of the game and getting better as a person. All the money in the world is no good if you've got no medals. It's an old cliché: put your medals on the table. I want my players to be winners. Winners for us this year would be tenth place. Win our own little league. That is our goal.'

I ask Pards how he came to read my previous book, *West Ham: Irons in the Soul*, during his gardening leave from Reading. Is it a sign of his thoroughness? I can't imagine too many gaffers reading books by fans: 'West Ham was such a strange environment to come into, because the old players love it, and the fans wanted someone from within. It was really important to understand as much as I could from the outside about West Ham, what makes it tick. I took a couple of fanzines home, looked at the website, did a lot of reading and looked at the history of the club. I tried to not get caught out on questions about "Who did we beat in the Cup-Winners' Cup final?" I was going to need protection. I was coming into a really precarious situation: no money, a team that had to be sold, with a fan base that wasn't really happy.'

Which brings me to the question of why did he take the job? At Reading there was nothing like the expectation at West Ham of automatic promotion. There, if he got them in the play-offs he was a hero, if not he'd been unlucky: 'I was touted as one of the best managers outside the Premiership at the time, so I put a fair amount on the line. It was a matter of principle. They wouldn't let me talk to West Ham, which I didn't think was right in the modern day. It was two things: the draw of West Ham and the fact that the employer wouldn't let me speak to another employer, and I don't accept that. Ultimately, I knew that if I was to progress as a manager, I needed to take on a big club.

'All my colleagues in the game told me not to take this job. Perhaps it was London, or the fact my friend had gone on and on about West Ham all those years I was growing up, so maybe that was an emotional draw. I wasn't a West Ham fan as a kid. I bounced around whoever was trendy, Fulham then Chelsea, Liverpool.

'The fan base attracted me, of course. I thought it was a club perhaps at the bottom, and although it's going to be sticky, if you get it going again it can be what you want it to be, because of the fan base. It can be an Arsenal. But there's a long way to go before we get there. But the fan base suggests it could be an Arsenal.

'The other beauty is it's a family club. It's passed through the generations. You can see a granddad outside the gates here with his great-grandchild dressed in a West Ham kit and the kid can't even talk yet. There's not many clubs like that now. Granddad, uncle, nan, mum, brother and cousin all come to the game. That loyalty that perhaps in the past has been taken for granted, but certainly it's not taken for granted by me.'

It was noticeable that he praised Terry Brown immediately after the play-off win and he clearly enjoys a good relationship with the reclusive chairman. Like most fans I've criticised Brown in the past, but Pardew makes a forceful case for putting the United back into West Ham: 'There's a misconception with Terry Brown, because he withdraws from the media. I don't think it's because he's hiding, it's because he's not comfortable with it. He loves this club. His home is like another museum. He's built one at the ground and he's built one at home!

'Perhaps his loyalty to the club blinds him to some poor decisions, and to be fair to him he's held his hands up, certainly to me. I think that makes him a big man, to say, "I made major errors." And yet, is that it then? We can't forgive him and we'll chastise him all the time?

'He's been good to me. Always positive. He's tried to be strong for me in his own way. I've said to him I think he needs to be more positive, more proactive with the fans and the club and I think he's taken that on board.

'I've made him buy a new car as well! He said "I can't buy a new car because the West Ham fans will resent that." And I said, "You can't live like that. Buy a new car, just go up the road!" It's a shame, because he's put all his life into this club. Everybody has their time limit to how long they can be a manager or chairman, but certainly he'll be a director of this club for the rest of his life.'

So, Alan Pardew really could make a non-used-car salesman. I mention the shot of him dancing with his daughters on the pitch at Cardiff and wonder if there's a lighter side to the man beneath the ambition to bring success back to Upton Park. 'People always accuse me of not smiling,' he says, a little miffed at the fact. 'In fact, I like to think I'm an amicable sort of guy. The fans might see a different side to me this year. But it was very difficult to mess around when it was such a serious situation we were in. It doesn't fit with me to be on telly smiling and cracking jokes with the media when we've been beaten by Brighton. Perhaps the image I portrayed wasn't me. I tried to be very serious, very honest, not to pull the wool over anyone's eyes, tried not to blame the players. But at least we're in the Premiership now and not under the same intense pressure to get out of the Championship. Maybe I'll enjoy it a little bit more. I'm looking forward to it.'

Is he tempted to do a spot of karaoke like José Mourinho at Chelsea? 'I'm not going to give away too many of our secrets. We don't do karaoke, although I'd put Jimmy Walker up against anyone in the Premiership on a karaoke machine. It's important to have a laugh; it's not all scientific textbook stuff, but I do like the training to be right.'

There is still a question worrying all fans. How can we avoid selling the next generation of young stars like Noble, Ferdinand, Ward and Reo-Coker? 'Well, financially we've got ourselves on a strong footing. We've got one of the lowest wage bills in the Premiership. In the Premiership it's not a bad debt; in the Championship it was a disastrous debt. This happened to me at Reading a little bit when we lost the play-off final. In the extra year you can iron out some of the energy-sappers and adjust the wages. Those two years of correction might do us a power of good.'

When Pardew finished his career at Barnet, and also when he was sacked as reserve-team boss at Reading, he worked as a glazier. Is that a sign of his strong work ethic?

'I couldn't sit at home, I'd go mad. After finishing at Barnet I was scouting for Aston Villa in the evenings, going in my work clothes and putting on a tie as best I could. Remember I didn't turn professional until I was 25. I was working on building sites doing structural glazing on tower blocks. I was on big sites with ardent Chelsea, Arsenal and West Ham fans – real hardcore. They read *The Sun* from front to back. It's a great debating paper. Anyone with the *Express* is labelled a bit of a snob. It's that sort of culture. I wasn't down to my last penny, but my family has always been the same. We're real hard workers. When I sit at home for an hour that's my lot. I have to do something, mow the lawn or watch a video of another player from Azerbaijan.'

Which brings us to his quest to sign a new striker. Pards has had no success yet, but he does not rule out signing some former players. 'There's a lot of negatives about past players coming back and I don't see that. I'm thinking of Lee Bowyer and Fredi Kanouté. People shouldn't get bogged down with what players did in the past, because they're coming into a new environment.'

He then uses a buzz phrase from *The Tipping Point* again. 'It's not people that change, it's culture that changes people.'

We move on to some specific players. One important close-season signing has been Tomas Repka, who has signed a new contract. Only doesn't he find Tomas, although clearly a good defender, a liability sometimes because of his temperament and sendings off?

'He was only sent off once last season, and [received] six bookings – a huge improvement under this culture [management team]. We've worked hard on him. Obviously he ain't ever going to be perfect, he's always got

229

that fuse. But if he played every Premiership game, I would expect him to be sent off no more than once. From where he was when I arrived, smashing balls away over the hills in training, getting angry with everyone, almost getting sent off every game, I think it's a huge step forward and I think the best thing he could have done as a player is re-sign for us.'

He must have been delighted that Hayden Mullins finally came good at the end of the season, too. 'Unfortunately for Hayden, he was my first signing. We were short of staff. He played right-back which is not his position, centre-back, different roles in midfield, in a struggling team. He was shuffled around, there was a lot of negativity around, the crowd giving us a tough time.

'People say to me, "I'm so pleased you got promoted and proved the fans wrong who wanted you out." Well, with Hayden Mullins you can put his name next to mine. He's had to do the same and it takes character. It was hard for him because he's on the pitch; it's easy for me. I once had a tough time at Palace, and I know how difficult that is. He should get a lot of respect from the fans for standing up to that. He never asked for a move or to be rested, he just battled on.'

And what about Bobby Zamora suffering from the pressure of being a West Ham supporter? Imagine the pressure on us fans too . . . 'It's different for different players. Bobby's a character who plays on his confidence. If he's super-confident, he's a different player. The negative effect of friends and family asking him why he's not playing so well, it gets to him. I suspect it ain't going to affect Konchesky, who's also a West Ham fan. They're different characters. He's a player who's going to have a big season for us in terms of "Come on Bob, you've had a go in the Premiership and it weren't so great, well, here's your time . . ."'

Pards has mentioned the West Ham fan base as providing the potential for the club to be an Arsenal. Just how far can the club go? 'Well, Everton were in dire straits, but by selling Wayne Rooney had huge success, so I don't think fans should ever get bogged down with that [selling players to make money]. You can hold on to a player for too long. I look at the Defoe situation. A lot of managers have said we'd have been promoted a year earlier if we'd held on to Jermain Defoe. Maybe, but I think there was a good chance we wouldn't have. He'd been sent off three times, he didn't want to play for us. He was carrying a lot of anger in his mind, he was difficult to reach. He wasn't doing his job in terms of the rules I gave him, in terms of how I wanted him to play for us. He was playing as a free spirit, and you can't have that as a team. You have to all buy into what you're doing. If you've got one player pulling in the wrong direction it ain't gonna work for you, as good as he is. It was the right decision to make at that time.

'But the question was when can we compete with Arsenal? You look at their training ground and the money they can spend on the team, and they're a million miles away. But against that there's a huge debt for the new stadium. Football is such a precarious business. If the TV money goes down, who knows what effect that could have on that stadium. We could find ourselves level-pegging with Arsenal just like that. That's the beauty of football. We've got to hope we're going to have success here in the next two or three years.'

It seems we suddenly found some team spirit in the run-in last season. Was this simply due to the emergence of younger players like Ferdinand, Ward and Noble? 'Results help, of course. In all honesty, I wouldn't have been manager if the spirit, and faith of the players in me, hadn't been there. The fact they believed in me and I in them – we believed in each other – it pulled us through. It looked greater at the end, but it was the energy of a winning team. If the directors asked me about team spirit last season I'd say, "Yes, we're shit. We're playing crap at the moment. But [we have] good spirit – we'll be all right."'

We've been allotted half an hour, 'Which is a lot for me,' says Pards. He announces, 'I'm finishing up now,' as I ask about his post-Cardiff comments about 'keeping myself in check'. 'It's important you don't get carried away by failure or success. Have you noticed coaches only ever write a book about success? Clive Woodward brings out a book about winning. I want to read Clive Woodward's book about this year's Lions tour, because it was a disaster! Anything can look good when you've won. Why did it go wrong, that's what interests me. Why did the most expensive Lions tour we've ever put together not work? There was more staff, more players: why didn't it work?

'I enjoyed Clive Woodward's book. There were a couple of things there, I thought, I'm having that – he's about doing things right on the periphery. But ultimately it's when rough seas come and how you deal with that . . .

231

'Some managers get a Premiership job and they've had no rough seas. Alan Shearer is mentioned for the Newcastle job. I can't see that, for the life of me. What management experience has he had? What psychological training has he had with a football team? Has he coached the youth team, worked with the reserves? My guess is, no. It's not as easy as that. Look at Mourinho: all those years sitting in the backroom staff at Barcelona, observing. What a lucky man he was to have had that!'

Pards is an impressive man when you meet him. Serious certainly, and driven, but you imagine the players must respect him too. He has the hunger of the self-educated bloke from the building site. ('It might sound arrogant, but all the bosses I've played under, I've always felt I could improve on what they did and that drove me on.') It's not hard to imagine yourself being motivated by him. But let's forget the psychology now. Has he been to Ken's Café yet, where the tipping point is 50p next to the brown sauce? 'I've been to the pie and mash shop a couple of times. I got grabbed for autographs and fans ask "Why are you playing him, Pards?", so it's difficult round the stadium. But one day, maybe I'll give you a call. Now I'm in the Premiership I feel I can go in there for a bacon sandwich!'

17

BACK WHERE WE BELONG

13 August 2005
*Premiership football returns to Upton Park . . . Yossi says gizza job
. . . Robbie gets Savaged . . . Nigel Reo-Coker has the Bobby Moore
Stand disco-dancing . . . Blackburn get Dickov on and off . . . and
West Ham go joint top of the league.*

My 46th birthday is on 13 August 2005. I feel fortunate that 35 years
after first visiting Upton Park, I can still look forward to the opening day
of the season. So many other fans have succumbed to the lure of Sky, DIY,
parenting and armchairs or they despair at the mercenary traits of modern
players and the mistakes of the board. Some have even got a life. But, as
Elton John put it, I'm still standing – or rather sitting since the Taylor
Report.

We've been staying at Nicola's mother's house near Bishop's Stortford
and as I buy my return train ticket to Upton Park I ask the ticket seller if
my Network railcard is valid. It will be cheaper, he announces, adding,
'Anything to cushion the blow of losing, eh?'

In *The Guardian*, sports writers Niall Quinn, David Pleat and Michael
Walker all tip West Ham for the drop. In the *Mirror*, Oliver Holt, Simon
Bird, David McConnell, Neil McLemen and David Maddock predict
relegation for the Irons. But what do they know? Pards appears to have

made good close-season signings, and in a move towards West Ham glasnost, Terry Brown has even admitted to some 'bloody cock-ups' in the *Standard*.

It's a day of heat and rain. Ken's Café is sweltering inside as Ken feeds the chip pan and Carol dispenses her numbered tickets. But before egg, chips and beans, two slices of bread and a cup of tea there's time to tell Carol that I'm still hopeful Pards will visit and maybe bring the players for some sports nutrition, too. On Green Street, fans are still wearing play-off-final T-shirts and carrying flags. It's going to be a celebratory day, whatever the score.

There's even a tabloid story that some Iranian-born geezer wants to invest £100 million in the club. Perhaps he would install a pistachio nuts franchise in Ken's.

In the Newham Bookshop, Vivian, a lifelong socialist, is exchanging political banter with Iain Dale, owner of Politico's Bookshop, Hammers fan, a beaten Conservative candidate in Norfolk and author of a new book on Margaret Thatcher. And all in front of a backdrop of books by Cass Pennant, Bill Gardner and a bloke from the Cockney Rejects.

At the ground the new credit-card-style season ticket works surprisingly easily, although oddly there's no cashback facility and the turnstile operator won't give me any Nectar points.

My fellow season-ticket holder Matt is in the Faroe Islands, taking in the EB/Streymur v. IF first division game at the world's most windswept ground and trying to find vegetarian dishes that don't include fish. Nigel's wife Carolyn, who only seems to come when West Ham lose but has slowly been consumed by Hammers addiction, is at the match today. I assure her that her status as a West Ham jinx has ended now we are entering a glorious new Premiership era. Fraser is carrying a complete packet of cigars in his shirt pocket. 'They're still wrapped in their cellophane,' he pleads in mitigation.

All the seats around us are full, unlike last season. 'Where were this lot last season at Rotherham?' asks Nigel. Yes, we were there through the dark days of wooden stands.

Just to wind up those whinging Preston supporters, there's a banner reading 'Back Where We Belong' above the players' tunnel. Jeremy Nicholas plays 'Bubbles' but then stops the CD after the first verse, and there's a neck-tingling moment as the crowd stand and sing the rest of the song unaided. Even the sedate Upper East Stand are standing and singing our hymn to faded dreams. It's all reminiscent of the 2004 play-off game against Ipswich. The stadium is positive and West Ham are united.

There's an unfamiliar look to the line-up. New keeper Roy Carroll is in for the injured Jimmy Walker. Teddy Sheringham is back in place of Bobby Zamora. Dailly is at right-back with Repka injured. Danny Gabbidon, the £1.5 million signing from Cardiff, has replaced Elliott Ward at centre-half. Paul Konchesky, bought for £2.5 million from Charlton, is at left-back instead of the departed Chris Powell.

Our £2.5 million signing Yossi Benayoun is playing on the right of midfield and with his slim build and black hair he looks like a hybrid of Eyal Berkovic and Alan Devonshire. I'm a little worried that Pards has changed a winning team, removing Zamora, Newton and Ward from the play-off-winning side. But a substitutes' bench containing Zamora, Noble, Newton and Ward is a sign of the progress the club has made in the last three months.

The stadium is buzzing, and on four minutes Reo-Coker receives the ball midway inside his own half, moves forward and plays a delightful through ball to Marlon Harewood, who outpaces two Blackburn defenders, only to scuff his shot wide from the edge of the box.

Blackburn have the better of the next half-hour, though, and start to dominate midfield. Robbie Savage brings down Benayoun early on to welcome him to the Premiership. Konchesky then heads a free-kick from Savage away from the line. From the resulting corner, Dailly half-clears the ball and it falls to Andy Todd who pokes home a soft goal. There's no defender on the left post as the ball trickles home. It's the sort of scrappy goal West Ham have often conceded over the past three seasons. Sod it. We did only finish sixth in the Championship. And this is where we find that Blackburn know too much for us.

'I guess we'll have to settle for the UEFA Cup rather than the Champions League,' I tell Fraser.

But the crowd is still behind the Hammers. There's another huge chorus of 'Bubbles'. In a way, it suits us to be underdogs, after being expected to win every week in the Championship. There's none of the discontent of last season.

Christian Dailly is out of position at right-back and has already made a couple of dodgy back passes. He's showing good fitness levels to get up and down the flank, but unfortunately most of our attacks, inspired by the skilful Benayoun and Nigel Reo-Coker, are being channelled through Dailly and his crosses are poor. Etherington on the other flank is hardly seeing the ball. But West Ham come back in the final ten minutes of the half. Sheringham has a low shot saved by Friedel and then just fails to make contact after the Blackburn keeper spills an Etherington cross. Paul Konchesky causes a fracas in the Rovers area by going in hard on Robbie Savage; a sure way of winning over the home crowd.

Come on! Don't they know the final chapter of my book is resting on this? At half-time we agree the final chapter about a home defeat, or perhaps a scrambled draw, will need much Alastair Campbell-esque spinning. 'Close. But no cigar,' suggests Fraser.

We take our seats for the second half. Immediately Yossi Benayoun makes a determined run from the halfway line, drifts through the Rovers midfield and plays a ball in to Sheringham. The ball deflects off a Rovers shin into the path of Teddy and the 39 year old brushes it home with the composure he's shown throughout his career. His celebration is even better: arms outstretched to the Bobby Moore Stand and then a sweeping run to the East Stand. Clearly he's been working on it pre-season.

We can't quite believe it. Pards must have told them it was my birthday. Fraser is lighting his cigar. 'It's for the first Premiership goal of the season,' he explains.

The crowd are full of belief now, and Blackburn can't cope with our pace. Marlon Harewood, working hard up front all afternoon, is allowed to turn and shoot just wide. Mattie Etherington is now beating Neill every time, and a run down the left sees Sheringham poke the ball tantalisingly wide. And Hayden Mullins is all over the pitch, tackling hard and also chipping through balls to Etherington in one of his best games for West Ham.

Then Etherington receives the ball from Marlon's throw-in, plays it across the box to Nigel Reo-Coker whose touch takes it across the defender and he thumps a ferocious shot into the roof of the Blackburn net. It's a marvellous goal and the Bobby Moore Stand becomes one mass of bouncing blokes in replica shirts, arms upraised doing their 'Nigel Reo-Coker, da-da-da!' disco dance.

I'm motioning for Fraser to get his next cigar out, but he's still on his first and says he can't smoke that fast. When Rovers do come back Anton

Ferdinand looks assured at this level, and Gabbidon puts his head and feet in where it hurts. Konchesky clears a Todd header off the line, but on 80 minutes Harewood is holding up the ball around the corner flag, before Emerton wins it and then passes straight to Benayoun on the right-hand side of the box. The little Israeli playmaker remains calm, and unselfishly plays the ball across the box to Matthew Etherington who taps home. Blimey. Fraser is still on his first cigar. He'll be smoking all evening and his lungs will have gone by the end of the season. And he's only got five in the packet.

Rovers substitute, that little irritant Paul Dickov, is sent off for a horrendous two-footed lunge at Konchesky. Even West Ham must be assured of victory at 3–1 with ten minutes to go against ten men. I'm thinking that it took newly promoted Palace and West Brom eight games to win in the Premiership last season, while Norwich were fourteen games into the campaign before they won. We didn't win a home game under Glenn Roeder until the end of January. If we win our first home game in the Premiership there's hope of much more than survival. 'As Jim Bowen said on *Bullseye*, it's the points on the board that count!' agrees Nigel.

'Can we play you every week?' sing the fans. And we're playing with style. Every West Ham pass is being greeted with cries of 'Ole!' Ten-grand substitute Shaun Newton, on for Sheringham, is causing Rovers numerous problems with his trickery on the right wing. He even goes close to scoring with a turn and chip. 'We are top of the League!' sing the Bobby Moore Stand. Maybe we really have reached Pards' tipping point. This could be the rebirth of West Ham

The Irons win comfortably, and after Jeremy Nicholas announces the other Premiership scores he adds, 'Ladies and gentlemen, boys and girls. As it stands, we go top of the league!' Actually, Charlton's late goal at Sunderland means we go second on alphabetical order, but at least we can cut out a league table in which West Ham are second in the Premiership.

Nigel is texting Matt in the Faroe Islands asking him where he was when West Ham went second in the league. As we walk towards Plaistow in the unseasonal rain, we discuss who we want to win when Wigan play Chelsea the next day. I suggest that we need Wigan to lose, but Nigel counters, 'No, you're looking at the wrong end of the table!' We need Chelsea to lose to maintain our challenge for the championship.

You can't predict anything in football. We may lose all of the next 37 games. But today it's been proved, once more, that the fans are West Ham. When the crowd are 'jumping', as Pards puts it, we can trouble any side.

The following day, the England squad is announced for the match against Denmark. It contains James, Johnson, Rio Ferdinand, Lampard, Cole, Carrick and Defoe, but it doesn't seem as hurtful as usual. For there are new heroes. With Harewood, Reo-Coker, Anton Ferdinand, Etherington, Konchesky, Zamora, Yossi and even good old Hayden Mullins there is something to build on. After two seasons of mediocrity, we have an ambitious young manager who talks the club up rather than down. We could win our own mini-league or we could yet be relegated, but today West Ham have played with style and flamboyance. We're back in the Premiership, and there just might be hope for all those with Hammers in their hearts.